Potters' Tips
Second Edition

A Ceramic Review Publication

Potters' Tips

Edited by Emmanuel Cooper and Robert Fournier
Designed and produced by Ben Eldridge

Cover image: Julia Harrison

Potters' Tips
First Edition   1990   (Edited by Robert Fournier)
Second Edition   2006

ISBN 0-9523576-6-6

Published by Ceramic Review Publishing Ltd,
25 Foubert's Place, London W1F 7QF
© Ceramic Review Publishing Ltd

Contents

Introduction

One of the hallmarks of *Ceramic Review* has been the generosity of potters in sharing their ideas and experiences with others, giving freely often hard-won knowledge. The column Potters' Tips was started some thirty years ago, and over the years has provided a wealth of practical and down-to-earth advice. Many are often brilliantly simple and sometimes quirkily individual, but all are useful. They throw light on the way potters work and think about their craft. Whether giving advice on recycling materials, making use of the heat from kilns or fashioning brushes from waste objects, potters prove themselves adept at self-sufficiency, devising inexpensive and often cost-free ways of making potting simpler and more efficient.

The first edition was prepared by Robert Fournier, who not only marshalled apparently disparate tips into a coherent form, but also added comments that enabled them to be read as a group or referenced for easy access. For this, the second edition, tips printed in the last fifteen years have been added. The presentation follows a similar format to the first edition, with the addition of a separate chapter on health and safety. In all, *Potters' Tips* contains some 600 pieces of advice, each one of which adds to our understanding of the way potters work. Long may these innovative ideas continue to inform, amaze and elucidate.

Emmanuel Cooper, Editor

Measurements

All measurements are given, for the sake of accuracy, as originally supplied.
Use the following formulae to convert from imperial to metric and vice versa.

Length
1 inch = 2.54cm
1cm = 0.394 inches
1ft = 0.304m
1m = 3.281ft

Area
1 square inch = 6.452cm²
1cm² = 0.155 square inches
1 square ft = 0.093m²
1m² = 10.764 square ft

Volume
1 cubic inch = 16.387cm³
1cm³ = 0.061 cubic inches
1 cubic ft = 0.028m³
1m³ = 35.315 cubic ft

Weight
1oz = 28.350g
1g = 0.035oz
1lb = 0.454kg
1kg = 2.205lb

Temperature
$a°C = (a \times 9 \,/\, 5 + 32)°F$
$a°F = (a - 32 \times 5 \,/\, 9)°C$

Chapter 1
Clay

Contributors to the *Ceramic Review* Tips column showed surprisingly little interest in clay bodies. The only clay recipe turned out to be a gentle joke by Frank Hamer who, after his visit to China, tells us:

 ● **THE CHINESE POTTER** is friendly, honest, helpful and inscrutable all at once. I asked for and was promised the recipe for the porcelain clay at the Wei Min Factory. As we left, this slip of paper (left) was handed to me at the gate. **FH**

More practically, two recipes for the specialised Egyptian paste were offered. From Tennessee a revision of her earlier recipe published in *Ceramic Review* by Sylvia Hyman which she considers will produce a more 'stone-like' quality, and from Alicia Felberbaum, notes from her experience of bead-making.

● **EGYPTIAN PASTE RECIPE** (Orton Cone 012 to 010)
Soda feldspar (or nepheline syenite) 39
Soda ash....................................4
Lithium carbonate 4
Bicarbonate of soda 4
Kaolin 6
Ball clay 6
Flint...37
+ Bentonite 2
+ Copper carbonate ....2 **SH**

● **THE FOLLOWING RECIPE** for Egyptian paste should be fired to 970°C – over this temperature the texture becomes more matt and the colour less bright:
Feldspar 34
Quartz 34
China clay 5
Sodium carbonate 5
Sodium bicarbonate 5
Bentonite 4
Copper ....3 (oxide gives a greener colour, carbonate a darker colour)

Other colours:
Manganese ....3 (mauve purple)
Chrome ....3 (apple green)
Red iron ....3 (salmon pink)

The powder is mixed with the minimum amount of water and used immediately; the great secret seems to be to touch the surface as little as possible to avoid removing the sodium bicarbonate. Hang the beads as soon as they are made to achieve an even glaze effect. Do not dry on the table. **AF**

On the subject of Egyptian paste, Bo Ratcliffe gives a method for 'neutralising' soluble salt.

● **WHILE AT AN** art foundation college a couple of years or so back, an exercise in ceramics was to make some Egyptian paste and then make up some jewellery. All done; I had myself a beautiful coloured bead necklace. There was one snag – the sodium salts contained within the Egyptian paste continually migrated to the surface of the rich (in this case turquoise) coloured beads, periodically leaving a fine powdery white film. Of course one quick wipe and you could wear the beads without any immediate fear of the film coming back. This started my cogs in motion – well the soda salts are alkaline, why not try to neutralise them? So I did.

All you do (a bit time-consuming but well worth it) is pop the freshly made Egyptian paste into a bowl of vinegar for a couple of days. The acidic vinegar has certainly worked for me and I suppose citric juice from lemons would work too. It is worth a try for anyone who makes Egyptian paste regularly. After the treatment, rinse in clean fresh water and leave in an airy space for a few days and the smell of vinegar disappears. **BR**

When we come to handling clay, however, there is much useful advice. The distinguished Australian Potter, Ivan McMeekin, suggests the use of a concrete mixer. The only potential snag is that hired mixers are very likely to be contaminated with dried concrete, which could get into the clay.

● **FOR THOSE WHO,** like Michael Cardew, consider wet mixing to be the best method of preparing clay bodies but have neither the space nor funds to install a blunger, the following cow pat slop system can be useful.

Borrow or hire a small cement mixer. First weigh out powdered ingredients, place in mixer and then leave to mix dry until thoroughly integrated. Empty out mixture. Pour sufficient water in cement mixer (proportions water to clay vary according to nature of clay mix, but a starting point could be 40 fl.oz water to 60oz clay powder). Add clay, start mixer and leave until a thick slurry has been achieved.

Empty out on to sloping board (the reason for the name is now clear) into a cloth-lined brick trough. Leave to dry out until right consistency. **IM**

The dewatering of clay poses problems in any workshop, as the following tips illustrate. Sheila Wood offers the simplest method, while Ruth Lehmann reports on the bag method of stiffening slop clay.

● **TO REMOVE EXCESS** water from, say, a bucket of clay you are reclaiming, all you need is a piece of damp sponge – it will pick up every last drop. **SW**

● **IT IS VERY** wet and rainy here in Nairobi where I live, and getting clay dry is a continual hassle. I pour the clay in a very wet slip state out into cloth bags and let the water drip out in a fashion much like that of cheese. After about five days the clay is in a reasonable state to then be transferred on to plaster or whatever system is used to get the clay dry from there. A marvellous space saver – the only nuisance is making the bags. **RL**

Depending on the extent of your wardrobe or the availability of jumble sales the following will be of interest. Dave White puts old trousers to good use, Pat Cormack takes this idea one step further, while Janet Lundie offers two methods of reclaiming clay.

● **THE FOLLOWING IS** a method of de-watering slip using old trouser legs – corduroy seems to work best. Sew the bottoms up and a cord into the top end to strengthen it. Fill with thick slip. After a couple of days the clay is stiff enough to be squeezed out onto plaster batts. This saves time and the plaster from becoming water-logged so after a day on the batts the clay can be removed and pugged. **DW**

● **A VARIATION ON** the bag made from legs of old jeans is to make a wider bag with cotton drill (seam on the outside) so that it can be used in a bucket. Pour in the wet clay, gather the top edge and tie firmly. Suspend over the bucket for about a week emptying the water away as necessary. Finally lie the bag on a thick wad of newspaper, preferably on a piece of chipboard. Cover with another wad of paper and another piece of chipboard. The paper can be renewed as required until the clay is of a removable consistency. Several bags of clay can be dried in this way by stacking. The wet newspaper can easily be torn into strips and used on the compost heap or dug straight into the vegetable garden – it is ideal for holding moisture for runner beans. **PC**

● **CLAY IS LOVELY** stuff when it first comes out of its plastic sack – perfect texture, all air pockets pugged out, no foreign bodies, ready for some energetic wedging or contemplative kneading before submitting to our will on the wheel or under the rolling pin.

Then, of course, the trouble begins; buckets and bowls full of lumpy slurry or piles of drying shards waiting to be reclaimed. It is not too much of a problem in a large working pottery or a college studio. On a dedicated bench, furnished with large plaster slabs or paving stones, mountain ranges of clay can gently dry out before going into the pugmill. But for those of us who try to pot in the nooks and crannies of our own homes, piles of wet clay are space consuming and undesirable. The following method works for me; others may find it useful.

PLAN A: The Pudding Cloth Method. Regular readers of Potters' Tips will doubtless remember the suggestion that slurry can be put in a sewn-up trouser leg and hung in the open air until the excess moisture evaporates out. Have you ever tried getting wet clay into a trouser leg? You need two hands to hold it open, and

12

unless you have a willing assistant to pour the slurry, most of it lands on the outside or on the floor. However, the principle is good – clay left to drip and evaporate out in the open air does finish up in good condition in a very painless way. If, instead of a trouser leg, you place a large square fabric (a piece of old sheet or curtaining for example) over a washing-up bowl and pour the slurry into the centre, the corners of the square can be tied together, carried out into the garden in the bowl (so no trail of drips) and the bag suspended from an appropriate bough of a tree. I have a loop of strong string hanging permanently from my tree, and attach the clay bag with an S-hook.

The time left hanging is, obviously, widely variable according to the weather conditions and the original state of your slurry, but if you give it a prod each time you pass, you can monitor its progress. Surprisingly, normal rain seems to make very little different to drying out, but severe frosts are a problem (see plan B). When it is ready, detach from the tree and examine the folds in the fabric for earwigs before taking it indoors and unwrapping, ready for kneading and wedging.

PLAN B: Batt and Bowl Method (if you do not have the sort of garden where blobs hanging from trees are acceptable, or when it is icy).

Buy a cheap smooth-bottomed plastic washing-up bowl from a Pound Shop; pour plaster of Paris in to about a quarter of its depth when set remove the slab (as it is a new bowl it should come out easily) and allow it to dry out thoroughly.

The reclamation method starts in the same way as Plan A – plaster batt in bowl – cloth over bowl – pour in slurry, but at this point wrap the corners of the cloth over the top of the clay and leave it. This method is quicker than plan A, and the clay is frequently ready the next day. If you produce large quantities of slurry, you could have two or three bowls on the go.

Remember to remove the plaster batts and allow them to dry out thoroughly before using again.

The advantage of this method is that the clay makes no contact with the plaster bat, and needs no handling until it is ready to knead cleanly. The credit for Plan A must go to my sister Heather Graham who pots in an incredibly limited space in Norfolk. Plan B is my modification of the original idea. **JL**

For another variation Mrs S Hardwick goes into the garden, as does Susan Bennett.

● **I USE AN** old wheelbarrow which has a few holes in the bottom and line it with denim from old jeans. I load it in my workshop with soaked scrap clay and push it outside. When the excess water has drained away and the clay is dry enough for kneading, or mixing with fresh clay, I wheel the barrow back into the workshop, pick the clay up in the cloth and dump it on to the wedging table. I find it a useful idea, anywhere. Children like the idea too. **SH**

● **SINCE DISCARDING OUR** plaster batts, reclaiming clay has been a problem: we had been tipping reclaim on to marine ply boards and leaving it to stiffen, preferably outdoors, weather permitting. This led to uneven drying.

To protect the clay from contamination I threw an old sheet over the heap one day and found it dried evenly, and remained clean. You could always peg some polythene sheeting over the cloth sheet to protect from showers when necessary.

If this method catches on some enterprising entrepreneur might like to 'undertake' the production of 'winding sheets' for 'clay bodies'! **SB**

More traditional drying techniques are explained and illustrated by Margaret Moseley, Ken Isherwood and Peter Dick.

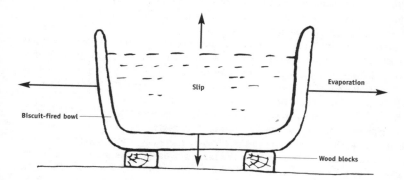

● **DRYING SLIP FROM** the wheel is a major headache, especially for the spare-time potter working in restricted space. I recently made myself a container for the purpose, using a well-grogged clay, and a deep rectangular washing-up bowl as a mould. The bowl was lined with newspaper to release the pot, which was roughly finished outside, but well smoothed inside, and biscuit fired. When this slip container is raised on blocks of wood slightly above floor or shelf level, evaporation can take place from all sides, and the slip soon dries to a workable consistency. **MM**

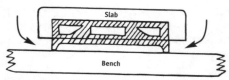

● **TO MAKE A** plaster slab with a very smooth surface, line a drawer with a strong sheet of polythene, surplus overlapping the rim, and pour in plaster. When set, the slab should lift out, usually with nicely rounded edges, and no damage to the drawer. If a large drawer is used a perforated plastic milk crate can be pushed into the plaster before set, and the rim of the crate can be left out of the plaster. This allows drying air to circulate under plaster slab. If all slabs are wet, or in use, use wads of old newspaper, cover with cloth, and place slip on the cloth. When the clay has set, the cloth can be picked up at diagonal corners and moved to another wad of newspapers to dry further.

To scoop clay onto a slab and spread into an even layer, place a plastic bag on one hand and hold round the wrist with the other hand. The slip does not run through your fingers, and you can just throw the bag away. **KI**

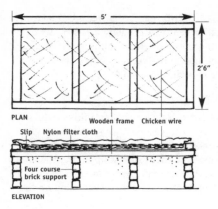

PLAN

5'

2'6"

Wooden frame   Chicken wire

Slip   Nylon filter cloth

Four course brick support

ELEVATION

● **A WOODEN FRAME** made as shown in the diagram, covered with chicken wire and rested on brick supports. One course of bricks is laid all round the top edge of the frame. Nylon filter cloth laid inside with a large overlap. Slip is poured on top of this and overlap laid over (this cloth speeds the drying and prevents a dry clay crust forming). **PD**

Ingenious devices come from John Miller and Peter Clarke; Bill Turner and Alan H Bolton successfully recycle redundant tea towels and net curtains respectively. Claire Hurford finds siphoning most effective.

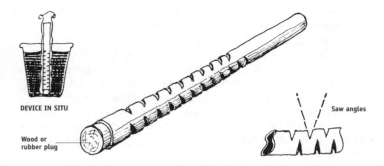

DEVICE IN SITU

Wood or rubber plug

Saw angles

● **SOME OF US** have thick but very wet slip standing around the workshop (particularly in winter where an outside covered trough is subject to freezing etc.), painfully long in settling and attaining workability – especially so when required as or in a clay body.

I use a length of plastic pipe (plumbers offcut) about 1½" diameter and long enough to stand a few inches above the surface when stood vertically in the bucket, in which I saw notches about ¼" wide and 1" apart in two opposing and staggered rows. A wood or rubber plug seals the bottom end, the top being left open (sawing the notches with, for example, an old tenon saw is a quick and easy operation).

The pipe is sheathed in a cut down nylon stocking leg, plugged end at the foot, and the whole stood upright in the middle of the slip and left. Each day or so I drop the end of a small-bore tube down the middle and suck or siphon out the seepage – which is quite considerable compared with settlement surface sponging. **JM**

● **I HAVE FOUND** that if you wet a two inch wide strip of horticultural capillary matting, dip one end into the slip of glaze and hang the other end over the side of the bucket surplus water will quickly be siphoned off. **PC**

● **OLD TEA TOWELS** make excellent cloths for drying clay slop. Unlike ordinary sheeting there are no loose threads of cotton to get entangled with the clay, which have a tendency to reappear during throwing. Incidentally, standing the slop, wrapped in cloth, on ordinary household bricks speeds up drying time; for potters not familiar with the use of a cloth, this draws water to the surface which is either absorbed or evaporates, preventing a hard crust forming on the surface. **BT**

● **AFTER BECOMING RATHER** untrusting of my plaster drying batts I started laying old net curtain (not cotton as this rots) over the batt first. This not only stops small bits of plaster getting in my clay as before but assists in lifting and folding the clay. **AHB**

● **HOW TO DRAW** off a large quantity of excess water from a glaze or a slop bucket without disturbing the sediment or swallowing toxic liquid.

Get a slip trailer and a metre length of clear plastic tubing from a DIY or pet shop. The inside diameter needs to be about 6mm for a fast flow of liquid. If possible, put the glaze or slop bucket higher than floor level. Take the slip trailer and push gently into the tube until it fits snugly. Before putting the other end of the tube in the liquid, expel as much air as you can from the slip trailer bulb, then put the tip of the tube into the liquid. Release pressure on the bulb and watch the liquid draw along the tube. Keep the bulb below the level of the liquid and as the liquid nears the end of the tube slide the trailer nozzle out of the tube to allow a free flow.

If you have no slip trailer you can insert a narrower tube in to the valve in the opening of a shower gel bottle – the type that hangs upside down. It is a bit trickier to pull the tube out as the bottle fills but otherwise it works well. The narrower tube is particularly useful for siphoning water from small quantities of glazes that are easily stirred up and do not settle out again quickly. **CH**

A simple physical phenomenon, not always appreciated, is the decreasing viscosity of water, to a quite remarkable degree, when it is heated. This is brought to bear on the problem of reconstituting clay by Eric Degg.

● **I HAD ALWAYS** taken it for granted that the correct method for re-constituting clay was to let it become bone dry, break it up small and sprinkle it into water. For years I did just that... and sure enough... it worked... given time... unless one was foolish enough to try to help the process with one's hands. The studio where I teach in Boston College of Further Education is very small. Technical help is minimal. We cannot afford to waste clay. We have both hot and cold water.

I now marvel at the fact that for a whole year I went on using cold water for re-constituting clay. One day it occurred to me to sprinkle the fragments of bone dry clay into hot water. The clay seemed to break down much faster. A simple test with two jam jars and two fragments of clay demonstrated the fact very conclusively. Cold water worked, but hot water worked very much faster. **ED**

Four final reclamation hints come from Jean Hamilton, Tony O'Donovan, Janet Cottrell and Bonnie K Holland.

● **AT THE END** of a night-school class I have found the perfect solution to the pile of wet, soggy clay discarded from the wheel, and the dried out clay left by the handbuilders. Place it all in layers in an empty plastic clay bag and jump up and down on top. By the following week the clay is soon ready after a quick wedging. **JH**

● **I PREVIOUSLY LET** trimmings dry and then soaked them down in an old sink. When thick enough it all came in on to plaster slabs. Now I have got rid of all that plaster, made more room for myself, and grow plants in the sink. The answer is two large beer fermentation buckets. As each layer of trimmings go in, I sprinkle them lightly with water. Do not overdo it or you will need the plaster batts again, but done well you will find you can turn the bucketful out, knead it, and use it straight away.

If you let some trimmings go dry, crush them, and put through a flour sieve – you have grog that can be fired in pots in your next biscuit firing. A variety of sieves will give you all the grades of grog you require. **TO'D**

● **I HAVE ACQUIRED** an old mincer, the sort that clamps on the edge of the table, through which I put all my scraps of 'precious' clay, for example coloured porcelain. The mince that results is easy to reconstitute with a minimum of water. **JC**

● **RECENTLY I HAVE** been testing and using several different stoneware clays, some of which look remarkably similar when they are being recycled. There is no problem in the reclaim and 'restored' bins because the bins are labelled, but I found it difficult at times when I had different clays drying out on plaster batts My solution to keep confusion at bay is to write the names of the clays on ice-lolly sticks and poke these into the piles of soggy clay being reclaimed. If I have mixed the clay, I put in sticks to represent the ratio of the clays combined. For instance a two-thirds buff/one-third white stoneware would have two sticks marked 'buff' and one marked 'white'. Simple but effective and stops one wondering 'did I get that right?' **BKH**

Preserving clay in reasonable condition is a perennial problem, especially in evening classes. Margaret Hinchcliffe, Jonathan Chiswell Jones, Janet Armstrong and Bill Jones give advice, while Susan Bennett deals with the bottom of the bin.

● **I SAVE ALL** my polythene bread wrappers, particularly the large sliced loaf size, turning them inside out to shake out the crumbs. These make excellent wrappers for small quantities of wedged clay, and can be thrown away after use. A fresh one can be used each time, without feeling wasteful, thus avoiding build up of dry bits of clay. **MH**

● **I HAVE FOUND** an old fridge with the shelves taken out, lying on its back, a most convenient way of storing pugged clay. It does not rust and is quite airtight. I have kept clay in there for six months and found it quite usable. **JCJ**

● **KEEP RAW MATERIALS** in plastic bags – well labelled in dustbins with a big label tied to the handle, listing the contents. I have two bins labelled 'A' and 'B'. These bins are stored under a worktable on plywood bases fitted with Shepherds castors for easy mobility. **JA**

● **SADLY, WE HEAR** of children being locked into discarded fridge freezer cabinets but potters can do something to help. An old fridge freezer cabinet, airtight lid, top-loading, is the ideal thing for storing clay, either in extruded forms or in pre-wedged state, and what is more you do not need to connect the mains. **BJ**

● **THIS TIP MAY** help teachers confronted with complaints that there is no clay left. How often has one discovered a great wodge of perfectly usable clay adhering obstinately to the bottom of the bin? No one seems to relish scratching at compacted clay, but someone has to remove it. I believe there is a tool designed specifically for the purpose. In the absence of this luxury, a tough wire coathanger works very efficiently as a 'loop-scoop'. **SB**

The rest of the clay tips are a mixed batch. Joseph Neville explores the preparation of paper pulp for incorporating into clay, while D Haig-Thomas gives some instructions on wedging.

● **HERE IS A** quick, easy way to prepare paper pulp to incorporate with clay, almost cost free and fairly effortless. I used it for the 12 years I was principal props maker to Merseyside Unity Theatre.

Large or small amounts of paper pulp suitable to blend with clay slurry can be speedily made using newspaper. Tear the paper, rather than cut, into rough squares and immerse separate pieces into hot water containing a little washing-up liquid. Allow to thoroughly soak for an hour or so, then roll balls of the sopping wet paper over a rough surfaced paving slab. Within a few minutes the paper will have disintegrated into an homogeneous grey pulp. No need to fret about trying to store wet pulp free from mould when the material can be made at short notice. **JN**

● **MANY DIFFERENT METHODS** of wedging need to be used according to conditions. Some of the following ideas may be useful:
1. Use a spade to chop clay into squares, turn over and chop again.
2. Punch clay with fist.
3. Stretch clay (again with fist) and move some of the top clay over by about a foot.
4. Powdered clay can be added to too wet clay and after wedging can be thrown immediately. **D-HT**

For slop-mixing bodies and glazes Philip Stanbridge and Edward Baker have advice on adding body clay and on the mixing itself, while Tim Ratcliffe offers an ingenious solution for shifting slurry.

● **FIRSTLY TO GET** your clay to a dry weighable powder, instead of bashing up slabs of body clay or unfired pots, let a lump of clay go leatherhard and grate it into small bits with an old cheese grater. When dry this can easily be weighed with the other dry materials. Secondly mix all the dry stuff (with a mask on) well before the addition of any water – and thirdly use very hot water to make the final mix. This way without too much effort the clay will go in without ending up as one cloggy lump to be forced tediously through a sieve. **PS**

● **SLOP MIXING IS** something I did years ago and it cost very little. I had the a two-speed drill, so I bought the longest ½" bolt, and a cutter off a butcher's mincer. I cut the head off the bolt, fixed the cutter on the other end with two nuts and there was the best mixer money can buy. I have used it in any bucket and I have never had to buy a piece of lawn since. **EB**

● **MANY OF US** have small studios and keep clay slurry in a large plastic dustbin to later recycle when time is with us. Problem: in a short while the bin becomes too heavy to move, putting pressure on studio organisation. Solution: get a trolley and put the bin on that. Problem: sturdy trolleys are expensive. Solution: make a trolley for next to nothing.
Here is how. Obtain that supermarket trolley which has been dumped in the river. (I have no problem with doing this. Once, I dragged six trolleys from a river and phoned the supermarket suggesting they come and collect them. They did not, as they could write them off against insurance.) Remove the four castors from the trolley. Next, go to your local scrap metal merchant and get a length, or four short lengths, of 2" angle iron. You will need four 16" lengths to make the trolley base frame. Many scrap merchants will give you such small pieces. Square cut the ends of your four lengths and take them to that friend of yours who can weld. Now you have the frame, attach the trolley castors to each corner. If the castors have a bolt/nut on top, drill through the bottom piece of the frame to secure each wheel. If the castors have a 2" flange projecting up from the wheel housing, have them welded directly onto the frame. Now, fill in the frame with strong wood. 6 inch wide by 2" thick offcuts from ceiling joists etc. are excellent. So go and have a natter with the carpenters on that local building site, as they

often throw away such offcuts. Finally, rub down the frame, respray it, and regrease the ball bearings in the castors.

Result: a strong trolley which you can move at any time. You can even pull it next to your potter's wheel and slop-out directly into it. So, if the pots are not selling, go into business manufacturing trolleys. **TR**

An ingenious graph which indicates the weight of dry material in a slip or glaze is contributed by Brian Sutherland.

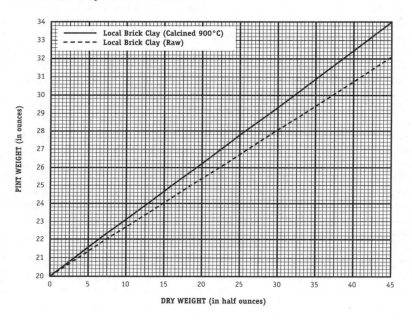

● **I WAS INTERESTED** to read in a recent issue of a method of calculating the dry material content of a slip or glaze of any pint weight. Not long ago I 'discovered' a very simple and accurate method of doing the same thing using graph paper (see diagram).

My method is to take 10oz of glaze or clay material (dry) and to add it slowly to half a pint of water until it is saturated. Then, after stirring I add water to make it up to exactly 1 pint (using a conical standard measure). This done, I then weigh exactly and record the liquid weight. The graph is numbered on its vertical axis, starting at 20oz and rising in ounces. The horizontal axis gives dry weight in half ounces.

Many of my stoneware glazes are blends of two local surface clays with additions of whiting, ash etc., and I have found my graph system invaluable for mixing up new stock from prepared slips which I keep in bulk. **BS**

Noirin Hobbs makes grog from clay bodies – good for colour and texture – while Joseph Neville recycles ceramic fibre blanket. The Association of Potters of South Africa put forward ideas for creating speckles in a clay body and a method of adding bentonite.

● **AFTER A TURNING** session on a clean dry wheel (basin), collect the clay shavings; and when bone dry, grind with rolling pin and sieve. I use three sizes of domestic sieve (no known size number) to give what I call coarse, medium and fine grog. The ground clay is placed for biscuit firing in any hollow ware – jugs, mugs etc. The grog-to-be can be used at this stage as bedding for pieces which will not fit rim to rim in stacking the kiln. Homemade coarse red grog can look very good when pressed on the outside of a thrown or handbuilt buff pot and glazed with transparent glaze. **NH**

● **OFFCUTS AND WASTE** pieces of ceramic fibre blanket can be used to grog clay bodies that are dunt-resisting. So far I have employed ceramic fibre, reduced to powder form, in clay used for handbuilding. To break up the blanket all that is required is to wet it, then tear it into pieces and grind it to a mush in a mortar; a surprisingly quick and easy process provided the material is kept wet. The ground fibre can be incorporated in plastic clay in its mashed form or, preferably, allowed to dry to a powder and then kneaded in to about two-thirds of the clay body in sufficient quantity to render the body rather 'short'. The remaining third of the clay is then added so as to restore plasticity together with a desirable feeling of 'tooth' to the mix. **JN**

● **IF YOU ARE** looking for added speckle in reduced darker clay, add some manganese oxide or granular ilmenite in a 20-40 mesh size. For a light stoneware body, iron flecks can be obtained by wedging in some coarse-ground manganese oxide. Light coloured glazes will further show off these speckles. A 3% addition of manganese oxide to a stoneware body can cause slumping and sagging of the body where the walls are thinner. The only way to overcome this is by running some lower firing tests to find the optimum firing temperature. Adding some nepheline syenite to the glaze will help lower the glaze maturity when firing.

Add bentonite in small quantities, about 1-2% only, to your dry clay while mixing it – mix it very well. Do not add it to wet clay as it is so extremely plastic, it might end up giving you unmanageable clay. **APSA**

'Reinforced' clay, for modellers especially, has been on the commercial market for several years and is used in many junior schools. It also has more ambitious and professional uses as Eric Degg explains.

● **IN THE EARLY** 1950s I attended a public lecture in Bath given by John Skeaping, very well known and respected at that time for his drawings and paintings of animals. He described a period of his life spent in a Mexican village where he worked with a local potter.

I wanted to know why those large intricately-formed and decorated low-relief designs in clay, which are so impressive a feature of Mexican popular art, did not fall apart when they were moved in the green stage. How could so fragile a structure be lifted and placed in the limited space of a kiln? The secret lies in the great reed mace, those large seed-heads on what are popularly known as bulrushes – the ones with the brown velvet-like covering. They are crammed with an amazing quantity of delicate fibrous material. One requires only a relatively small amount of this fibre thoroughly kneaded into the clay to produce forms which at the green stage would normally be far too fragile to handle. The following advice should prove helpful.

Do not try opening a bulrush head in your living quarters; the fibre may come out in a rush and you could find yourself living with bulrush seeds for a long, long time afterwards. Open the head in a large bag but do not make the mistake I once made and store a year's supply in a plastic bag. There must have been some moisture in the heads because they all went mouldy and I lost the lot.

The fibre is best teased out onto many thin slices of clay which are gently placed together and then thoroughly kneaded. If you hold your batch of clay up to the light and very gently pull a small fragment away you should be able to see the amount of fibre present as the clay begins to come apart. If you cannot locate a source of supply in the countryside any keen flower arranger should be able to give you useful information.

An alternative to bulrush heads is hairy sacking, which can be pinned with drawing pins on a piece of wooden board and used as a wedging board. If it does not yield enough fibre simply brush the hessian gently with a wire brush from time to time.

I have tried using fine fibreglass strands but found it far less successful than either of the methods described above. **ED**

A dangerous state of compression can be set up in a fired glaze which shrinks less than the body of the clay on cooling, causing it to peel or shiver from the surface, especially on rims. Darwin Turner suggests a cheap cure.

● **SHIVERING, THE OPPOSITE** state of a glaze and body to crazing, is not as rare as one may think. One answer is 'change the clay'. This may or may not correct the fault depending on the choice of clay. Try adding nepheline syenite to the glaze 5% at a time (i.e. 5% first, if not correct add a further 5%). 10% is usually sufficient to correct the fault but it does lower the maturation temperature. It has the advantage that it is cheap. **DT**

The health menace of clay dust is well known but often ignored by potters. In the Health and Safety chapter advice will be found on keeping dust to a safe level. In the meantime, Susan Bennett discusses clay dust in connection with pierced ware, as well as outlining, with Earl Hyde, a refined version of this tip.

● **WE ARE ALL** aware of the hazard to our health posed by the ingestion of clay dust and other toxic materials. When teaching I actively discourage rubbing down of dry ware and in my own studio keep it to a minimum and wear a mask whenever necessary. However, I produce a great deal of filigree ware which I need to smooth over with an abrasive pad, and find it difficult to remove dust from every crevice. There is a great temptation to blow it out – thus creating clouds of dangerous dust. Loosening with a brush helps, but the best solution I have found to date, especially on bisque, is to hold the fine nozzle of a vacuum cleaner as close to the surface as possible. Any more persistent particles can be loosened with a brush while operating the machine, and as a final precaution the pot can be lightly dabbed with a damp sponge.

Be warned though, the filter on the vacuum cleaner will not prevent the finest particles from re-circulating, and it is still advisable to wear a mask and work in a well ventilated area.

If one could organise the weather it would be ideal to do this work outdoors – on a dry day of course – it would not do to electrocute oneself while trying to avoid a long, slow death from silicosis. **SB**

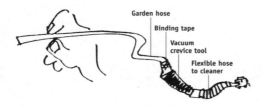

Garden hose
Binding tape
Vacuum crevice tool
Flexible hose to cleaner

● **SOME TIME AGO** I recommended using a narrow nozzled vacuum cleaner for removing dust from bisque or green ware. Recently, I needed to prepare 150 small filigree pots that were full of residual dust from rubbing down, for glazing. I found the weight of the tube heavy and awkward to handle, and the nozzle too large and inflexible for the task.

We solved the problem by inserting a length of garden hosepipe into the end of the vacuum nozzle and binding them together with strong adhesive tape. The suction was still powerful and the pots were cleaned efficiently in a very short time.

To reach the very small awkward areas one could further refine the appliance by the addition of smaller nozzles – such as rubber tap extensions – whatever works best for your needs – just suck it and see. **SB/EH**

Finally a brief idea with cold clay from Anna English.

● **DURING AN ARCTIC** spell of winter weather we discovered another valuable use for our microwave oven – it defrosts frozen clay beautifully. **AE**

The extrusion of clay, the use of the pugmill in weighing clay for throwing, and other tips in connection with the working of clay will be found in the following chapters.

Chapter 2
Throwing and turning

There was quite a lot of useful help from readers for this chapter on throwing and turning. To start with the wheel itself, Susan Green and Edward Dawes send two photographs of simple, and in the first instance truly primitive, potter's wheels.

1. INGLEBY GREENHOW This is a very primitive wheel we built three years ago in North Yorkshire. It is constructed entirely from wood and rope with no nails or screws. The place was forestry land and we stayed for three weeks digging clay, making pots and firing them in raku and bonfire styles.

2. CHILTON POLDEN This is a kickwheel we built here in Somerset; it is somewhat more efficient, though not much more sophisticated than the Ingleby model: the fly-wheel is cast cement. We think both photographs are self explanatory. **SG/ED**

With more detail Alan H Bolton describes the building of his wheel. The idea of a 'free' lower end to the shaft is ingenious and obviates the necessity for a crank. It may be better to take the kickbar support back to the leg it swivels from to give a smoother movement.

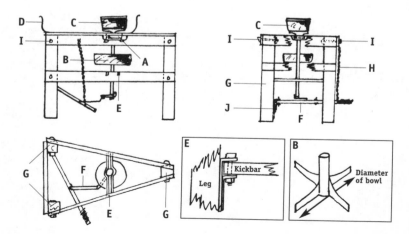

● **BEFORE I BOUGHT** my Alsager Electric Wheel I happily used a home made kick-wheel. The following hints may help anyone contemplating the same:

A Old half-shaft with bearing and mounting from local garage. Although worn from use on the road I found absolutely no movement. The mounting can be fixed directly under the top board thus taking the full weight of the wheel-head, fly-wheel and shaft.

B Fly-wheel. Made by using an ordinary kitchen bowl as a mould for concrete; the centre shaft fixing was the centre leg of a typist's old chair with the four spokes cut off to fit into the bowl.

C Concrete wheel-head of any suitable size. This can be secured by bolting a ply-wood disc through to the half shaft.

D The wheel tray consisted of a plain white Mothercare baby bath. It was very strong, the perfect size and very easy to drill for wheel-head hole and drain hole.

E Two metal bars span the wheel frame to grip the lower bearing. As the upper bearing does all the supporting the lower bearing is merely to stop flapping.

F Because the fly-wheel is just under the wheel tray the cranking is made easy. One bar bolted to the end of the shaft bolted to another that in turn swivels on the foot push bar.

G The wheel frame consisted of three 4 × 4" legs bolted together by six lengths of 4 × 1". Over the top was laid a solid surface of 1" wood.

H Chain to support kickbar.

I Corner bolts to hold frame together. I also used wood glue.

J Two right angles of metal bolted through into the leg leaving a large enough gap for the kickbar to swivel in.

Unfortunately because of lack of space I have since dismantled this wheel. Most books advise getting a kiln before a wheel. I disagree; get or make a wheel and throw lots and lots of pots and just slake them down again. **AHB**

A simple, handy addition to the wheel is offered by Susan Bennett; an economic way with bearings by Jonathan Dring; a somewhat odorous non-slip drive from Pete Brown; a method of adjusting wheel height from Richard Mason, a recycled splash tray from Andy Burt; and an extra turntable from Lyn Hudson.

● **ANYONE WORKING IN** a small studio where floor space is at a premium might like to copy my idea of making the wheel serve as extra shelving, leaving ample space for buckets underneath. I have screwed two short lengths of metal bracket supports to the wooden side of my Alsager wheel. I cut a piece of blockboard to a suitable shape and screwed two brackets on, so the shelf can be removed if not required but is quite stable when in use.

I use it to stack throwing batts, for tools, extra water etc. leaving the integral shelf free for balls. It is a great help when repetition throwing and also when decorating as I no longer have to reach across the pot. **SB**

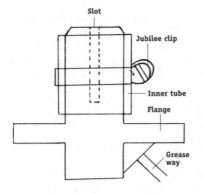

Slot

Jubilee clip

Inner tube

Flange

Grease way

● **HERE IS A** tip for those with Fulham-type electric wheels with badly worn top bearings. These bearings are the sleeve type, made in phosphorus bronze. Re-sleeving is possible if you have the facilities but failing that try the following.

Cut four slots down into the top half of the bearing, quartering it almost to the flange (remove any burrs with a file). Slide a piece of bicycle inner tube over the slots to prevent grease coming out and slip getting in. Now put a jubilee clip around the inner tube loosely.

Put the bearing back on the wheel and adjust by tightening the clip; the play in the shaft can be eliminated altogether and any future wear taken up by again tightening the clip. **JD**

● **TO CURE SLIPPING** friction drive belts, etc. on wheels, hand check that this is not caused by water, apply a small quantity of Stockholm tar, and run the device to distribute a thin film over the whole drive surface. Leave for a few hours before using. Thereafter your workshop will smell like HMS Victory. Stockholm tar is obtainable from old-fashioned ironmongers and farmers' suppliers. **PB**

● **I WAS GREATLY** intrigued by the drawings of potters working on the wheel in ancient Greece which I think are depicted on vase paintings – one sitting on the floor, the other on a seat. I have not yet managed to work on the floor, but I have found that standing each of the legs of my electric wheel on a brick has elevated it sufficiently to make it easier to use – particularly for decorating. Simple but effective. **RM**

● **A SHORT TIME** ago my Alsager packed in after twenty-five years of trouble-free operation. I bought a Shimpo wheel, which is fine, but I could not come to terms with the split tray. I found it messy, unstable and time wasting.

The picture shows the Alsager tray with the centre hole enlarged to take the top of a plastic bucket and form a skirt. Three holes were drilled into the top of the Shimpo casing. Plastic spacers between the tray and the wheel raised the tray above the motor and bearing bolt heads. What a transformation. Feels good; looks good and is so simple. If I can find another discarded Alsager tray I will buy it and fit it to my other wheel, a Brent which is begging for similar treatment. I feel certain no practising potter was involved in the design of the split tray. **AB**

● **WHEN I BOUGHT** my last wheel I also purchased a 'Lotus type' wheel-head to use for shallow items not easy to lift off the wheel-head. At the same time I had made a turntable base, on which to keep the head not in use. The spare head never gets mislaid, and the extra turntable is very useful, besides being cheaper than a complete whirler. **LH**

So much for the wheel itself. Quick and semi-mechanical ways of obtaining accurately weighed balls of clay for throwing exercised the minds of Rein Follestad, John Harlow, John Dix, Susan Bennett and Ruth Lyle.

● **I HAVE BEEN** potting for 14 years and have never seen anybody use my simple method. I put the extruded clay on a small trolley (I used some of my children's wooden toys) and fixed a harp to the wall with a hinge so it could only move vertically, and then drew a line on the table under the harp. After marking a scale on the trolley you can move the trolley under the harp and cut with regular intervals. (I made the harp from a piece of wood and a stick). Cutting this way you can repeat any weight exactly. **RF**

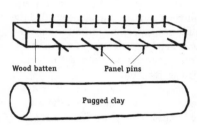

Wood batten   Panel pins

Pugged clay

● **WEIGH A MEASURED** length of pugged clay. Divide into sections according to weight required. Measure sections and put panel pins into a wood batten at corresponding intervals. Differing measurements can be put into other three sides of batten. Press pins into length of pugged clay then cut with harp where marked. **JH**

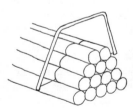

● **I HAVE NOTICED** a few people cutting extrusions from a pugmill to obtain the correct weight. I do much the same apart from stacking the clay completely wrapped in polythene for six to eight weeks, to sour it, before cutting with a harp as shown. The lumps are used without preparation for all of my small flower pots. It saves a lot of time. **JD**

● **INGENIOUS SUGGESTIONS HAVE** been made regarding measuring lengths of extruded clay to make balls of equal weight. A word of warning, however, when using reclaimed clay like this.

The more clay is recycled the 'shorter' it seems to become. For delicate hand-work in school I always give the children clay fresh from the packet. The same type of clay recycled through the pugmill produces ragged edges, cracks, easily crumbles and demoralises the students. From my own work, when using 8-12oz balls straight from the pugmill ragged edges occur on my rather thinly thrown ware. Wedging the pugged clay before dividing into balls usually seems to alleviate the problem. In short, when recycling, wedge before you weigh before you throw! **SB**

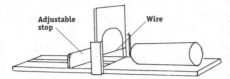

Adjustable stop

Wire

● **HERE IS A** simple method of measuring lengths of clay from extruded lengths. Once the adjustable stop is set, lumps of clay can be cut off with ease and very accurately, even for very small balls. **RL**

David Huddy contributes an ingenious and economical method of hand kneading to obtain clay suitable for throwing.

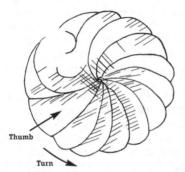

Thumb

Turn

● **I HAVE NEVER** seen this method of kneading used, described, taught or even heard it mentioned. Having used it myself for some time I cannot imagine how I ever managed with out it. It is suitable for weights up to about a kilo.

Holding the clay in the right hand, place the left thumb at the top of the outside rim and push into the centre. Turn the clay in the right hand a small amount and repeat. Soon the distinctive kneading pattern will emerge (see diagram).

A good deep drive into the centre aids the speed of mixing. If the clay is too firm a little water in the well in the centre will soon mix in and soften the mass – if it gets too wet add a little drier clay. Hard lumps can be pinched out easily; fully dried unbreakable lumps can be pushed through the wall and returned to the bin. In five minutes or so the most intractable mess can be reduced to a smooth throwing consistency.

Leave all throwing slops to dry and hand knead. Put all dried turnings in a bowl spray to soften and hand knead. From the slops and turnings I now recycle nearly all my throwing body and return very little to the bin for reclaiming. One word of warning: it is easy to knead air into the clay – so be careful. **DH**

Wheel batts of many materials are contributed by Alan H Bolton, C R Brampton (wood), K A Mitchell (Perspex), Peter A Lee (Masonite), Stephen Grieve (clay), Paul Reid (plaster) and from Joseph Neville self-centring detachable batts.

● **IF READY-CUT PLYWOOD** batts are too dear, my 7-ply standard plywood batts coated in polyurethane have lasted four years so far and there is still no sign of the plys lifting. If you do not have a band saw or get fed up cutting them (as I did), cutting as shown does just as well. Mark off in thirds; repeat if a more circular effect is desired. **AHB**

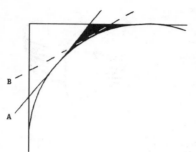

● **WHEEL-HEAD BATTS ARE** expensive when professionally made, so try this alternative. I find ³/₈" ply and ³/₄" chipboard quite suitable. Cut the material into suitable squares, make the great circle and cut off corners, as at A. Now cut again along B to remove the small corners, then mount the batt on a ring of clay centred on the wheel-head. A surform file held at 45° followed by glasspaper will then remove all roughness. **CRB**

● **IF YOU MAKE** your own wheel batts try this. Instead of making them out of plywood that always seems to warp and splinter, use ¹/₄" thick Perspex. You can get the Perspex quite cheaply from the offcut bin at plastics shops.

Advantages include: absolute flatness, the non-absorbent surface seems to reduce the tendency for pot bases to crack, less wear on the fitting holes and generally will withstand much more misuse throughout a longer life. The only disadvantage seems to be that they should not be left on top of the kiln.

To improve the grip, the high gloss surface can be scored or grooved like a record in a few seconds with coarse glasspaper whilst the batts are revolving on the wheel. **KAM**

● **HARDBOARD (MASONITE) BATTS** can be made to last longer by using a builder's metal float as a scraper. This has a thin springy blade that conveniently removes the section of clay left after cutting-off, does not scratch the surface and polishes the surface. There is no need to wash the batt as the polished coating of remaining clay protects it. **PAL**

● **THE BEST BATTS** I have used are simply made of bisqued clay about ³/₄" thick. They stick well to a pad of clay on the wheel, lever off easily and dry the bottom of the pots out nicely; pots must of course be cut through with a wire before putting aside. In the past I have used both asbestos and wooden batts and I find clay batts much superior. They should be made of an open clay (I used a lot of fireclay) and dried very slowly to avoid warping and then bisqued fairly hard but not beyond a good porosity. The snag is of course that you need batts to make them on. After use I scrape the clay off and dry on the kiln overnight ready for the next day. It is so obvious for potters to make their batts from clay and yet I have never heard of others doing so. **STG**

● **I HAVE FOUND** that a good way to make a circular plaster batt for the wheelhead is to use a polythene washing up bowl as a mould. Simply mix your plaster, pour into a bowl to a depth of about 20mm and ensure that the plaster sets while the bowl is resting on a horizontal surface. The plaster batt will have a nice rounded top edge and if your bowl is a good one, will be fine for use on the wheel. **PR**

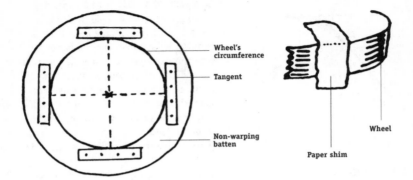

Wheel's circumference

Tangent

Non-warping batten

Wheel

Paper shim

● **NO NEED TO** modify a plain wheel-head, much less master the skill of slapping batts on to a clay covered wheel. Instead, cut out accurately a disc made from marine ply or high-grade blockboard conveniently wider in diameter than the wheel, locate the centre and scribe a circle whose diameter is precisely that of the wheel itself. Glue and pin four tangents of square section batten (preferably hardwood and at least 20 × 20mm thick) at the four cardinal points on the scribed circle. Seal the entire batt with thinned polyurethane varnish.

Initially the tangents may grip the wheel-head without any tendency to slip, but a positive secure grip can be guaranteed by placing a strip of newspaper at each cardinal point before applying the batt. Such strips are no hindrance when the batt is lifted off the wheel. I have used DIY self-centring batts for the past twelve years and found them utterly reliable, although I cannot recall any pottery manual describing their low-tech design. **JN**

For the easy removal of tapered shaft wheel-heads, Hugh Watson offers his own very original recipe.

● **HAVING TRIED VARIOUS** greases for the spindle of my Morse taper wheel-heads – seeking a balance between easy removal and lack of slippage when centring – I now use an old laboratory recipe.

Spread a few grams of grease on a tile, and add about a third by volume of rubber solution. Mix well with a spatula, and leave spread for an hour or so to allow the rubber solvent to dry. The resultant should be very tacky, and of decidedly limited aesthetic appeal. I store it in a container in the dark, on an assumption that the rubber will be degraded by light. A few grams lasts for months; a smear, or what is almost a winding of the tacky threads around the taper, is sufficient.

I use a general purpose lithium grease, and have used 'cow' gum or rubber solutions sold for cycle tyre punctures with apparent equal success. Rubber emulsions, such as Copydex, will not work.

Safety note: the solvent from the rubber solution is likely to be inflammable. **HW**

Anne Hughes gives advice on avoiding bubbles under the base when slapping a ball of clay down on the wheel. Stephen Grieve gives help on the difficult task of centring large pieces of clay, while John VEG Mitchell outlines two useful throwing aids.

● **WHEN YOU ARE** measuring clay into balls for throwing, try rocking each ball backwards and forwards on the table a few times before putting it on the wheel-head in order to make the base of the ball slightly convex. In this way you avoid trapping difficult air bubbles under the base of your pot. **AH**

● **WHEN I WAS** learning to throw, a repetition thrower from Govan Croft Pottery, Glasgow, taught me these useful habits. To centre large amounts of clay for big ware e.g. say 30lbs clay – divide this up into whatever weight of clay you find easy to handle – say three lots of 10lbs: centre the first ball spreading out the bottom well, then add the next ball and so on – easy!

The other point is that for larger weights of clay it is often better not to throw this on the wheel as advocated in many books, but just hold the clay under pressure on the middle of the wheel while it rotates until it sticks – this helps to prevent bottom cracks and saves your wheel bearings. **SG**

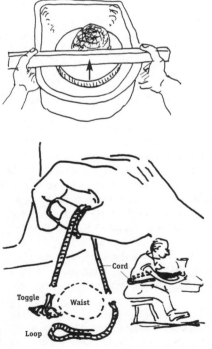

● **IF YOU CANNOT** centre the clay on the wheel, you cannot throw a symmetrical pot. If you have weak arms and fingers, this will help.

Get a batten of wood about 50 × 25mm. Clamp it to the sides of the tray with your fingers and then slide it slowly into the side of clay to be centred. **JVEGM**

● **YOU ARE THROWING** clay on the wheel... all of a sudden the right knuckle following the revolving 'sticky' clay wall... DIGS IN! This tip offers more control of the right arm and lessens the chance of this happening.

It is just a loop of cord around the waist and a loop around the right thumb as shown in the figure. The length of the loop is adjusted to allow the thumb just to reach the centre of the wheel. My cord has a toggle and eye for easy tying. **JVEGM**

Dennis Holloway from Henley and Edwin Todd from Jamaica both stress the value of a mirror for giving a different perspective on your pot during throwing; Susan Bennett offers a new slant on the tea ceremony, Hugh Veater shows how to prevent the same tea (or water) soaking your trouser leg, Colin Cooke avoids 'spinners', John Neville outlines a method of throwing a large teapot, while John VEG Mitchell offers a way of 'seeing how it is done' and describes how to throw an oval casserole.

● **SITTING AT A** wheel with one's head above the pot being thrown it is easy to misjudge its shape due to the foreshortening perspective. I use a mirror, in my case a jumble sale shaving mirror, fixed to the front offside of the wheel housing to bring it just above the level of the rim. A quick glance gives me a good side elevation view without moving hands or body. **DH**

● **PUT A SLANTED** mirror on the potter's wheel behind your pot and you can easily see the profile without gymnastics. **ET**

● **OBJECT – HOW TO** use less water when throwing very fine pots which tend to collapse through over-saturation.

METHOD – throw with a cup of cool tea in which 2-3 teaspoons of sugar have been dissolved. I discovered this in the middle of throwing a large batch of very thin candleholders with flyaway rims that often sit down minutes after they have been thrown. I ran out of water and the slip in the wheel would have spoiled the smooth surface, but someone had left their cup of tea within reach – so that went into my bowl. From then on my fingers flew like magic over the clay. The sugar makes the water silky, and you need far less to throw for longer.

RESULT – smoother, faster throwing of thin pots, less incidence of collapse through saturation.

INFERENCE – I imagine the tea can be dispensed with, and sugary water used instead. It would be an expensive addition for large outputs, but useful to try on fine objects. I was using Moira stoneware; I think porcelain would be easier to throw with this method too. **SB**

● **TO STOP THAT** persistent dribble of water that always seems to run down the right arm (when throwing) and eventually on to the right knee, fit a tennis sweat band around the right wrist. **HV**

● **I OFTEN COME** across 'spinners' – pots with a flat base that have sagged slightly in the firing so making a 'spinner'. This can simply be avoided by tapping flat bottoms into a concave while still leatherhard and the arch so formed will hold its shape well during drying and firing. **CC**

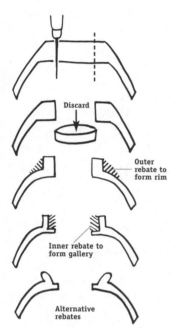

Discard

Outer rebate to form rim

Inner rebate to form gallery

Alternative rebates

● **TO THROW A** large teapot – throw two bowls equal in diameter, the upper part with a thick base. Flatten and slightly flange both rims. Turn both bowls to ensure they are thinly potted. Then with the upper pot on the wheel, cut out a disc using a needle, removing what would have been the centre of the base of a normal bowl: this aperture will form the teapot's mouth. Now turn an outer and then an inner rebate to provide a neat rim and gallery for the lid. Centre the lower bowl on the wheel, held securely in a clay chuck. Score and slip the flanged rims of the two bowls and lute them together. Marry and smooth the outer flanges with a throwing rib, and introduce a Japanese-style 'question mark' rib stick or the curved edge of a wooden kitchen spoon to deal with the internal flanges.

This technique is child's play compared with the task of throwing a big but thinly potted vessel in one go, and then embarking on the tricky business of 'splitting and sinking' a thickish rim to make a gallery for the lid. **JN**

● **MOST PHOTOS OF** potters throwing on the wheel are taken looking at the potter. If you are beginning and want to copy the position of the potter's hands, just turn the book upside down (forget about the pot) and you will see the hands as the potter sees them. **JVEGM**

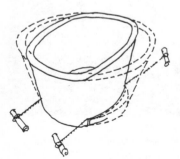

● **TO THROW AN** oval casserole:
1. Throw a circular vessel.
2. At just above the thickness of base, make two horizontal cuts with a taut wire. The wire starts on the outside and goes in for about one sixth of the diameter of the base.
3. Ease the two cut sides into an oval.
4. Cut off the two surplus parts of the base.
5. Weld the joints with a wooden tool.
6. Wire the casserole off the wheel. **JVEGM**

Jean Morse and Dick Shattock deal with pot gauges; John Miller helps in gauging the thickness of a pot base during throwing; John VEG Mitchell puts forward a remedy for a thin base and a tip on throwing big bowls; Jan Bunyan offers a different solution and suggests an alternative use for a toilet brush.

● **A SIMPLE POT** gauge can be made using a 1" spring clip, 16" length of broom handle and 16" length of ¼" dowel (shaped to a rounded point at one end).

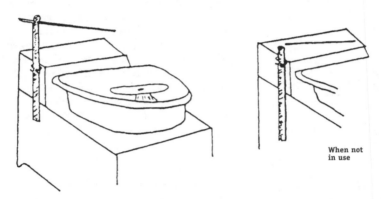

When not
in use

Drill a ¼" hole through broom handle approximately 1¼" from rounded end, to take dowel. Screw spring clip at a convenient point at left of wheel shelf. Push broom handle into clip and insert dowel into drilled hole. Adjust broom handle up or down for height of pot, and adjust dowel for pot width (dowel can be removed and broom handle pushed down when not in use).

A record of pot sizes can be kept for future reference by marking broom handle and dowel with felt pen in appropriate places and recording in notebook by a given number for each pot size. **JM**

● **ABOVE ARE TWO** photographs which I hope are self explanatory. The pointer can be adjusted to any position and could be adapted to hold more than one pointer. **DS**

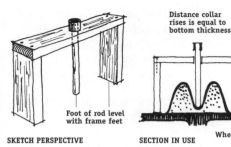

Distance collar
rises is equal to
bottom thickness

Foot of rod level
with frame feet

SKETCH PERSPECTIVE   **SECTION IN USE**   Wheel-head

● **I NEVER TAKE** chances with bottom thicknesses when throwing, having been faced on more than one important occasion at the turning stage with an unhappy denouement. I now use for each and every piece thrown – and later in its turning – this simple do-it-yourself wooden bottom-thickness gauge, made out of almost any handy pieces and to the span and height best suited to one's own production. Mine is framed in 2 × 1" (nominal) whitewood with a ½" diameter dowel rod running in a slightly oversized hole, the rod fitted at the top with a ½" collar of plastic hose as a 'stop'. It adds only seconds to processes and gives enormous confidence, especially in repetition work where varying bottom thicknesses can, after turning, upset the uniformity of a finished range or set. **JM**

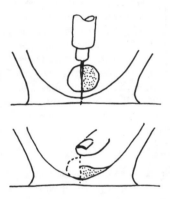

● **YOU CAN FIX** the base of a bowl that has been thrown too thin – if it is discovered soon enough. Start by drying the inside bottom of the bowl with a dry towel. Form a piece of firm clay into a ball and impale it on a needle. Poke the needle through the centre of the bottom of the bowl, then with finger and thumb press this clay down and out from the centre, with the wheel turning very slowly. Then continue throwing – and you have avoided the weighing out of more clay, more kneading, more centring. Next time remember to needle the base sooner. **JVEGM**

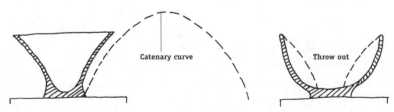

Catenary curve   Throw out

● **BIG BOWLS THROWN** on the wheel often 'relax gracefully' (slump). If you start by throwing the 'bowl shape', it is more than likely to happen. Start by throwing a 'funnel shape' to the correct diameter then turn the 'curve' inside out, as the last operation. The 'funnel shape' should approximately follow a 'catenary curve' (see illustration). If the throwing is 'sloppy' wait for the funnel to dry out before finishing to the bowl shape. **JVEGM**

● **IF, LIKE ME,** you occasionally throw a pot with too thin a base, stand it (when it has dried a little but is still pretty damp) on to a piece of Masterboard or another absorbent flat surface and pour in a little body slip. Shake or tip the pot so that the slip runs evenly over the base. Leave until ready. **JB**

Hugh Allen and Nora Kay explain their methods of pot measurement and recording for repetition throwing. Clay weights could usefully be added to Hugh Allen's compact card.

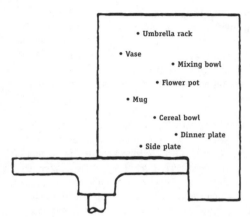

● **LIVING IN AFRICA** for much of the last 15 years I have had little opportunity to read *Ceramic Review*. This tip was given to me by John Harlow of Bridgwater. It concerns obtaining consistent weights and heights for pots, and involves the use of the card illustrated. By marking the rim position of each pot on this card a pointer is precisely re-set to the same position in a moment, when the card is set with its stepped edge butted to the edge of the wheel-head. This method eliminates the need for a notebook, or several cards, and is best made from marine ply, which can be easily bored at the appropriate positions. **HA**

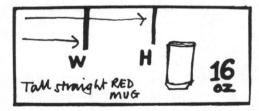

● **SO FAR, I** have not found any other potter using this method, but as it is so simple and easy, many others must have already devised it for themselves.

Having experimented and found the exact weight of wedged clay needed for throwing any particular shape, throw this shape on the wheel. Then take a piece of stout white card – about 8 × 3½″ – and mark off, clearly with a good black felt-tip pen, the width and height of the shape.

Add a note of the weight of clay, a brief description and a small diagram of the shape. Finally, cover the entire card with transparent plastic film.

This makes a durable, long-lasting working measurement-gauge; damp clay smears and smudges are easily wiped off, and a collection of these gauges take up little room and are easily stored. **NK**

Elana Morris heads her diagram and note, 'Repeat throwing off a hump made easy'. A little optimistic perhaps but it would certainly help to maintain uniformity. Jane Cullett, Mike Rawlinson, Susan Halls, D Metcalff and Hugh Veater suggest ideas for throwing ribs. Peter Godfrey raids the garden shed for his shaper and former.

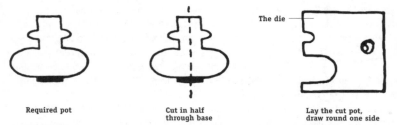

Required pot

Cut in half through base

The die —

Lay the cut pot, draw round one side

● **YOU CAN MAKE** a die out of wood (similar to throwing ribs). When your pot is nearly ready, put the die against it to check required shape and size.

See above diagram for details of how to make the die. Smooth the curves with sandpaper. **EM**

● **FOR MANY YEARS** a delicate six inch plastic ruler was my favourite throwing rib. Imagine my distress as I watched it slowly wear away and eventually become too flexible for robust everyday use. Kind providence, in the form of the NatWest Bank urging me to destroy my obsolete Access Card, provided a shining, gleaming substitute. No doubt any other unwanted credit card would be equally serviceable. **JC**

● **WHILST TIDYING THE** bathroom recently I came across some wonderful curved throwing ribs which I immediately requisitioned for the workshop.

Some time later a somewhat irate partner informed that they were actually for removing unwanted body hair – apparently there is one in every box of hair-removing cream. Boots' own brand is recommended for its efficacy and the excellent design of the accompanying throwing ribs. **MR**

● **PLASTIC PHONE CARDS,** which are frequently left lying around in telephone booths, can be cut and shaped (using scissors or scalpel) as throwing-ribs, mark-making tools and general scrapers. **SH**

● **LONG-LASTING THROWING RIBS** can be made from clay, unglazed and vitrified. I have made some from porcelain, burnished, and these work wonderfully. They are very hard-wearing, and, if used carefully to prevent chipping, will last for years. **DM**

● **REMOVE TOP AND** bottom of discarded beer cans, the tube remaining can be cut into light-weight flexible metal ribs/scrapers, etc. **HV**

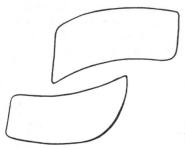

● **THE SHAPERS AND** formers available commercially seldom quite fit the design of one's own pot, bowl or dish. A simple solution can be found – in the common (or garden) plastic flower pot. These are thin, semi-rigid and curved, which when made into formers sit very comfortably in the hand.

Illustrated are two shapes I use but anyone can quickly make one-off shapes cheaply and easily. Take a plastic flower pot and split it – standing on it is as good a way as any – like all great ideas I accidentally did that and lifting the three pieces ran about with the famous cry of 'eureka!' on my lips.

Draw the shape you want with a marker pen on one of the pieces of plastic. Cut off rim and base. Remember this material is brittle; there will be splitting as you do this and therefore wastage. I use kitchen shears which have a better bite than scissors. Cut with care slowly. File pointed ends into curves and sandpaper the edges of your new tool. That is all there is to it. Make them as you need a particular shape for the pot you are making.

Even the rigid curved rim is useful as a check on handbuilt work or for the rim of a pot gone slightly oval by robust removal from the wheel-head. **PG**

Cutting and releasing the thrown pot from the wheel can be a tricky job and welcome advice comes from Jean Maffey, John Dix, Lyndon Thomas, Ron Payne, Elana Morris, Nicholas Homoky (submitted by Edna Weldon Davies), Ann Parkhouse and Charles Stileman.

● **HOW OFTEN DO** you find yourself searching for that wire, which seems to have a mind of its own, when you are ready to cut a pot from the wheel or batt? Why not fix a wire to the wheel tray directly opposite the thrower? This must be done on two levels enabling the wire to be used for cutting off the wheel or batt, the distance between the two levels being dictated by the thickness of the batt.

The wire can be pulled taut with one hand as the wheel revolves and the wire pressed down onto this with the fingers of the other hand. **JM**

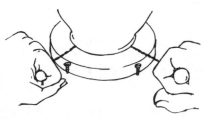

● **I HAVE BEEN** practising a sort of potter's yoga; knee up against the bench, batt against the knee and cut the pot off. Very awkward it is too and (for me anyway) cuts holes in far too many bottoms for my piece of mind. There must be an easier way...

Two well-spaced nails in the edge of the bench hold the batt firmer than my knee and I can watch what I am doing. The only disadvantage is that it makes the bench uncomfortable to sit on. **JD**

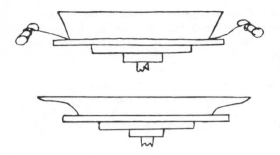

● **WHEN THROWING LARGE** plates and bowls on batts I find it advantageous to cut the base before flattening the rim. Cutting at this stage is more easily accomplished and is less likely to damage the flattened rim. **LT**

● **POTTERS WHO SLIDE** their pots off the wheel onto a tile are later faced with the problem of hacking them off again. This can be avoided by wrapping the tile in a strip of polythene cut from a clay bag.

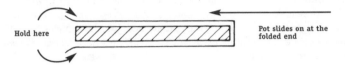

Hold here

Pot slides on at the folded end

When the pot is leatherhard the tile can be slipped out and the plastic peeled off the pot, leaving it flat and smooth. Even if the clay dries completely it is unlikely to split and may not need turning.

A ³/₄" ribbon of the same plastic is a useful tool for shifting pots which are reluctant to slide. **RP**

● **TO LIFT BOWLS** without batts:
1. Cut square pieces of newspaper to fit the top of your pot.
2. Go round gently with your finger over the paper along the rim to make sure it is stuck.
3. Cut and lift. The pot will stay tight and round. **EM**

● **NICHOLAS HOMOKY REMOVES** a pot from the wheel having first placed a sheet of paper over it to prevent distortion. **EWD**

41

● **I HAVE A** Pilling pottery wheel with a pegged wheel-head to take asbestos throwing batts. I have aimed to throw certain pots with thin bases and to turn off the excess from the bottom sides when I throw the pots to avoid turning at the leatherhard stage, thus economising on time and maintaining spontaneity of form as the whole shape is completed in one process.

So far so good; I release the pot with the twisted throwing wire to give the attractive shell pattern underneath. At this stage the pots are too wet to pick up. That is what the pegged batts are for. However here is the difficulty; when the pots are firm enough to pick up they have re-stuck themselves to the clay on the batt.

I had been advised that I should always make sure the throwing batt is free from excess water as moisture gets underneath the pot making it re-stick. But I did this anyway. The right answer suddenly hit me the other day – do not cut the pots free when they are thrown, but wait until they are leatherhard, then put them back on the wheel-head and release them. Simple. **AP**

● **ON THE ODD** occasion when a pot has not been wired off after throwing, it can be difficult to remove from the batt without ruining it by forming a very irregular cut. One solution is to pull the wire very slowly and cautiously under the pot while the wheel-head is rotating extremely slowly, if necessary moistening with a little water to soften the clay. This can result in a clean even cut. **CS**

Franz Westerveld and Alison Clarke illustrate systems for fixing batts to wheel-heads; Heather Chambers a method for releasing them.

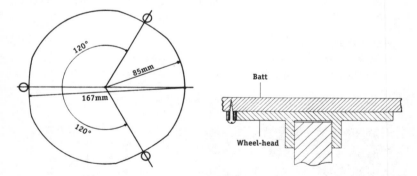

● **THERE HAVE BEEN** one or two tips concerning the fixing of batts to wheel-heads. This made me come forward with a solution that I worked out some years ago and which gave me entire satisfaction. The diagram shows my wheel-head to have three 'flats' machined to it. In reality the flats have a circular curvature for smoother operation. The underside of my wooden batts have three studs, bushings held by a wood screw. When the batt is placed on top of the wheel-head with the studs in the positions indicated and the batt is given a slight twist, the studs wedge up against the flats and the batt sits tight. To remove the batt, untwist. Even if the batt comes loose with a jerk, this will not tend to throw over a soft tall pot.

When the wheel-head is accurately machined – any decent machine shop will do this – it will accurately re-centre when taken off the wheel for a while, such as when throwing pots in sections. The positioning of the studs on the batt is not critical in this respect. To put the studs in position on the batt, centre it on the wheel-head and, keeping it there with one finger, rotate the wheel slowly while trailing a pencil along the edge of the wheel-head, copying the outline off on the underside of the batt. Then screw down the studs just clear of the outline.

Above a certain minimum diameter, the size of the batts can be freely varied. It remains possible to throw directly on the wheel-head without using a batt. This method might not be advisable with aluminium wheel-heads, as this is a soft metal and the studs might indent the wheel-head, causing loss of recentring accuracy. **FW**

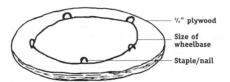

● **DRAW A CIRCLE** on a batt the same size as the wheel-head. Nail the staples just outside the line. Batts can be made in various sizes. Secure with a small lump of clay to prevent spinning. **AC**

Labels on diagram: ¼" plywood — Size of wheelbase — Staple/nail

● **AS THE WEATHER** became colder I experienced some difficulty in changing the batts in my Lotus wheel-head. Now I keep the kettle handy. Pouring hot water onto the metal rim of the wheel-head causes it to expand and the batts slip in and out easily. **HC**

The idea of using newspaper under thrown pots occurs to Mike Rawlinson, Jane Fairbanks and June Linsley Hood. Janet Cottrell prefers a firmer support.

● **THE PROBLEM OF** what to put freshly thrown pots on to seems to be a perennial one. I finally came up with the following system.

For ware boards I use floor-grade chipboard. This has a smooth surface, is fairly porous and remains flat when wet, so that the pots stay round when placed on them. I have found that there is only one material to place on top of the boards and that is the paper from good quality Sunday colour supplements. This is sufficiently porous to allow the bottom of the pot to dry quickly, so that you do not get a pot with a dry rim and a squishy base to deal with. It is also sufficiently smooth and strong to enable it to be peeled off the pot when it is dry enough to handle (unlike other papers which fall apart and stick to the pot).

The only major disadvantage is that it is too easy to start reading them when one should be working. **MR**

● **I USED TO** find it difficult to remove thrown pots from pot boards when ready for turning until a friend suggested newspaper. What I now do is to place pieces of newspaper on my pot boards and then place the freshly thrown pots on to them. There is then no difficulty in lifting up the cheese-hard pots and peeling the newspaper from underneath. **JF**

● **I HAD BEEN** having trouble with large slip-decorated plates which cracked across the base during the drying process: and also with double flowerpots which split at the rim just beyond the part where they were joined together. Slower drying helped, especially if the pot was covered loosely so that the rim did not dry before the base, but I concluded that the real problem was the inability of the wide base to move freely on its batt as it contracted in drying.

The answer was to stand the pots on a couple of sheets of newspaper. This has two advantages: it absorbs some of the moisture, and it is able to contract with the pot, so that by the end it is as wrinkly as Mr Toad's fingers when he was pretending to be a washerwoman. This can be done at a very early stage by reversing them carefully, like cakes from the oven, onto a spare batt and then back onto a newspaper-covered one. **JLH**

● **GOOD QUALITY CARTONS** made of corrugated cardboard with brown paper on both sides can be cut to suitable sizes and used as disposable 'tiles' for thrown or small slabbed ware. **JC**

Two quick-drying schemes from opposite sides of the globe. From Magic Mud, Hong Kong (Margaret Kneer) and Kendall (Judith Palmer). Meanwhile, the Midland Potters Association offers tips on preventing cracking when drying plates, and Charles Stileman looks at drying platters.

● **IN THE WINTER,** whilst having difficulty getting the bottom of wide-based pots such as casseroles and pie dishes dry enough for turning, I discovered a quick easy way. I keep a large thickish slab of biscuited clay in the airing cupboard, so it is always warm and dry. Then I lift the dampish pot carefully on the slab, and leave for about half an hour; the base is then ready to turn. Several pots can be hardened off this way before the slab needs re-drying. **MK**

● **HAVING GOT A** rush order for coffee mugs during a very hot and humid spell, where it was taking over a week for anything to get leatherhard for turning, I hit upon the idea of speeding up the drying time by using my microwave oven. Brilliant! A one minute whizz at high or two minutes at medium resulted in lots of steaming mugs that were thrown, turned with handles put on within a day. I found that a couple of short blasts of microwaves at intervals worked better than a longer intensive time where certain areas dried too fast and cracked. But it is worth experimenting to get the ultimate timing. **JP**

● **PLATES MUST BE** dried very slowly and evenly for a minimum of two weeks and wrapped in plastic to control the drying. Dry on wire racks or pegboard to allow airflow. If your racks leave marks, use fibreglass screen door screening on the racks, or place small objects under the piece to prop it up and allow the foot and bottom to dry at the same rate as the top and sides. You might want to make some small bisque pieces for this purpose. Uneven drying can set up stresses that do not show themselves until the final glaze firing. To control drying so that the centre dries faster than the rim, cut a round hole in the plastic about 3-4 inches in diameter over the centre of the plate. Water-based wax can be painted onto the rims to prevent them from drying too quickly.

The general process is: throw the plate, wire it free from the batt, and set on a shelf.

When running a wire through a large plate it is bound to rise up in the middle even if you pull tightly, so make sure your plate is thrown very thick and plan to trim a lot. An alternative is using plaster batts, which will release on their own. Dry slowly and evenly, so as not to let the rim dry out first. As soon as the bottom is hard enough to support itself, sandwich a batt on top and flip the platter over. Take what was the throwing batt off and let the plate dry open to the trimming stage. After trimming, place on a shelf rim down and cover to dry

Another innovative solution to the above problem, besides using plastic batts, is using oiled masonite batts, 1.3cm thick (so that they are completely inflexible). The clay then releases itself from the oiled surface. **MPA**

● **I THROW PLATTERS** with up to a 1″ thick base to allow for turning of supporting rings. Frustratingly one must often wait many days before the base is sufficiently dry for turning. However, once the walls are firm I undercut and slide the platter onto a sheet of 6mm water absorbent masterboard. This dries out the base quickly, enabling it to be turned within a day. **CS**

On turning techniques, Tony O'Donovan uses a ruler to deal with unevenly dried pots; G Hunt suggests a tool for turning at the throwing stage; Nora Kay, Pam Williams and Kathleen Hunter discuss centring the leatherhard pot on the wheel; Eric Degg and L E Wells give valuable general advice on turning; Susan Bennett advises on keeping fingers dry; and John VEG Mitchell gives a method of checking the internal profile.

● **UNEVEN DRYING DUE** to wind, sun or night-school radiators results in a pot that emulates the leaning tower of Pisa when inverted ready for turning.

To level it quickly take a straight wooden ruler, or similar, and hold it flat across the bottom of the pot a little beyond centre. Tilt the furthest edge up slightly, and the edge nearest to you will start cutting the high side of the pot away. Hold the ruler level as the cutting is on the right side only and if you tilt the ruler that way you will finish up with the pot high in the middle. Once you have got the hang of it you can try something sharper than a ruler if you like, but be warned, it becomes a very instant process then.

More speed (of the wheel) and a gentle touch – though be firm – is better than too much pressure. **TO'D**

● **A TRIANGULAR TURNING** tool can only be used with difficulty to turn the bottom of bowls immediately after throwing – because the clay very quickly builds up in the right angle of the tool and needs to be cleared frequently. A more continuous flow of clay can be turned at the wet stage by the use of a dessertspoon ground and cut to an angle of 60° or less. The probable useful lower limit is 45°. If held vertically or less, the top edge of the spoon will cut into and remove the clay, which flows more or less continuously towards the handle and has to be cleared much less frequently. By tilting the spoon into the clay (i.e. at an angle less than 90°) then the effective angle at the base of the bowl between the clay and the wheel-head can be considerably reduced – even to 40° when using a ground 60° spoon. This tilting action cannot readily be effected with the triangular turning tool – except of course if the base of the bowl is at the very edge of the wheel-head.

The force required is minimised if the axis of the spoon relative to the spinning clay is 30°/60° – although 90° is achievable but two hands will probably be required. For beginners, the tool can be used to clean up the base of a centred mass of clay. l have used an old nickel silver spoon, but an old stainless steel spoon would be equally satisfactory. **GH**

● **MY OLD KICKWHEEL** once had grooved circles marked on its wheel-head, but most of these have gradually worn away. When wanting to centre pots for turning and decoration I use a piece of ordinary blackboard chalk, held slightly edge-wise, and make a few concentric circles. These are easy to do, clear to see, and easily wiped off. **NK**

● **IF YOUR WHEEL-HEAD** has no circular grooves marked on it, which are a useful aid when centring for turning, make pencil circles by holding your pencil point still on the wheel-head for a few seconds as it rotates. Mark one or more circles slightly larger than the diameter of your pot. **PW**

● **IN ANSWER TO** Pam Williams's tip on centring. I am surprised that anyone aspiring to be a competent potter should waste time marking the wheel-head with pencil rings. Time could be spent more wisely by practising to 'tap the pot to the centre of the wheel'. This is a great time-saver and a much more professional way of approaching the problem. I have been doing this for over twenty years, and was very grateful when my tutor taught me how to do it. **KH**

● **A TEACHER AT** Boston College of Further Education for many years, I have taught many school teachers and other mature students. Most of the techniques they have learned previously have been pretty standard but, every one, without exception, had learned to turn pots by securing them to the wheel-head with pieces of clay. I learned that particular method myself from James Tower at Bath Academy of Art in 1953 and continued to use it until 1962 when Derek Emms at

Stoke-on-Trent College of Art taught me a superior method, which I have used and demonstrated ever since.

The wheel-head is well wetted. The inverted pot is held against the moving wheel-head and rotated in an anti-clockwise direction a little faster than the speed of the wheel. This flattens the rim of the pot slightly and helps it to grip the wheel-head. As the rim begins to grip remove the hand supporting it and sharply tap the fullness of the side of the pot towards the centre of the wheel. If it should grip the wheel too tightly before it is 'on centre' grab the pot to dislodge it, run the rim around in the moisture on the wheel-head and tap it again in the centre.

Once the pot sits 'on centre' apply the point of a wooden skewer to the edge of the pot to secure it firmly in place. The great advantage of this method is that one has a completely uninterrupted view of the profile of the pot. When turning is complete, I 'stop' the pot with both hands as the wheel turns and it should easily lift off. The same method can be used to centre the pot on its base while one turns off the extra thickness left on the rim when throwing, to facilitate this method of turning.

I like my students to learn this method of centring by first practising the 'tap to centre' method with an inverted biscuit or glazed pot on a dry wheel-head. They then go on to try centring tea plates, saucers, plastic yoghurt pots, fifty pence pieces etc. until they become really proficient. To date, no student learning this technique has ever wanted or needed to revert to the old method. A little determined practice is all that is required. **ED**

● **IT SOMETIMES HAPPENS** that when preparing to turn the foot of a pot one finds that the waste to be removed is not concentric with the pot proper, and may even have considerable roughness due, for example, to finger pressure dents if there had been trouble in removing the pot from the wheel. It then becomes very difficult to turn off the uneven parts, as the turning tool will tend to bounce and chatter. A very effective solution is to use a needle in a manner similar to trimming a rim.

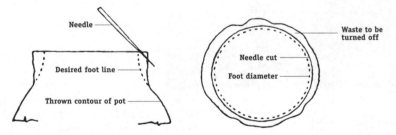

After first turning the bottom flat (starting at the centre and working outwards) take a needle and insert it at an angle, just outside the desired finished foot diameter, and gently thrust it through the clay as the wheel turns at a moderate speed. This will cut through inside the rough contours, leaving a clean circle ideal for starting off a smooth cut with a conventional turning tool. **LEW**

● **ANOTHER TIP WHEN** turning pots using the method of sticking the pot on to a dampened wheel-head. When turning large batches at high speed, I used to dip a sponge into a bowl of water to wet the wheel-head. I found it irksome to have to dry my fingers each time before commencing turning – and I was always losing the sponge! Now I simply dip a small paintbrush into water, or slip and apply it as required. This is a faster, more accurate and cleaner method. I can even enjoy my tea and biscuits in comfort – but no more sponge fingers. **SB**

● **POTTERY CAN BE** turned to a finished size, with confidence, if there is a method of copying and comparing the internal and external profiles. Soldering wire can be used for this purpose since it does not spring away from the pot when it is pressed against it.

The inside profile is copied as a reference and then compared with the changing external profiles as the turning progresses. This will still work even if the opening into the pot is smaller than the general diameter of the pot.

Carefully close the internal profile so that it can be extracted... then open it out so that the 'opening in the profile' matches the measured diameter of 'the opening in the pot'. **JVEGM**

At the South Wales Potters Conference Colin Pearson demonstrated his double calliper used for checking the thickness of clay during turning (below). D Metcalff and Peter Clarke suggest methods of making your own.

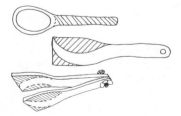

● **QUICK AND CHEAP** callipers can be made from two flat beechwood spatulas, which can be obtained cheaply from Woolworths' cooking ware section. Cut the wide end of each spatula into a curve, then fix both together with a butterfly nut and bolt through the holes usually there for hanging purposes. **DM**

● **VERY OFTEN IT** is difficult to judge exactly the thickness of a pot wall when trying to thin it down during turning. A pair of equal callipers can easily be made out of stiffboard or, with a bit more effort, by fretting out of thin ply or plastic sheet. Illustrated is the set I made recently which gives, at the outer end, the exact thickness of the wall inside the pot. **PC**

Many potters use chucks for turning. Alan H Bolton, Tom Westman, and Pauline Beresford have suggestions, while John VEG Mitchell outlines a turning aid.

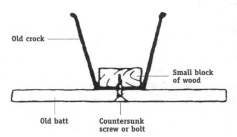

Old crock

Small block of wood

Old batt   Countersunk screw or bolt

● **AFTER THROWING NUMEROUS** chucks at the same time as throwing bellied pots I found the chucks were invariably too dry or too damp. I then started using an old pottery crock (flowerpot) bolted to an old batt and have since done the same with various sized crocks so I now always have the right sized chuck ready to hand. **AHB**

● **WHEN PLACING A** pot upside-down onto a clay chuck for secondary throwing, for example when throwing the base of a goblet bowl or foot-ring, the upturned pot has a maddening tendency to adhere to the chuck. Despite all efforts to throw as dry as possible, some water always trickles down and gets between pot and chuck in defiance of the laws of centrifugal force.

Adhesion can be prevented by interposing a piece of cloth between chuck and pot. Examination of the type of cloth found most suitable for the purpose revealed it to be a thin cotton-type material which in better days had been part of a garment of ladies' night attire.

To sum up. First throw your chuck to the appropriate size and shape to receive the upturned pot. There is no need to wait until the chuck is leatherhard. (If thrown on a batt, batt and chuck can later be removed, wrapped in polythene and stored almost indefinitely.) **TW**

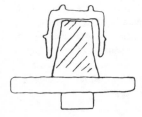

● **THE ILLUSTRATED METHOD** of turning repetition-thrown cylinders has many advantages: in supporting the base rather than the rim of the pot it helps prevent sagging, it can accommodate slight variations in size and is particularly helpful if the pots have dried out slightly more than required. It is, I believe, a traditional method in some Japanese potteries. **PB**

● **USE A LENGTH** of 16mm diameter dowel rod to help control the turning tool while working the foot of a pot. Place the end of the dowel on the bottom of the tray. Grasp it with the left hand approximately level with the base of the upturned pot. Rest the wrist of the right hand holding the turning tool on the thumb and extended first finger of the hand grasping the dowel as shown. Adjust the position of both hands together to find the best position for turning. **JVEGM**

A variety of hints associated with turning have been submitted by Elana Morris, Ellen Curran, Susan Bennett, and Lakshmi Murthy.

● **WHEN TRIMMING SOFT** pots, in order to prevent the base from sinking in, use any lids like jam jars, any size, as needed. Put on top of the base. The lid helps to spread out the finger pressure without sinking. **EM**

● **I HAVE FOUND** that 12 × 12" acoustic ceiling tiles work very well for handling and stacking flat plates and low bowls that are awkward to handle by themselves when trimming, etc. They are lightweight, smooth on one side (or both) last as long as one takes care of them and one on the top as well as the bottom of a plate helps to equalise the drying. **EC**

● **THIS IS A** tip I learned while attending a porcelain workshop at Wobage Farm. An unacceptably high proportion of the flat-based porcelain bottles and filigree candle-holders I was producing were cracking – sometimes not all the way through, often just a series of fine surface cracks that could not be disguised by smoothing over. It was suggested that turning might help. I now turn all thrown porcelain and the problem is solved. As an incidental bonus, the look and feel of my work has improved too. **SB**

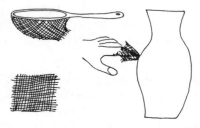

● **FOR FINISHING ARTICLES** in the green stage, sandpaper is of course widely used, but the paper wears away very quickly and a fresh piece is always required. A better solution I have found is using broken sieves. Once a sieve gets torn, I remove the mesh from the frame and save it. The mesh is now further cut up into little bits – squares of about two inches. These can easily wrap around the forefinger and finishing of products becomes very easy. Different mesh sizes could correspond to different grades of sandpaper. Mesh also lasts much longer than sandpaper. **LM**

A simple method (as most good methods are) of correcting rim distortions, comes from Tony Wells. The only trouble is that clay likes to go 'out of shape' again once it has been there – see, for example, Michael Cardew's chapter in *A Pioneer Potter* on clay memory.

● **WHILST FIXING HANDLES** on large numbers of thrown beakers, to be ready for a Christmas order, I found that quite a few suffered a slight distortion on the rim which was not easy to correct accurately by eye. I had a conical pot made for a test glaze to hand and found that I could quickly correct the distortions on the rims by inserting the pot into the beakers, and giving a slight twist. With care so that the rims are not split by excess pressure this became the final check for accuracy on all my beakers, and of course the conical shape allows the implement to be used for a wide range of rim diameters. After the original pot was broken it was a simple matter to throw another one. **TW**

The making of turning tools from scrap attracted several contributors. Some of these are to be found in the tools, equipment and materials chapter but here are three unusual ones from Australia (C M Grieve), China (Mary Rich), and from L E Wells.

● **AN INEXPENSIVE TURNING** tool can be made from a bobby-pin and the outside case of a Biro. Open the bobby-pin and reshape with pliers. Place the two ends in the small end of the Biro (after removing the writing part). Use a match to heat the plastic and while hot and soft squeeze over the bobby-pin with a pair of pliers. Various shapes can be made to suit all manner of turning needs. **CMG**

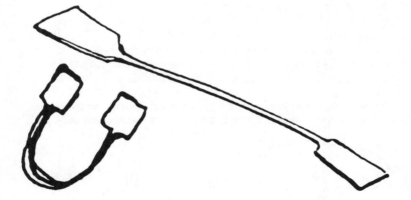

● **THE ABOVE TURNING** tool is cut from very wide bamboo. Heavier, chisel-shaped ends with thin flexible middle used as a hooped turning tool, approximately 7" in length. **MR**

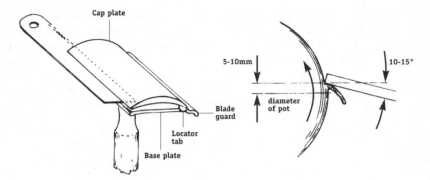

● **BY MODIFYING AN** old-type safety razor a holder for a variety of cutting blades is produced, giving a most versatile turning tool (see the rough sketch, which is not to scale). Cut off the locator tabs at both ends of one side of the cap plate, and also the blade guard along one side of the base plate. The cutting blade, say a short length of a broken hacksaw blade, or one of the disposable blades now easily available in DIY shops, is positioned and clamped by screwing up the razor handle. If the handle feels too short, a little inventiveness should find a solution – I have an old cistern chain wooden handle bored out to take the razor handle drive-in fit.

Caution – the disposable blades being of hard steel keep their edge well and are really sharp, so take good care until you are fully used to them.

They are quite brittle, so the shape can be modified by snapping off small pieces with strong pliers – protect your hands with thick cloth. The new edge is then cleaned up on a grindstone, but keep very cool by frequently dipping the blade in cold water, otherwise the hardness (temper) may be lost. This applies also when grinding hacksaw blades.

The cutting edges of tool intended for turning clay should be ground to 45°; but in fact as many potters will already know, a square edge (e.g. the back of a hacksaw or the edge of steel strapping used on packing cases) will cut quite well if applied to the work with a reverse rake (see the enlarged sketch). **LEW**

Finally, noticed by Mary Davies in Yixing, an unusual casserole shape (similar to our cake or savarin mould) which will test your throwing and turning skills.

Chapter 3
Finishing and handbuilding

Avoiding lips and spouts that dribble back down the body of the pot when used for pouring is a perennial challenge. A fairly sharp, well turned-down lip helps and two more elaborate suggestions come from an anonymous potter in Stevenage, and from L E Wells of Northampton. John Harlow shows an ingenious gadget for cutting teapot spouts, while David Lloyd Jones ensures they are cut straight.

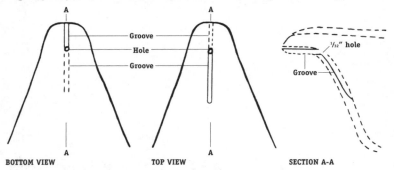

BOTTOM VIEW   TOP VIEW   SECTION A-A

● **HERE IS AN** intriguing solution to the dripping spout problem. The spout is on a factory-made German porcelain coffee pot made by a pottery called Melitta. I have tried to make it drip but failed.

A small hole about $1/32$" is drilled through the spout and two grooves are gouged out from this hole. One on the underside to the edge of the lip and the second from the hole down the inner side of the spout. **ANON**

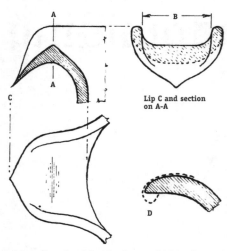

Lip C and section on A-A

● **WHAT SHAPE CONSTITUTES** the perfect jug lip? Indeed can good fluid control be obtained from an aesthetically pleasing shape of lip? In the hope of deriving sound advice from experienced potters, I have roughly sketched out what appear to me to be the theoretical essentials for good pouring.

1. Adequate width of throat, B, for the amount of fluid to be poured.

2. A well defined weir, section A-A, to cut the flow as the jug is returned to the vertical.

3. A very sharp lip, C, affording the minimum of horizontal area upon which a drop can form, and with a sharply rising back up which a drop cannot climb, as can occur in a lip shaped like D.

A lip made to this design would not be very pleasing to look at, and also would be extremely fragile. I wonder whether a guaranteed non-drip lip is possible in ceramics. (Compare with the shape of the lips in stainless steel teasets.) **LEW**

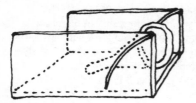

● **CUTTING SPOUTS TO** fit teapots: nail two pieces of plywood to wooden base and make curved saw cut through both walls. Place thrown spout inside as shown in the diagram and pull a fine cutting wire down the saw cut to shape spout. **JH**

● **IN THE PAST** I have lost many teapots because the spout has not rotated the correct amount in the glaze fire however carefully one may judge the offset when cutting the lip in the raw state. I overcame this by throwing the spout with the wheel going anti-clockwise then clockwise in more or less equal amounts. This neutralises the throwing tensions in the clay and the spout lip can be cut straight. **DLJ**

Four aspects of lid fitting are dealt with by Sheila Tyas, Sheila Wood, Alison McKay and Murray Cheesman.

● **LIGHT 'SAFE' LIDS** for tea and coffee pots. **ST**

● **IF, LIKE ME,** you find that your good-fitting lids fit a little too well, having been dried in situ to keep the shape, and at leatherhard stage get stuck, try piercing a hole with a needle in the base and blowing in it. The top pops off as if by magic, and a small amount of clay rubbed over the hole seals it without trace. **SW**

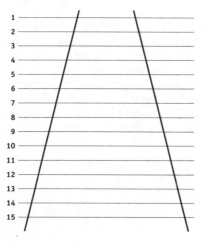

● **THE PROBLEM I** have come across with lidded pots is that sometimes at the lid turning stage, the lid breaks or I am just not pleased with it. To then throw a new lid to fit the old pot has in the past for me been guesswork because the pot has shrunk an unknown amount. However I came across a simple but fail-safe way to ensure my newly thrown lids would fit yesterday's pots by making a graph. I used A4 lined paper for ease. The angle of the diagonal lines is personal choice. The graph hangs on the wall near my wheel. Now when I throw I number each pot with its calliper reading from the graph. **AM**

● **WHEN THROWING LIDDED** jars, the temptation is to leave making the lids until the batch of jars is finished, which, if the batch is of any size, can become a chore. My suggestion for an alternative approach is to 'grub' (or weigh out) sufficient clay to make both pot and lid, treating the central lump as one would the cone when throwing off the lump, and making the lid specific to each jar.

It is arguably easier to adjust the size of the jar than it is the lid, but if one prefers the reverse method one simply makes a jar first and then starts the above process, throwing the lid for the previous jar each time and measuring in the usual way. Once the lid has been cut off, the lump may need re-coning, but this method has the advantage of minimising the risk of spiral cracking in lids thrown off the lump in quantity, as well as providing an interesting and challenging way of working. **MC**

Water dripping down one's arm is as aggravating when pulling handles as when throwing (see page 34). Shelley Talbot has a simple solution, while Murray Cheesman is inspired by George Curtis's method of pulling handles.

● **FOR ASPIRING HANDLERS** who dislike water trickling down their forearm and dripping from their elbow, here is a simple remedy, which I worked out after a couple of trial runs. Use a piece of ½″ foam plastic about two inches wide and only just long enough to reach round your wrist. Wrap around it an old towelling face-cloth leaving a free end to overlap. Sew into place and then sew two large hooks and eyes to secure it fairly tightly. This is easily rinsed out and dried. **ST**

● **THOSE WHO HAVE** seen the BBC documentary on George Curtis (*Big Ware*) may have noticed his technique for pulling handles, which is in essence to roughly roll out a lump of clay, dip the pulling hand, clay and all, into a bucket of water, and ram the butt of the handle onto the pot, with just a couple of pushing strokes to weld it on, before pulling proper (which, if memory is to be believed, was accomplished in three or four strokes).

Doubtless the level of finish would be too crude for many tastes, but this is not inherent in the technique, and having tried this method (albeit in somewhat ham-fisted fashion), it seems to work equally well for stoneware. Perhaps the lesson to be learnt, apart form the sheer facility of the traditional potter, is that the deciding factor in whether a handle stays on a pot or not is that the clay for the pot and handle should be as close in consistency as possible, an equation that runs something like: pot as soft as can possibly be handled without distortion, handle clay soft enough to allow the maximum of plastic expression without cracking in drying. **MC**

Denis Hopking and M M Crump suggest a novel way of making oval dishes and a variation on the old method.

● **THIS IS A** quick and simple way of cutting a form into an ovoid, besides the 'leaf from the middle' method. It is done on a flat board 10″ square and an inch thick. Two screwing hooks are fixed in one end and attached to them is some two feet of very thin wire, as illustrated.

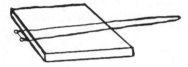

Place the leatherhard pot onto the wire, hold the pot down with the left hand and simply lift the taut wire up through the pot (lid and all). Join the two halves together with slip and soft clay. **DH**

● **THOSE WHO MAY** find it difficult to get back to their pots when they are just the right consistency for cutting and making oval should try cutting and altering them before they are removed from the wheel as follows:
1. Throw pot on batt.
2. Wet batt and wire through.
3. Cut out leaf shape.
4. Wet batt and wire through.
5. Ease dish oval.
6. Smooth small coil over scar and sponge with wheel turning slowly.
7. Wire through dry and remove batt. **MMC**

Stan Allman provides an entry for 'pinching'.

● **WHENEVER I TAKE** my old dog for a slow walk I also take a piece of clay to pinch into a small pot. During a very frosty spell of weather I found that by having the lump of clay wrapped in cellophane my hands were much warmer, and now I always 'start' a pinch pot this way whatever the weather. This also retards the cracking and flopping. **SA**

The rolling, cutting, handling, affixing and drying of clay slabs inspired entries from Jean Emmett, P H Rattray, John VEG Mitchell, Sylvia Hyman, Ted Pitman, Peter Dixon, Danny Honig, Kenneth Breese, Karen Roskell, Dean Coates and Jeanett Grube.

● **TO ROLL A** very large piece of clay use canvas, rolling pin and gauge sticks in the usual way. When the clay becomes difficult to spread because it is adhering to the canvas take away the batons and roll a second canvas lightly over the clay making a sandwich. Then seize hold of both canvases together using both hands, either on the right or at the front, and flip over with confidence. Peel off the top canvas which was the one to which the clay had previously stuck and using the gauge batons, re-roll. It will be found that the clay spreads readily. Repeat as necessary. **JE**

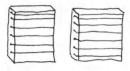

● **TO MAKE GLAZE** test tiles, I suggest that having wedged your clay and beaten into roughly the right shape as required for the finished article, then cutting is very simply done with two blocks and a nylon cord or a wire tightly stretched between them, either by using a harp or stretched by hand.

Each block is drilled at intervals of ³⁄₈″ giving six drillings equally spaced. A saw cut is made to each drilling to allow the wire to enter the drilling. The blocks are made at least 2″ square to provide an ample base when being slid along while cutting and avoid toppling over. **PHR**

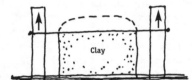

● **I USE THE** handles of a cut-off wire as thickness guides when cutting slabs of clay. The wire is attached to the handles off-centre (see diagram, above). The amount the wire is off-centre determines the thickness of the slab. For the first cut the handles are reversed to point down. It is very quick. **JVEGM**

● **I HAVE FOUND** Pellon interlining to be the ideal surface for all slab work with clay. Since it is a non-woven fabric it leaves no textural imprint on the clay. It is tough, practically non-absorbent, almost wrinkle-proof, washable in a washing machine, and therefore can be used repeatedly with different kinds of clay. I use it on my Bailey electric slab-maker for rolling out large slabs of clay and also under all work-in-progress as it allows the work to shrink freely without clinging. The roll of Pellon I have was given to me by a clothing manufacturer but I think it is available in most fabric stores. It is available in several thicknesses but I prefer the thickest and also the widest which, I believe, is 46 inches. It is easily cut with scissors. It is a perfect surface on which to place extruded or pulled handles before applying to the pots, if that is the method used. In my studio Pellon has completely replaced the use of newspaper or canvas and has made possible some techniques which were not possible before I discovered its many uses. I understand that a similar fabric, Vilene, is available in the UK. **SH**

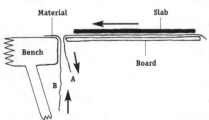

● **TO MOVE A** slab of soft clay which might tear or distort if lifted by hand, place the board with slab or clay (or material) close to the end of the bench.

Pulling down at A will cause the slab to move on to the bench where it will pick up the piece of material B carrying it with it on the bench top. **TP**

● **I RECENTLY HAD** cause to join a large number of slabs at an angle of 60°. This makes butting impossible. To avoid the tedious cutting of slab edges for mitring I made the following device.

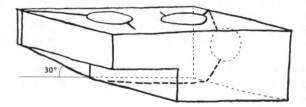

Cut a piece of wood as shown incorporating the angle required – in this case 30°. Unwind a single strand from a steel cutting wire and stretch it taut around one end of the block as shown. To fix the ends down wind the wire round drawing-pins and hammer them down hard. Make sure that the wire bites into the wood at the two places circled so that it does not pull away when cutting.

The method of use is fairly obvious. The tension on the wire can be increased by pulling the wire sideways on the back surface and holding it with another drawing pin. I found that the single strand was quite strong enough to cut leatherhard clay although a stronger wire may be needed for coarsely grogged clay. The loose ends, which can be painfully sharp, can be cut very close with a pair of scissors. **PD**

● **FOR (FREQUENT) SLAB** makers who do not use a mechanical slab roller, you can roll out any thickness from 2-10 millimetres by using knitting needles instead of slats of wood. If you make your slab on a separate board, you can lay the knobs at the needles' ends over the edge, thus achieving uniform thickness. For a longish slab you can move your needles from one side of the board to the other, moving them along the clay. **DH**

● **IF YOU SAVE** your plastic washing up liquid containers, then fill them with clay slurry using a funnel, then replace the plastic top, it will keep your slurry moist for ages. It can then be squeezed out in a controllable jet for joining clay together at leatherhard stage. **KB**

● **WHEN ROLLING THIN** pieces of porcelain and stoneware clays, I find rolling the clay on the cotton-coated side of a PVC apron gives an excellent non-stick fine grain; just bung the apron in the wash and it comes out perfectly clean for the next rolling session. **KR**

● **DRYING CLAY SLABS** quickly without warping is best achieved by allowing air to circulate underneath and on top of the slab allowing even drying. There are several ways to do this but one innovative method I have come up with is to place partially dry slabs onto bubblewrap, bubble side up – the gaps between the bubbles allow air circulation beneath the slabs, providing more even drying. **DC**

1 2 3

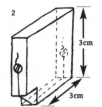
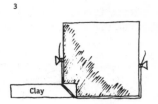

● **INSTEAD OF CUTTING** slabs with a knife you can fashion a tool that makes it easier for you. You need a piece of hardwood, a small saw, two small screws, a screwdriver and a piece of cutting wire.

Saw the wood into a square 3 × 3cm and make a little notch in one of the corners (see figure 1). This notch must be as wide as your clay slab is thick. For example, if you have a clay slab that is 0.5cm thick you make a notch of 0.5 × 0.5cm. Make a groove to insert your cutting wire and screw in your screws in the places shown (figure 2).

Cut your slab as shown in figure 3. **JG**

Tilemaking is associated with slabbing, and suggestions come from a book on William de Morgan by Jon Catleugh, and from Peter Crotty.

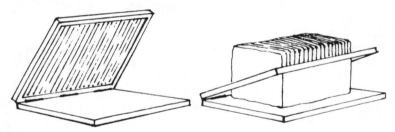

● **THE ABOVE DRAWING** of William de Morgan's tile cutting harp is taken from *William de Morgan Tiles* by Jon Catleugh, published by Trefoil Books, 1983. **JC**

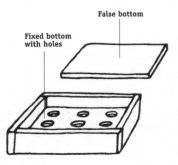

False bottom

Fixed bottom
with holes

● **TILE MAKING BOX:** To make a 6″ tile, construct a square box as diagram, allowing for shrinkage. Place false bottom in box and sprinkle interior with fireclay, having oiled the sides with linseed to stop tile sticking. Press clay into box working from centre outwards. Make sure clay is proud of the top of the box then scrape off excess with metal rule. Place a batt on top and invert the box and push down on the false bottom through holes in the base to remove tile. **PC**

Ian D Smith uses slabs for making coil pots, while John VEG Mitchell has a solution to prevent sagging coil pots.

● **AS WITH MANY** of the best tips and wrinkles, I cannot remember where I came across the following method of coil making. It may even have been in an ancient copy of *Ceramic Review*. I am a teacher of pottery dealing with groups of between ten and thirty pupils and I find the illustrated method of coil pot making to be much simpler than the traditional making of sausages of clay into coils. This method has also been used successfully with night-school groups and children in special schools.

Roll out the clay in a slab or sheet to the required thickness for the wall – using roller guides. Cut parallel strips across the clay; the distance between the cuts is equivalent to the height of each coil. Join the coils to the base and each other in the usual manner.

There are a number of advantages with this method in my situation as a teacher. Less drying out of the coils due to less handling; a more rapid rate of production in limited lesson time; and a more uniform width and height to each layer. Admittedly, handling the clay is an advantage to the pupil and the more traditional methods of coil production can give a more distinctive individual appearance to pots. However, these aspects can be concentrated upon at a different stage – especially after the successful completion of a first coil pot. **IDS**

● **WHEN MAKING LARGE** coiled pots, striving to get height in the minimum of time, too many coils are placed on top of each other – the pot sags. To save time, coil the pot in two or three sections, then join them together at a later time, when they are firm enough to support the weight of each other. When starting the second or third section, aim to have a thicker coil at the base, then the sections can be luted together without thinning the joints. **JVEGM**

A small but varied group of tips connected with handbuilding comes from Bob and Paula Winokur, Phyllis Beeching, Audrey Blackman, John VEG Mitchell and Brenda Angel.

● **WE HAVE FOUND** that an ordinary hand-held hair dryer is very useful for drying strategic parts of handbuilt sculptural objects which need to be stiffened to enable further work to be carried out. **BW/PW**

● **I USE AN** ordinary india-rubber eraser for getting into corners etc. where fingertips cannot – and it leaves no nail mark. **PB**

● **FOR ALL THE** years that I have been making pottery figures I have found it progressively more difficult to move the dry work from board to batt – earthenware, stoneware and now porcelain, which needs so many props. Long ago I tried building direct onto the batt but the base, which must remain moist, stuck to the rough batt. Yvonne Cuff solved my problem by suggesting newspaper on the batt. I visited Mildred Slatter and found she had broken one of her elaborate and historically accurate trains (taking weeks to make) in moving it. As it has taken me decades and Mildred years to arrive at our solution, I feel it may save others if we pass on this tip. **AB**

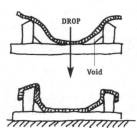

● **THE CLAY HAS** been rolled out into a thin sheet and with an impressed texture. It has been draped over a wooden mould to form a shallow dish or tray.

How do you get the clay to follow the contours of the mould into the corners? If you use a rubber kidney to smooth the clay, your texture will be lost. So instead, drop the clay and the mould flat on to the floor. Drop it three feet or more – the clay will spread into the mould. **JVEGM**

● **AS A HANDBUILDER** I am constantly looking for ways to keep the rim damp while the rest of the pot, built by coiling, stiffens up. I have now found that a layer of cling film is highly effective. Once smoothed into place, it really does prevent moisture from escaping, and has proved a boon. A friend now uses it for thrown pots, wrapping the stiffened pot up completely until required. **BA**

Advice on plaster of Paris and a note on the use of wooden moulds comes from Christa Reichel, Jean Emmett, Douglas Eaglesham, Tony O'Donovan and Eileen Lewenstein. Brief notes from Janet Cottrell and Kenneth Breese look at a simple hump mould (balloons come in many shapes and sizes) and a method of guaranteeing easy release.

● **I HAVE BEEN** making pottery in the south of Ireland for many years, and found when I first came over from London that I could not get potter's plaster or fine white Italian for making press-moulds.

In my remote farm situation all I could get was builders' plaster, or common 'hard wall' plaster, so I decided to try and use it. I made moulds of flat ware, dinnerplates, breakfast plates and seven sizes of oval dishes. I produced dishes from these moulds weekly and daily, hundreds and hundreds over six years, then sold the pottery with the moulds. Three years later and those very same moulds were still going strong. The extra bother and a bit of patience when making them – as builder's plaster obviously is not as easy to handle – is well worth it. They never chipped or broke and I could make three dishes off a mould in a row before the plaster got really wet. I dried them on boiling hot kilns, and did all the things one is not supposed to do, and they still survived. **CR**

● **WHEN MAKING PLASTER,** I find it helpful to just line the bucket with a plastic bag. When the job is done it becomes a simple matter to get rid of spare plaster as the whole lot goes into the dustbin, bag and all – none at all down the drain because there is no need to wash the pail. **JE**

● **THERE ARE TWO** well-known methods for determining the relative quantities of water and plaster required to make a satisfactory mixture for moulds. One can sift in the plaster until it just breaks the surface of the water or, for more accuracy, one can measure the volume or weight of water and then calculate the amount of plaster to be weighed and added. The first method requires considerable experience for one to achieve uniformity; the second is time consuming and necessitates the use of a scale. In place of these a new method is suggested as described below. It requires neither arithmetical calculation nor measurement of weight or volume.

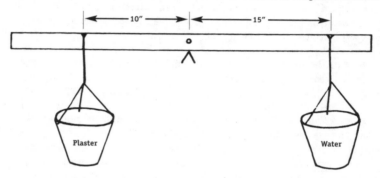

Turn a wooden yardstick into a balance by drilling a hole in the centre and driving a nail through for a loose fit to attach it to an upright support. The nail becomes the fulcrum. Now make a notch along the upper edge 10" left of centre and another notch 15" right of centre. From each notch suspend a container such as a plastic pail. Label the left notch and container 'Plaster' and the right ones 'Water'. Since one container is closer to the fulcrum than the other there will be a lack of balance if they are equal in weight. Correct the imbalance by taping a small bit of metal (such as a few nails) to the appropriate pail.

Now the balance is ready for use and no weights are necessary. Simply put any desired quantity of water in the water container and then put sufficient dry plaster in the other container to balance it So long as the suspension is from the notched areas the proportions will be in the commonly used ratio of 1lb of water to 1½lbs of plaster. Alternatively one can of course choose any quantity of plaster and balance it with water.

What will be the volume of the mixture? By test 1 part of water added to dry plaster in the above proportion becomes for practical purposes 1½ parts of liquid plaster. Accordingly one can extend the usefulness of the apparatus by estimating the volume of the mixed plaster required and using two-thirds of this figure for the volume of water needed. Put this quantity in the water container and balance it with plaster. When mixed the proportions will be correct and the total volume will be sufficient.

Should one require a plaster harder than that given by the above ratio cut the notch for the water container further from the fulcrum. By this means a larger amount of plaster will be put on the balance for a given quantity of water. If a softer plaster is desired move toward the fulcrum. One inch in either direction will make a substantial difference. In each case balance the empty containers as described.

Most households have the materials necessary for construction of the balance. Those handy with tools will no doubt devise their own method of construction. A lath or other straight stick will do instead of a yardstick. Plastic tubs commonly used for food products such as ice cream serve very well as containers for the water and plaster on the balance. Suspend them with string or wire as in the diagram. The support for the balance can be a board attached to a bracket jutting out from the wall, or a length of 2 × 2" board extending vertically from a base wide enough to prevent tipping. One can improve the stability of the apparatus by cementing a wooden spool over the hole in the yardstick to make a better bearing for the nail put through it. So long as the balance moves freely the results will be consistently accurate. **DE**

● **IF PART OF** the rim and side of plaster moulds is painted with wax, slip does not adhere when poured out so saving the trouble of cleaning up. Any type of mould, such as those for slip trailed work can benefit from this. **TO'D**

● **IN TUNG KWAN,** China, wooden moulds were lined with fabric to ease their removal. The wooden mould of the giant jigger and jolley in which blanks were formed for final shaping by paddle and anvil was lined with a cloth sack into which a batt was dropped for each pot. When the jolleying was completed two potters, one on either side, lifted the clay form by the edges of the sack up out of the mould and on to a waiting stand. The cloth lining, now an outer skin, was dramatically peeled down and the pot was lifted still on its batt by the aid of two lengths of rope made fast under the batt to the yard outside.

I have previously lined all sorts of bowls and objects with newspaper for press moulding, but find fabric a useful alternative. **EL**

● **BALLOONS INFLATED TO** the required size make excellent hump moulds – to release simply pop the balloon. **JC**

● **FOR EASE OF** clay release when using plaster moulds, dust the cast with a small amount of talcum powder applied with a soft brush. **KB**

Penultimate in this section are two notes on making holes: a 'free' tool from Maria Jones (more ideas for hole-makers can be found in the Tools chapter); and cider jar taps from Ray Finch, a potter with much experience of these handsome pots.

● **TO MAKE A** neat round hole on the sides of curved pots such as cheese shakers etc. press a metal lipstick tube and turn to remove plug of clay in slightly under leatherhard pot. To finish to size – push in cork and turn until desired depth is achieved. The plug of clay will shake out during general clean up of pot. To glaze, replace old cork and dip. **MJ**

● **FIXING CIDER JAR** taps:
1. Jar taps must be fitted in cork.
2. Make the bung hole in the jar to take the size of cork you intend to use. After firing this gives a good driving fit.
3. Bore the cork to fit the tap. This is best done with a circular rasp bit, of the correct size, in a power drill, (preferably in a drill stand). Hold the cork when drilling, with a pair of grips, NOT with your fingers.
4. Ease the bored cork onto the tap, first wetting both, and drive gently into the jar with a wooden mallet. **RF**

Finally a system of base levelling from L E Wells.

● **PARTICULARLY IN SLAB,** coiled, sculptured or any non-thrown work, it can be difficult to make the piece stand firm and true. Glass or sandpaper will work but quickly clogs. A very useful 'levelling board' can be made by affixing a piece of mild steel expanded metal sheet of ¼" or ⅜" mesh upon a heavy ply or block-board base. (Not the aluminium variety of mesh used for loudspeaker grills – it is too soft.) It is the material often used by builders as a base for plaster work; and your best chance of obtaining a small piece (say 12" to 18" square and flat) will be to approach your local builder. Use it with the sharp side of the mesh upper-most. The work should be at least leatherhard, and could be completely dry. Hold the piece steady with both hands and move it with a rotary motion over the surface of the mesh. The high spots will quickly disappear. **LEW**

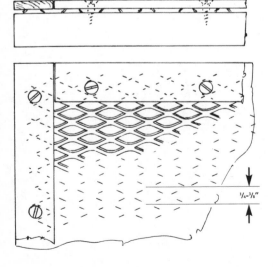

Chapter 4
Decoration

Contributions concerning the tools and techniques used in the decoration of pots and dishes are varied. Potters' seals are included in this section as they can be very decorative in their own right. The few tips on brushes come from Tony O'Donovan, Alan H Bolton, David Frith and Alan Ashpool; Susan Bennett discovers the benefits of petrol, while Anne Duffy suggests an alternative for drawing fine lines.

● **A LONG LINING** brush, because it is floppy, is difficult to use: a short one does not hold enough colour to go round a big dish. So take a large conventional brush, and shorten the outside hairs, as per diagram. You now have a short manageable brush with a large reservoir. **TO'D**

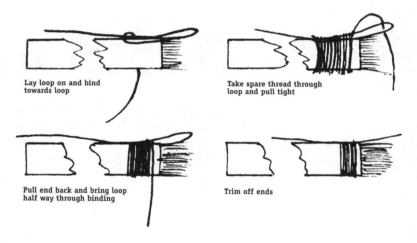

Lay loop on and bind towards loop

Take spare thread through loop and pull tight

Pull end back and bring loop half way through binding

Trim off ends

● **IF YOU HAVE** had trouble with the hair end of Chinese brushes splitting and therefore odd hairs sticking out at unwanted angles, try binding them with waxed twine or button thread as shown above. This method loses the ends. **AHB**

● **THE BENT WIRE** rack that David Frith has devised for resting brushes over hot wax. **DF**

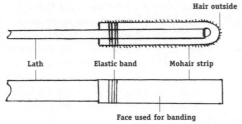

Hair outside

Lath Elastic band Mohair strip

Face used for banding

● **SIMPLE BANDING BRUSHES** can be made by cutting narrow strips of varying widths from a mohair painting pad refill, folding them over a lolly stick or short length of lath so that the hair is on the outside, and binding them to the sticks/laths with an elastic band as shown in the diagram. The strips should be about 10-12 centimetres long. After use the strips can be easily removed for washing. **AA**

● **I HAD ALWAYS** understood the Brushwax I used for resist work was water soluble and therefore cleaned my brushes in warm soapy water. However, after a while beads of wax clogged up the hairs and they became unfit for use – a sad fate for Chinese and Japanese calligraphic brushes.

I was cleaning up recently after a lustre session using petrol – which works brilliantly by the way (I keep the petrol in a safe container and well away from the studio and decant a small amount as I need it). I tried dipping a stiffened, clogged-up wax brush in the solution. The wax seemed to dissolve, and the brush became malleable again – a great relief and a great saving. Do not be stuck up – try it yourself. **SB**

● **TO MAKE THIN** lines for writing/patterns with slip a good alternative to a slip trailer or brush is a large darning needle. Dip the 'eye' in slip and use as a pencil or pen. **AD**

Lyndon Thomas reminds us of the virtues of the ancient Chinese inkstone.

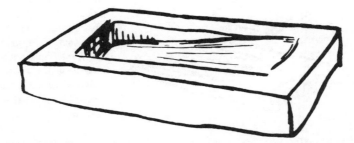

● **AN IDEAL PALETTE** for oxide decoration is a chinese ink stone, now readily available in Britain. Alternatively one could be easily made from a slab of fairly smooth clay. The great advantage of the ink stone is that the greatest concentration of colour is collected on the tip of the brush giving a brush stroke of graduated tonal quality on the surface of the pot. **LT**

E M English, Susan Bennett, Bolton Technical College, Anne Leon and Cynthia Wardley deal with moulded relief, filigree, combing and texturing respectively.

● **HAVING HAD SEVERAL** frustrated attempts to free pressed clay from shallow plaster moulds to create relief decoration, one of our keen students has found an easy method.

1. Cut a suitably sized piece of plastic from an empty washing-up liquid container.
2. Spread clay into mould and smooth with palette knife to level of plaster.
3. Press piece of plastic firmly onto clay.
4. Lift plastic, and clay relief should come away from mould attached to plastic.
5. The edges of relief may then be trimmed with needle point smoothed with damp fine textured sponge or damp paint brush and pulled away from plastic to fix onto clay shape with slip.

N.B. a piece of polythene is too flimsy to be effective. **EME**

● **IF YOU HAVE** recourse to wielding a scalpel to produce fine filigree work, here is a tip specially 'cut out' for you.

I produce a great deal of filigree work in both stoneware clay and porcelain. The consistency of the clay at the moment of incision is crucial to the success of the designs. A Cheddar cheese hardness is ideal. However, sometimes, especially with porcelain, the surface forms a thin crust and the sharpest blade produces a crumbly edge instead of a clean cut. Try dipping the blade in olive oil – it helps to prevent it from tearing the clay, and produces a crisper, smoother edge. I am told that George Owen, who used to produce fine filigree pieces for Worcester, employed this trick to make the tiny waste fragments adhere to his blade, thus preventing them from falling between the pierced surface and the inner wall of his pieces. **SB**

Glue together

● **A SIMPLE AND** elegant device for combing patterns in clay may be made from Boots' toothpicks, held firmly together by gluing a piece of plywood across the flat facets at the handle end of these picks. **BTC**

● **BEFORE THROWING OUT** rusty wire whisks, potato peelers or other potentially useful texture tools, spend a few minutes pressing them into clay. The handles of whisks that are wrapped with wire give fossil-like indents; the opposite end of the whisk gives a star. Potato peelers with a slot running down the middle of the blade make feather-like marks if pressed into the clay several times, side by side. Incidentally, try pressing a firm slab of clay into a cut glass bowl before making a slab pot. **AL**

● **MAKE A ROLLING** pin from soft clay, roll it with the palms of the hands over the surface of textured rock or bark. Allow to dry. When rolled over clay the imprint re-creates the original texture. The rolling pin may be biscuit-fired but lasts a good while just as it is. **CW**

Further ideas for texturing clay come from Ian Grant and Martin Cowley.

● **I RECENTLY DISCOVERED** in my garden shed a sheet of frosted Perspex, evidently intended for a window pane. The frosted effect was achieved by a pattern of deep indentations on one surface of the sheet. It struck me at once that this might be useful for texturing leatherhard pots.

One simply rolls the pot over the indented surface to produce a banded or all-over pattern, according to the shape of the pot. The depth of the pattern, of course, depends on the amount of pressure one can safely exert on the pot. Care must also be taken, for obvious reasons, not to apply the glaze too thickly. Transparent glazes, or those which pool well, would probably be most effective. My sheet of Perspex was a lucky find, but I imagine it can be bought at a builder's merchant. **IG**

● **HAVING SPENT MANY** hours making rollers and roulettes out of bits of dowel with Meccano handles, it is a pleasure to discover a ready-made version for use in the classroom or studio. Castors from old items of furniture can be used to imprint designs; the small ones are best, and if the surface is made from rubber, plastic or wood, designs are easily carved into it. The ends are often threaded, and it is a simple matter to make and fit a handle. **MC**

Two similar ideas for cheap slip trailers from Adrian Phelps and M A Hatfield; Joseph Neville has a suggestion for avoiding splattering when trailing slip, Freda Earl suggests an ingenious dotter, G W A Newton offers his own version, and Bill Jones has a simple but effective idea to ensure slip stays mixed.

● **A SUITABLE ALTERNATIVE** to purchasing slip trailers is to recycle used nasal spray bottles, such as Vicks Sinex and Otrivine. These can be used as very effective slip trailers, and the nozzles can be easily adjusted to any required diameter by inserting a pin or small nail. **AP**

● **THE PLASTIC APPLICATOR** bottles supplied in home perm and home hair colourant kits make very good slip trailers when thoroughly washed. **MAH**

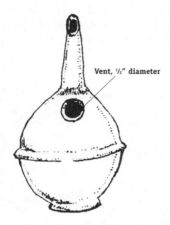

Vent, ½" diameter

● **THE DRAWBACK OF** the conventional bulb slip trailer is that, once pressure relaxes, the nozzle fills with air, and bubbling and spattering occur when the bulb is squeezed again. Obviate this defect by cutting a circular vent, about ½ inch in diameter, in the bulb. Seal off this vent with the index finger's tip while pressing the bulb, and lift away the finger when trailing stops. Air thereby enters the bulb via the trephined hole, not through the nozzle. And it is easy to fill, empty and rinse a bulb syringe by way of a vent. Such syringes have quite another practical use: aspirating supernatant water from glaze suspensions, either directly or by initiating siphonage by connecting the bulb to the end of the siphon tubing. And a trephined bulb can be left in place once siphoning has been established, provided the bore of its nozzle is sufficiently wide. **JN**

● **A GLASS EYE-DROPPER** from a bottle of eye drops (many old people use one a month for glaucoma) will produce a series of identically sized dots of slips or glaze for decoration. The bottle will protect the glass dropper when not in use. Be sure to rinse well after using as the tiny neck cannot be cleaned once it has blocked. **FE**

● **THERE HAVE BEEN** several designs for slip trailers, but no apologies for yet another. Three items are required:
1. A used (or new) wine cork.
2. A plastic bottle that takes the wine cork in the neck and is flexible. There are a range of these from used shampoo to sauce bottles.
3. A standard 3.5ml micro pastette.

Pastette

Cork and pastette

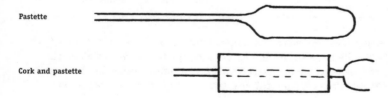

A nail is pushed through the cork so that the pastette tail can be pushed through with the bulb on the inside of the bottle. The bulb is cut in half and the tail cut to a suitable length.

The advantage of this device is that the slip can be stored in the container using the original stopper, the cork is inserted when required and washed after use. Pastettes (catalogue number LW4020) are available from: Alpha Laboratories, 40 Parham Drive, Eastleigh, Hampshire, SO50 4NN. Website: www.alphalabs.co.uk. **GWAN**

● **TO KEEP SLIPS** mixed in a squeezy bottle or slip trailer insert a ball-bearing or glass marble in with the slip. The trailer can then be shaken and stirred. Alternatively a rolled and fired ball of clay may be used instead. **BJ**

Resist techniques continue to intrigue potters and various aspects are discussed by Pauline Ashley, Bolton Technical College, Eliza Grummett, Borax Fritz, Briglin Pottery, David Hobbs, Krzysztof Buras, Ben Bates, Jane Searle (two methods), Bruno Manini, Nirmala Patwardhan, Pat Southwood and John VEG Mitchell.

● **FOR SOME TIME** I have been raw glazing using wax resist as part of my decoration. Recently I placed some green ware previously decorated with wax resisted slip on top of my hot electric kiln and found that very quickly the wax (two parts candle wax to one part paraffin) burnt away leaving a receptive surface for raw glazing. Works well with reactive slip and glaze from Taggs Yard. **PA**

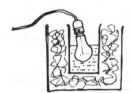

● **FOR FLAME-FREE MELTING** of paraffin wax resist mixtures, try this idea borrowed from a batik artist. A 2lb size tin is supported by crumpled newspaper insulation inside a larger tin. Heat from a 60W bulb melts wax without over-heating. My light bulb has not suffered from repeated heating and cooling, and happily stays in the tin with hard wax when not in use. **BTC**

● **AFTER MANY YEARS** of dangerous living with a lighted candle underneath an upturned flower pot, itself poised on castellated kiln props, supporting an old coffee tin bubbling smokily with hot wax, I have at last found a safe substitute.

A baby's electric feeding bottle warmer is ideal for keeping wax paraffin mixture at the right temperature. A slight adjustment to the thermostat screw underneath was the only thing I had to do to make the warmer operate at the higher temperature. **EG**

● **IF WAX RESIST** dribbles or splashes on to biscuit where it is not wanted, there is no need to biscuit fire again to get rid of it – just burn it off with a gas torch, let the pot cool and then try again (carefully this time). **BF**

● **HOT OIL/WAX RESIST** material can be tricky to control. If the wax is too hot or the brush is too heavily loaded, a run of wax from, say, the foot of the pot can occur.

If the pot is leatherhard, this run can usually be lifted off by carefully using a knife. The wax does not seem to penetrate the pores of leatherhard clay. However, if the run occurs on a biscuited pot the wax will be absorbed, and scraping or abrasion will not eliminate the now resisting surface streak.

This fault can be eliminated, however, by rubbing the affected part with a cotton bud dipped into petrol. A perfect elimination of the fault should be achieved.

Note: It is best to do this in the open air – certainly not in the studio when the kiln is operating. **BP**

● **WE FIND THAT,** despite the extra bother of heating the pot, paraffin wax is by far the most efficient for resist work. Not only does it dry instantly but it effectively resists the glaze. For some time we used household candles which worked out to be quite expensive, but we have now found that Meade-King, Robinson & Co Ltd (501 Tower Buildings, 22 Water Street, Liverpool L3 1BL, Website: www.mkr.co.uk) will supply sheets of wax at much more competitive rates. Incidentally we dilute the wax roughly half and half with paraffin (UK) and keep it hot on an electric food warmer. We bought a 25 kilo carton, which is a lot of wax, but several potters could club together. **DH**

● **A USEFUL TIP** for those who use cut resist designs is to stick them on with an emulsified glue. Plastic sheet can be used instead of paper and is useful because it does not tear. I raw glaze with a basic clear glaze which is applied to a bone dry pot over which a plastic stencil has been placed. This is then sprayed with iron oxide stain. The emulsified glue I use is called Pritt Stick and comes looking like a lipstick. The back of the plastic design is smeared with Pritt and gently padded onto the pot. This will hold under the jet of the spraying system, and burns cleanly away in the kiln. Paper designs can also be stuck, and an advantage is that this method is not messy and the glue has a pleasant and rather fragrant odour. **KB**

● **I HAVE FOUND** an effective, reusable masking material: Blu Tack. It can be used repeatedly, and without detriment to it, or the ceramic work to which it is applied, and enables one to build up, by spraying or dipping, an interesting variety of glaze overlays and textures. It works particularly well on the coarser clays, which can be awkward to mask out adequately with more conventional methods. Pinching the material between the fingers, drawing it out and thinning it at the same time, the warmth from the fingers enhances the adhesion when applied to the object. Having used Blu Tack it can be removed when the glaze layer has dried, washed under the tap, dried and used again. It has proved easy to obtain, versatile and flexible in use. **BB**

● **WHEN WISHING TO** dip a pot in glaze and avoid glazing a modelled addition try this. Wrap the modelled area in clingfilm, which will protect it from the glaze. This method can only work if there is sufficient undercut to hold the clingfilm, which is removed after glazing. **JS**

● **I HAVE RECENTLY** been painting geometric designs in slips, on a white slip background, the pattern being drawn in pencil on the leatherhard pot. I have observed that the pencil line acts as a resist, and it is possible to flood an area with a fluid slip, which goes up to the line but not over it. However, the slip easily covers any lines that you wish it to. **JS**

● **WAX RESIST HAS** a bad habit of going lumpy and however much it is cleaned it keeps on caking up. If a piece of stocking is put round the lid and carefully held on by an elastic band it will then flow out like milk. **BM**

● **WHEN I WAS** learning batik – resist-decoration on textiles – spoilt cloths were put into petrol to remove the wax. When further pieces of cloth had been given the same treatment, the petrol became 'liquid wax'. I now collect all the dripped wax from Diwali candles and put this into a bottle with petrol and within an hour this too dissolves into a 'liquid wax'. When brushed onto a pot the petrol evaporates, leaving a thin layer that effectively resists glaze. But remember: petrol is highly inflammable, so do not use near a naked flame. **NP**

● **WHEN THE PAPER** part of paper resist has disappeared due to over-drying or over-slipping it can magically be found and removed by lightly spraying with a plant mister. **PS**

● **WET NEWSPAPER, APPLIED** to leatherhard clay, makes a very good resist, with crisp edges when covered with glaze. It seems natural to remove this resist by lifting the edge of the newspaper with a needle. This will spoil the edge of the design. Instead, stick the needle into the newspaper about 12mm from the edge, then lift. The design will remain sharp and the needle mark will be clear of the edge for an easy repair. I use raw oxides mixed with clay and water for the glaze, dabbed on with a natural sponge which has been cut to get the spongy texture. I find that newspaper is the best paper to use for resists, better than heavier paper. However, wet newspaper is very difficult to control so build up the design in small sections. **JVEGM**

Two surprisingly simple systems for reproducing and repeating a design or motif are described by Susan Bennett/Earl Hyde, and Peter Dixon. These are similar in essence to methods used on Chinese porcelain in the Qing period.

● **TRANSFERRING A COMPLICATED**, or even a simple repetitive design on to clay from the drawing board without the use of transfers, sprigging, or a stamp can be a painstaking and difficult process. Here is one simple and effective method.

Draw the design as you wish it to appear on your clay surface on a sheet of tracing paper. Then, with a free-running felt-tip pen, go over the outline on the reverse side. When you are ready, simply press the paper down on your pot, which should be slightly damp, and the ink will come off the paper cleanly and clearly.

You can go over the original drawing as often as you like, or prepare any number of designs in advance.

This method is well-suited to tile decoration, depictions of scenes or characters. You can paint with oxides, use ceramic pens, sgraffito or inlay – the possibilities are limitless and give scope to the imaginative use of all sorts of decorative effects. We used the illustrated repeat caricature of ourselves on promotional items. **SB/EH**

● **IT IS POSSIBLE** to photocopy on to thin sheets of plastic using modern photocopiers. Glue the edge of a sheet of bin-liner plastic (or similar) to a piece of paper and the copy will be made on to the plastic provided you put the sheet in the magazine the right way up. The plastic does not crinkle provided it is reasonably tight. The ink will not smudge but it will come off on to leatherhard clay – given a little rubbing – cleanly and clearly. **PD**

Three tips explore some of the possibilities of printing onto clay. Ken Palmer of the Midland Potters Association gives a clever method for monoprinting using slip and newspaper, Robin Colville outlines a technique for creating photographic images on clay, while Carol Wheeler gives recipes for printing 'inks'.

● **AN AREA OF** slip is painted on to a piece of newsprint, and allowed to lose its glossy sheen. The paper is placed on the clay, slip side down. The desired decoration is drawn on the back of the paper; it can be as fine as a biro or as coarse as the end of your finger. The paper is carefully peeled off and there on the pot is your pattern in slip. A bonus is that the paper now holds a negative of your design that can be applied somewhere else on the pot or to another vessel. A variation is to transfer an area of colour – square, round, oval – and work within that area, say with sgraffito or brushwork.

A second innovative method of decoration is the painting or trailing of slip on to the inside of a plaster slip-casting mould. When the mould is filled the coloured slip is incorporated into the body of the pot. One drawback to this method is that any decoration that goes over the seam is liable to be damaged at the fettling stage, but the spot decoration is fine. **KP**

● **I HAVE RECENTLY** experimented with placing black and white photographic images onto clay.

The first stage is to determine the type of image you want. Porcelain creates a very clearly defined image but with a heavily grogged clay the liquid emulsion washes off the tips of the exposed grog leaving a flecked image.

Take clay tiles to bisque before coating them with a white glaze and firing them up to stoneware. Apply a couple of coats of yacht varnish (available from DIY stores) and leave to dry. Now coat the tiles in Liquid Light emulsion (stocked by Firstcall Photographic, details www.firstcall-photographic.co.uk) under red light conditions, seal them in a light-proof box and leave for several days to allow them to completely dry. The liquid light emulsion has to be heated slightly to improve its fluidity, so using a hairdryer to dry the tiles is not recommended.

The dried clay can now be used almost exactly like black and white photographic paper with standard darkroom equipment. Determine the exposure time required by using spare tiles as test pieces. Care must be taken when putting the tiles into the chemicals as the emulsion will wash off if rocked too vigorously in the chemical tray. When washing the tiles after exposure use a very slow trickle of water, ensuring they are not directly under the flow of the water. Washing should be extensive to remove any chemicals left on areas that remain unglazed. Once the clay is thoroughly dry another coat of varnish seals the image but is not essential if the piece is strictly decorative.

This is not precision photography due to the high number of variables in the process. However, a little patience and willingness to experiment will provide a high quality image. **RC**

● **FOR ROLLING INTO** lino, I use equal parts copper oxide and cobalt oxide, combined with acrylic medium (amount varied according to desired translucency). For screenprinting I use Potterycrafts' dark blue slip for varying proportions of cobalt oxide, black iron oxide, red iron oxide and a white slip base, sometimes adding screen printing medium. For glazing, some use earthenware translucent white vellum and fire to around 1110°C. I use stoneware white tin glaze and fire to 1240°C. **CW**

Four contributors suggest ways of dividing the surface of a pot into sections for decorating: Ken Jones, Darwin Turner, Paul Barron and C M Grieve.

● **THE USE OF** paper or thin card can provide a simple and quick method of marking segments or quartering a wheel-head for decorating purposes. Cut a circle of paper, slightly smaller than the wheel, fold it in half, quarters etc. depending on the number of even segments required. If a small circle of paper is used take care to fold it in individual sections (not quarters, eighths etc. on the same folding).

For a platter or bowl, use a slightly larger circle of paper than diameter of the pot, so that the segments are visible against the rim.

Vases and other forms; band a line around the inside or outside surface, a thin strip of card is placed on this line and cut where the ends meet to give the exact circumference. The strip can then be evenly folded into the widths required and marked against the banded line. **KJ**

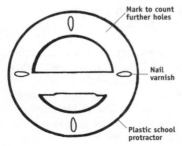

Mark to count further holes

Nail varnish

Plastic school protractor

● **I THROW CROCUS** and herb pots and have to set out the holes for cutting with a needle.

I use a child's school protractor with the cuts marked in with nail varnish. I place the protractor on the wet rim as soon as I have thrown the pot so it gets very muddy. My wheel is always clean and clear to read. I throw the pots on a batt to avoid distortion after they are cut and reduced in strength. **DT**

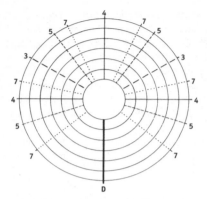

● **OFTEN SEEN IN** the decorating shops in the potteries, this simple device is not so often found in studios. Best painted in distinguishing colours on a cork table-mat with the datum-line in black, it can be centred on the banding wheel when painting or used on the bench when marking out for fluting, etc. This is the perfectionist's version; a simpler version, one giving 3, 5 and 7 would probably be adequate for most purposes, 'halvings' being done by eye. **PB**

● **A SIMPLE WAY** to mark even divisions around a pot is to string plastic drinking straws together – 5 or 3 or however many equal sections are required. The straws can be cut shorter. It is easy to mark the position for holes, or lugs, on a hanging planter by simply placing the straws on the rim of the pot and making a mark. This tool can be used to lay out an even design on a platter or bowl. **CMG**

Potters' seals or stamps have been included in this section as a decorative addition to pots: David Leach, while at the Leach Pottery, St Ives, used giant-sized seals as the sole decorative feature on the sides of casseroles. Various original ways of making stamps are suggested by Alan H Bolton, Don Witts (who both have a similar idea, though metal type will not be as readily available today), Graham Carey, Judy Glanville, J H Wood and Rosemary Metz. Tlws Johnson describes a rubber stamp which she used for repeat decorative lettering.

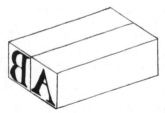

● **I READ RECENTLY** of someone who wished to hear of an alternative to biscuited clay or plaster for making seals etc. I had the same problem but solved it by scrounging the appropriate letters I needed to make my initials and town from a printer I know. I have found printers' type gives a very sharp impression and as there are so many different typefaces available it is possible to obtain the size and design to suit any seal. **AHB**

● **YOU CAN EASILY** obtain from printers, typographers, and some college printing departments, old used type of the metal (lead) kind. Most people use their initials, so you are not begging material of too great a value. You can either glue the ends together. or mount them in a sort of wooden handle, or as I do, use a soldering iron to melt the top (non-face end) of the letters together. This makes a very good seal with a crisp impression. If you are lucky or persuasive enough you can get hold of some really interesting and elegant typefaces. **DW**

● **A SEAL CAN** be made very simply, by casting the raised letters on a credit card in plaster or clay. **GC**

● **AN EASY WAY** to make your own potter's stamp. Incise your initials in firm clay as you would like them to eventually appear, either in relief or the reverse, slightly larger than you will require. Allow the clay to dry then press a piece of fresh clay into the mould leaving neat edges. This should then be dried and fired. Several can be made at once. **JG**

● **IT IS OFTEN** desirable to have stamps of various sizes to match the proportions of different pots. If your seal is of a rather intricate design it may prove difficult to make a smaller version. This problem can be eliminated by making a pressing from your large seal into a piece of clay that has a high shrinkage rate, porcelain being ideal. This is then fired, and a new seal made by using it as a die. Your new seal is thus a small replica of the original. This process can be carried out several times until the desired size or sizes have been obtained. **JHW**

● **THERE IS ONLY** a limited choice of lettering stamps suitable for various ceramic tasks. Why do ceramists not make and sell this commodity? An extensive range of 'masters' may be obtained from sign writers who can offer various methods of cutting the required letters for mould making. Ask to have letters 'reverse cut' and chamfered. When it comes to making the moulds, silicone rubber is very durable, but expensive. A cheaper alternative would be blue Gelflex. Both materials are flexible and allow for easy release. For the actual casting, try Alpha plaster mixed with polymer. Experiment is recommended.

File edges or they will register on clay work

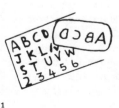  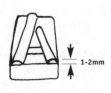

1-2mm

1   2   3   4

Materials needed include:
• Plastic lettering stencils from most office suppliers
• Buttery clay similar to T material
• Emery boards
• Fine dental tools, or similar

Method to make 'masters' and letter stamps:
1. Use the lettering impressions from sheets of plastic lettering stencils made for drafting purposes (see figure 1). Different fonts and sizes are available.
2. Roll out sheet of clay to 1cm thick; clay is best used when pliable but firm.
3. Press clay sheet gently into stencils, taking care not to press clay through to other side of stencil. A light sprinkle of talc on stencil surface helps to release clay.
4. Ensure the whole stamp is at least 1cm thick for durability. The letter will stand out from clay background surface by 1-2mm (figure 4).
5. Peel clay from stencil carefully.
6. After clay sheet is separated, trim letter (see figures 2 and 3). Do this carefully, leaving the narrowest of margin.
7. File the edges of the cut letter stamp when leatherhard. Unfiled background edges may otherwise register when stamp is used.
8. Construct a comfortable handle to be held between thumb, first and second fingers.
9. Fire unglazed clay letter stamps to stoneware temperature for durability. **RM**

● **I WAS RECENTLY** asked to make twenty-four executive gifts with the words 'BUCKINGHAM FOODS' included in the design. My prototype had the lettering in underglaze black which I painted on with a brush. However the space was very small and I found it difficult to fit all the lettering in. The black which I chose for its reliability seemed to dominate. In thinking about alternatives I decided to try a rubber stamp. I phoned a company in the yellow pages and discussed size and lettering type with them. They sent me the finished stamp by return of post. It worked perfectly. I let the porcelain dry slightly before I pressed the stamp in. This tip might be useful for anyone who has to add small neat lettering to their work. **TJ**

Very different aspects of decoration to conclude: a 'millionaire's resist' from Bolton Technical College, 'useful reflections' from Alice Bree, from Veronika von Nostitz a way of transcribing patterns, and the Japanese Mokomai technique from M M Crump. A trio of tips on the use of lustre come from Susan Bennett, Joseph Neville offers advice on adding rope patterned coils to heavily grogged clay, while Martin Cowley suggests a source of sprigs. Hannah Arnup proposes an alternative medium, a stamping aid comes from Bill Jones, and ceramic crayons are explored by the Potters' Society of Australia.

● **GOLD LUSTRE CAN** be removed with a mixture of strong nitric acid and table salt. This vile mixture will strip lustres off in a few seconds but areas to be protected can be safely shielded with wax resist. A possible decorative technique for millionaires? N.B. use this mixture with great care. **BTC**

● **IT OCCURRED TO** me recently how useful mirrors are. Not only to admire one-self in, but also to work with. I have an old dressing table mirror attached to the wall in front of my wheel. At a quick glance it is possible to get a long view of the pot being thrown without having to get off the wheel. Also, when pack-ing the glost kiln a small pocket mirror held behind pots will show you whether they are touching, but perhaps most interestingly one can use a mirror when designing decoration.

You make your drawing of whatever it is that attracts you and then hold a mirror against it at an angle of 90°. You can place the mirror on any part of the drawing, trying various positions to find the most interesting double image of the various shapes you have drawn. I used this method originally for embroi-dery, but no doubt it can be useful say in decorating dishes or bowls. It is really quite exciting – even the most arbitrary marks look quite presentable when doubled up. **AB**

● **SOME TIME AGO,** I hit on the idea of incising wet or damp clay slabs by placing notepaper with the planned design or inscription on the ware and then tracing the pattern with a blunt pencil. The result: no pesky burrs or sharp edges.

On small or awkward surfaces, however, this procedure is less satisfactory. By the time these can be handled, they are too dry to allow the paper pattern to stick and so too much slippage results. Plastic crumples and also slips.

I discovered that the cellophane windows in business mail envelopes solve small surface problems very well indeed. They provide a see-through surface, which accepts ballpoint, held all around by stiff paper. Large windows can of course be self made. **VN**

● **THE JAPANESE METALWORKING** technique of *Mokomai* may be adapted as a decorative technique for use with coloured clays. Virginia Cartwright suggests that one might sandwich together more than one coloured clay and roll it into a flat slab in order to join and thin the colours. Lay the slab on a foam rubber surface and prod it all over with a blunt tool so that the underside has bumps on it. Build a pot with its bumpy side outward. When it is dry, wear a dust mask, sand down the bumps to reveal rings of colour. **MMC**

● **LUSTRE IS SO** expensive one cannot afford to waste a drop let alone lose a great quantity by inadvertently knocking over an open container.

I have reduced this risk almost entirely by means of my instant, universal lus-tre bottle holder'. Simply take a lump of stiffish clay, stick the container into it and place on your working surface wherever convenient. The damp clay should also stick to that, providing double indemnity – it even works for tiny containers like lids.

Taking the idea further you could use a lump of clay to hold tools in current use, to keep brushes from rolling about or even stick individual brushes in the lump containing a particular colour thus avoiding confusion. My favourite is to use a lump of clay to hold my champagne glass steady as I celebrate the great sav-ings brought about by this idea. **SB**

● **I USED TO** accumulate numerous pots, often with a strong form but lacking liveliness in the glaze – dull, in other words. When I ran a stall I sold such pots cheaply to clear the decks, but experimenting with lustres provided a quick and not too expensive method of retrieving these lost souls, and enabled me to obtain a far better return on my work.

If you are not strong on design try painting the veiny side of leaves with copper, platinum or a contrasting colour to your base glaze, and carefully press on to the surface of your pot. You can print several times before re-coating – the image will vary, giving a freer effect. Try different types and sizes of leaf, try sponges, crumpled rags for a marbled effect. The possibilities are endless. Warming the ware first will help prevent the lustre from running, and should enable you to use it a bit thinner which is also a saving.

Lustre over the lustre – you can keep re-firing and adding to your design, or fire it out altogether and start again. Anything is better than 'dull' pots.

Another word for 'dull' is 'lacklustre'. **SB**

● **I HAVE ALWAYS** tended to be a bit of a fast worker. This has advantages in terms of output, but can be inappropriate for some processes such as applying lustres, especially when thinned down, which I find helps to prevent a 'lacklustre' effect. Great care must be taken to prevent dripping and thinning out, or bleeding.

Recently, in a hurry to get a kiln on, I worked on pots hot from the kiln and found that the lustre dried quickly and did not spread. I popped them back into the warm kiln to dry off, and in a short while it was easy to handle them, enabling me to pack a lustre kiln at once without the usual long wait until the pots were safe to handle.

To recall this tip – a new proverb: 'hot pots make short work'. **SB**

● **WHEN CLAY COILS** are used to embellish ceramics, such effects as barley sugar twists, cable, rope and plaits can be achieved by twisting a flattened ribbon of clay, or by plaiting, or by extrusion through a suitably rifled die bolted on to a wad box or pugmill. However, to be successful, all these methods demand a highly plastic body clay.

Fortunately a rope/cable/braided effect can readily be obtained on even 'short' or heavily grogged clay by simply rolling a length of clay coil over expanded metal, that mesh or basket-like material used both by plasterers and car coachworkers engaged in plastic surgery for dents. Rope patterns will vary according to the direction the coil is rolled – whether longitudinally, laterally, or obliquely. **JN**

● **MOST LARGE DIY** shops or woodwork shops stock a fairly extensive range of wooden mouldings, ranging from floral motifs to fancy friezes for application to fire surrounds etc.

Fill any undercuts or roughness with clay and use the mouldings to produce a set of sprig moulds for use in school or college. (Particularly handy for overworked teachers who have not got the time to design their own.) **MC**

● **FOR A CHEAP** and readily available medium, for suspension and application of powdered enamels, use 7-Up drink, allowed to go flat. Mix, as with other media, with a palette knife to painterly thickness. This has proved very successful for me in recent architectural works. **HA**

● **WHEN USING STAMPS** or cutting tools lubricate with WD40, thin lubricating oil that will fire out. This prevents drag when cutting and enables the stamps to function cleanly. **BJ**

● **CRAYONS CAN BE** used as a rather novel method of decorating pots – ideal for the young at heart.

A universal base recipe to make ceramic crayons (to be fired under a glaze on earthenware or stoneware) is as follows:

China clay 50
Silica 30
Whiting 20
Metallic oxides......................................±40%

Mix well in a dry state (taking care of the dust) by placing the ingredients into a strong plastic bag and shaking. Then add small amounts of water and mix until you have the correct plastic consistency, before coiling into pencils.

Dry pencils can be wrapped in paper or masking tape for added strength and used directly on biscuit ware – as well as raw clay – if the surface of the clay is first painted with a solution of wallpaper paste and then completely dried. A subsequent glaze firing will show the colour in the final pot. **PSA**

Chapter 5
Glaze and glazing

There is a wide spread of help and advice from potters on glaze making and application. Keith Parry uses baby scales to weigh his materials.

● **WE ARE A** medium-sized business employing three throwers and three others. Although our clay is a proprietary mixture, we have developed all our own glazes, which we are able to mix very accurately using some baby weighing scales. These scales are in old imperial weight measures, and were being thrown out by a local health centre. The procedure is simple.

First a bucket is placed onto the pan and the scale 'zeroed', then the required weight of the material is set, the bucket filled and when the scale balances exactly the contents added to the mixture in the glaze bin. The scale is accurate to less than ¼oz and will weigh up to 40lb – perfect for small- or medium-sized glaze mixing operations. **KP**

The tedious business of sieving glazes and keeping them smooth and useable is addressed in the following tips from Gary Marconi, Peter Naylor, Margaret Hinchcliffe, Veronica Lee, Darwin Turner, Ian Doyle, Susan Bennett (two hints, the second with Earl Hyde), Michael Montague, William Martin, Chrissie Bentley, Joseph Neville, Richard Baxter and Belinda Swingler.

 ● **WHEN SIEVING SLIPS** or glazes, use triangular shaped slats; the liquid runs down into the bucket or bowl and not along the surface on to the floor or table as it tends to do when flat sticks are used. **GM**

● **WITH THIS CHEAP** and efficient way of sieving, my glaze mixing has been reduced from a day's hard slog to two hours including weighing out 100lbs of various powdered materials.

Assuming that most potteries are equipped with some sort of electric drill find a piece of car aerial rod about 1½ft long (preferably not vandalised off someone else's car) or similar piece of metal that does not bend easily. Buy a 3" or 4" plastic propeller from an aeromodelling shop, fix this to the end of the rod with plastic padding or Araldite, making sure that no metal is prominent on bottom side of propeller (i.e. cover it with glue), and fix other end of rod into drill. Increase the height of your lawn (sieve) to the same length as the rod or make one like Jan van der Tas (see p148) using whole bucket instead of half. Pour in glaze to the top, place in propeller and switch on. The glaze will disappear through the sieve at an alarming speed. When the glaze starts to splash, top up again. Wash out filtrate when the glaze starts to slow up. You also have the added advantage of no mesh wear if the propeller is kept from contact with sieve. So you have the efficiency of a £100 vibrator and an ideal slip-stirrer. **PN**

● **I HAVE FOUND** that an ordinary plastic washing-up brush, the type with a round head, makes an excellent brush for sieving glazes. **MH**

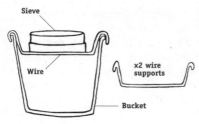

Sieve

Wire

x2 wire supports

Bucket

● **TO STOP GLAZE** splashing everywhere when sieving it from one bucket to another I use two wire coat-hangers bent as shown. Placed either to form an 'X' or side by side they allow the sieve to drop below the surface of the bucket, thus the glaze does not splash. Speeds up the sieving operation too. **VL**

● **A VERY EFFECTIVE** glaze stirrer for an electric drill can be made from an old wire coat hanger bent to form a simple paddle. **DT**

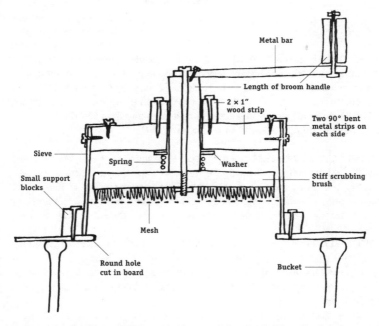

Metal bar

Length of broom handle

2 × 1" wood strip

Two 90° bent metal strips on each side

Sieve

Spring

Washer

Stiff scrubbing brush

Small support blocks

Mesh

Round hole cut in board

Bucket

● **I FOUND THE** illustrated dry ash siever quick to make from junk lying around and marvellously efficient: 24lbs of ash finely sieved in 2½ hours compared to 5lbs in a day previously. A longish metal bar will give good leverage for ease of turning. The overlap on the walls of the sieve catches on a wooden support block, which stops any spinning. A touch of light oil on the broom handle spindle prevents squeaking as it turns. N.B. Use a face mask to avoid breathing in dust. **ID**

● **IF YOU HAVE** trouble passing ash through a fine mesh sieve it may be clogging due to moisture retention.

Try baking it in shallow containers in your domestic oven until it turns light and powdery. If the timing is convenient you can, of course, use heat from your kiln to similar effect. This will save you time, elbow-grease and aggravation. **SB**

● **A SMALL DOMESTIC** hand-held electric whisk makes light work of preparing small quantities of glaze that have settled in their containers.

Decant glaze, place in suitable vessel and whisk until the required consistency is achieved. This method is especially useful for brush-on glazes that have coagulated – try it on lumpy slip, or to mix two colours together evenly – for anything that does not actually require sieving for technical reasons. Add water as necessary.

Make sure you wash the whisk meticulously, unless you wish to poison your guests with cobalt blue meringues. **SB/EH**

● **NO MATTER HOW** much I mix the glaze slop after it has been standing for some time it never seems to get as smooth and even as when I put it through the sieve, which is a time-consuming and slow process. I have found a quick, but not instant remedy in the form of an ordinary kitchen galvanised metal sieve – the sort with a long handle and open mesh. If this is swirled round the glaze for a minute or so it helps to mix up the slop to a creamy state. Furthermore, it has the advantage of collecting any lumps in the glaze which can be put on one side and sieved properly. **MM**

● **KEEPING GLAZES LUMP-FREE** is a problem. I have found that even after a good mixing with the hand, glazes which have stood for some time are difficult to get smooth. The use of any ordinary metal or plastic kitchen sieve such as the sort for straining vegetables, swished round and round the glaze a few times, will break up lumps and mix the glaze really well. A cheap, quick and efficient remedy. **WM**

● **IN THE FREEZING** winter months in most of our unheated workshops, there is nothing worse than being up to the elbow mixing up ice-cold glazes.

I use a cheap long-handled washing-up brush to mix mine, swizzle it about then use the tough nylon bristles to scrape up that stubborn residue at the bottom of the bucket.

Much more efficient than a stick, easy to use, and also very good for passing glazes through sieves, particularly the fine mesh type. **CB**

● **'BENTONITE, AND EVERY** night!' Such was Harry Horlock Stringer's slogan in one of his invaluable hints. Advocating the routine incorporation of this form of montmorillonite in glazes, he pointed out its two virtues: as a powerful suspending agent, and so adhesive once a glaze has dried that the ware can be handled with virtual impunity while being set out in the glost kiln. The sole drawback lies in bentonite's obstinate reluctance, once wetted, to merge with rest of a glaze recipe. Instead, it forms a viscous mass that reforms as porridgey gobbets after sieving, and resists stirring. The simple remedy is to grind the bentonite and most thoroughly disperse it amongst the other dry glaze ingredients before stirring the total dry mix into water. **JN**

● **SPECIALLY MADE GLAZE** sieving brushes are expensive, trap the last lot of glaze you sieved in them and shed hairs. In a rare moment of insight I tried a cheap hardware shop washing-up brush made of plastic – very easy to clean completely and virtually indestructible too. **RB**

● **TO STOP THE** glaze sieve sliding off the slats/guides, balanced on top of a bucket and splashing glaze everywhere, I have recycled a plastic-coated wire shelf from an old fridge. Bend the central few wires downward into a slight 'V'. This is placed over the bucket and the sieve placed on top. The sieving can then commence, in safety. **BS**

Five further hints on de-watering and mixing glazes from J R Dowling, Maureen Standring, Susan Bennett, Murray Cheesman and Barry Winslow.

● **WHEN MAKING UP** a batch of liquid glaze, the prepared glaze usually ends up too thin to use immediately and a few hours have to pass before it has settled out sufficiently to decant off the surplus water. Plaster cast blocks dipped into the glaze readily absorb the surplus water allowing you to rapidly adjust the viscosity of glaze for spraying or dipping almost as soon as it has been prepared. Any glaze clinging to the plaster block is easily removed so that the efficiency of the plaster in absorbing the water can be maintained. One plaster block approximately 2½ inches square by 10 inches long will absorb about half a pint of water. **JRD**

● **I ALWAYS KEEP** my glazes in 4 litre ice cream containers. After they have been standing a while some glazes settle at the bottom and are very difficult to mix up again, so I pop the whole lot in the microwave and warm it up for a few minutes and then it mixes up quite easily. **MS**

● **IN THE MIDST** of glazing a rush order, I found the crucial bucket of glaze had dried out completely forming a hard cake. I tried to break it up by hand in order to prepare it for soaking and sieving but realised it would take too long. In desperation, recalling previous triumphs with stiffish glaze and a hand blender, I wondered if my Kenwood food processor would be capable of breaking up really hard dry lumps the size of walnuts downwards.

I half-filled the beaker with dry lumps of glaze and added water until it was two-thirds full. After a short sharp blast of power to make sure the motor would not burn out – it sounded fine – I turned it up to maximum and reconstituted about a gallon of glaze in a few minutes.

I cannot guarantee this method would work with all makes of blender or food processors. With less powerful motors you may need to make the lumps of glaze smaller, but it would be worth a try and could save you a lot of time and trouble. Slip could be produced in the same way.

Do make sure you clean the beaker thoroughly to avoid poisoning your guests when you next whizz up avocado soup. **SB**

● **WHEN MIXING UP** glazes it is often beneficial to dry mix the materials prior to soaking them, and one way to do this without undue exposure to dust is to weigh them out into a strong polythene bag or sack (e.g. the type in which clay is supplied). The mouth of the bag can be restricted around the upper arm whilst the raw ingredients are given a rough mixing. This also has the advantage that the mixed materials can be added to the bucket or container for soaking with the mouth of the sack under water, thus avoiding further dust. Obviously, a face mask should be worn at all times. **MC**

● **SOME GLAZES SETTLE** like rock at the bottom of the glaze slop if left undisturbed for a week or so. Avoidance is better than cure. Stir such glazes regularly (once a week) and add 2% bentonite to help prevent it happening. I find that removing water, drying out the glaze and reconstituting is better than the laborious alternative of breaking up the lump with a knife. **BW**

Mary Davies has a hint derived from the Tung Kwan pottery, David White suggests an unusual glaze binder and G L Reeve outlines a method of checking glaze thickness.

● **BECAUSE CRANK CLAY** absorbs a great deal of glaze, one could coat the surface of the pot with ball clay slip to reduce the amount of glaze 'pulled' into the body. **MD**

● **LOOKING FOR A** suitable binder for glazes whilst having problems learning to raw-glaze, I discovered that half a pint of white emulsion paint added to about six gallons of glaze slop is ideal. When dry the surface is hard and tough enough to resist quite rough handling and cracking on sharp edges. Being mostly titanium based, this paint should have a slight beneficial effect on the solubility of lead glazes. There is no noticeable difference to fired results. **DW**

● **BEFORE GLAZING ANY** pots, I always dip a small biscuit fired mug that I keep especially for testing the thickness of the glaze. I can then tell whether the glaze needs to be thinner or thicker before dipping any new pots. **GLR**

A variety of suggestions will help glazers to grip their pots with a minimum of scars. A simple wire hook is sufficient for most occasions but Keith Wallis, Janet Kovesi, Alan H Bolton, Darwin Turner and Kenneth Breese suggest alternatives.

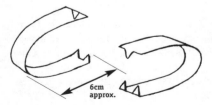

6cm
approx.

● **TO IMPROVE THE** glazing of plates etc., try making a pair of these spring-steel clips. One clip held firmly on each side of the plate whilst immersing into the glaze will give an even coating which requires very little further attention. **KW**

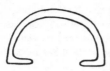

● **THE FOLLOWING GLAZING** aid was demonstrated by Shiga Shigeo, a Japanese potter living in Australia. It is very useful for glazing small- to medium-sized pots without a foot or other convenient gripping point for holding them upside down to dip into the glaze.

A piece of fencing wire (or even a wire coat-hanger) is bent round into the shape shown in the diagram and used as a kind of carrying handle, the ends supporting the rim of the pot.

One has to arrange one's fingers so that some are looped under the wire and others press on the base of the pot to keep the whole thing in tension. The pot can then be dipped in the glaze, and the only marks left by the carrying handle are a couple of tiny extra drips on the rim. Two fingers of the other hand can be rested on the inturned ends of the wire to give extra support as one turns the whole contraption right way up after glazing. It is sometimes a little tricky to lift the wire off and away before putting the pot down on the shelf, and a dress rehearsal is probably advisable.

These wire holders seem particularly useful for glazing beginners' pots, which often seem to be unfooted bowls. **JK**

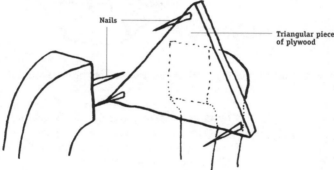

Nails

Triangular piece of plywood

● **INSTEAD OF PAYING** over the odds for a glaze claw I converted an old pair of laundry tongs as shown above. **AHB**

● **GLAZING HOOKS TO** fit the thumb and first two fingers can be made for nothing from old wire coat hangers.

If one first waxes the base of the pot, the inside and outside can be glazed simultaneously giving equal thickness inside and out. This is essential where glaze colour changes with thickness and uniform colour is required. **DT**

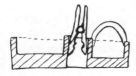

● **TO GLAZE CANDLESTICKS** and bottles I use clothes pegs to hold the piece, as shown in the sketch.

First I wax the base then dip in the glaze; the job is finished in one and is even all over. **DT**

● **TO GLAZE POTS** that are difficult or too heavy to hold and that have a drainage hole in the base, use a traditional corkscrew and two wine bottle corks. Place one cork well up on the spiral of the corkscrew, feed through the hole then fix the other cork inside the pot then lower into glaze, raise and spin. This allows for a very fine accuracy of the glaze level. **KB**

Further, rather more elaborate schemes are contributed by M Young, Vivienne Foley, Bruno Manini, Tony Valintine, Terence Turnbull, Anne Leon and Les Jamieson.

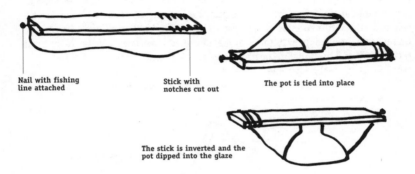

Nail with fishing line attached

Stick with notches cut out

The pot is tied into place

The stick is inverted and the pot dipped into the glaze

● **A TECHNIQUE TO** make the glazing of awkwardly shaped pots easier is illustrated above. **MY**

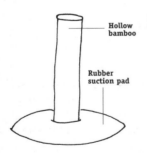

Hollow bamboo

Rubber suction pad

● **I WAS IMPRESSED** by a suction device used for glazing the outside of shallow dishes at the Shihwan tableware factory near Canton. All the glazing I saw was applied to raw ware.
1. Glaze inside of dish.
2. Dry.
3. Pick up dish with suction pad inside (sealing top of bamboo tube with thumb).
4. Dip bottom of dish in glaze.
5. Wipe feet. **VF**

● **ONE WAY OF** dipping small, awkward to hold pots is to attach the bottom of the pot to the suction end of a vacuum cleaner and then gently lower the pot into the glaze. Particular care must be taken not to suck the glaze into the cleaner as this would be dangerous and would ruin the machine.

When dipping small pots without a foot-ring I find it quicker not to wax resist, but to dip bottom first into the glaze and wipe – whilst glaze is wet – on a clean wet sponge with a twisting motion. By using the right amount of pressure you can also clean slightly up the side at the same time. **BM**

● **I HAVE FOUND** the following method a useful way of holding pots for stoneware dip-glazing:

1. After bisque firing the pots are inverted and their bottoms waxed.

2. When the wax has hardened, a lump of softish clay is firmly worked on to the waxed surface and shaped to give a good hand grip. (The greater the contact area the better the grip.)

3. When the glaze is dry enough after dipping has been done, the pot is held gently but firmly and the 'handgrip' removed from the pot.

I do not know what the limit would be but I have used this method successfully on pots up to ten inches in height. Make sure the clay is well worked on to the waxed surface or the weight of the pot will pull it off. **TV**

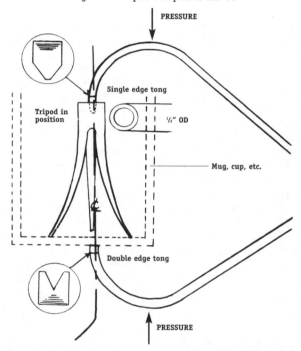

● **THE CHALLENGE HERE** is to once glaze dip a domestic range of pots, maximum size 1pt, leaving no exterior tong marks. As the above diagram shows, a length of ½" OD stainless steel tube is cut to form a tripod. The legs are bent to allow sufficient clearance for easy exit. Tongs cut with a single edge or point rest in the tripod top and a double point rests on the underside of the pot. Simple hand pressure then holds the tongs in place. With practice the tripod or prong method has proved very fast and only three faint blemishes remain on the inside at the bottom, leaving the outside glaze surface free from any unsightly and unprofessional marks.

Although slightly longer than the traditional single dip methods, I think the end result justifies the trouble. **TT**

● **IT CAN BE** difficult to hold some round-shaped pots upside-down while dipping them into a glaze. By throwing the pot with a ⅝" – or deeper – bottom, and turning the base as follows, a good grip is possible.

Leaving the desired width for a foot-ring (A) – ⅜" minimum is required – trim the well to a depth of at least ⅜" (B) and slope the inner wall of the foot so that it is undercut (C). On larger pots a deeper foot and well should be made.

When the pot is bisqued – and after glazing the interior if you do not use the double dipping method – place the fingertips of both hands under the rim. At this stage your knuckles should be facing each other, and your hands should be pulling in opposite directions. The pot can then easily be lifted. Keeping the pot level, lower it into the glaze. For large pots your thumbs can be placed on the foot-ring in order to help push the pot down into the glaze. After lifting the pot out, keep it upside-down and gently roll it so that any drops of glaze will even themselves out on the rim. Then turn the pot the right way up and slide it onto a table without touching the wet glazed area. If the glaze container is on a perfectly level surface, and the pot is held steadily, a perfectly level layer of glaze can be applied and a clean foot as small as a ¼" can be achieved. There should be no glaze on the bottom of the pot, and no fingerprints. This method is also useful when applying a second layer of glaze, whether a straight line or an angle dip is desired. Quite large pieces can be dipped this way, depending upon the strength of your fingers. **AL**

● **THESE ARE TWO** photographs of a device I have made to enable me to dip pots into glaze. As a beginner I find it very difficult to hold pots curving towards the base when trying to dip into glaze. The device consists of a block of wood through which a ¼" diameter rod is slotted. The wood can be slid up and down the rod to hold the pot securely. I find this more convenient than to totally immerse and then have to wipe off glaze from base and rim. **LJ**

For pouring and dipping both J B May and L E Wells hit upon the idea of using a funnel as a 'chuck'; Sue Parish finds a use for a chip basket, S Hayes releases the pressure and Hank Harmeling from Massachusetts is 'on the level'.

● **FOR POURING GLAZE** on the outside of a pot I found the two-bar method of suspending it over a bowl awkward to set up and it left bare spots on the rim. I invert the pot over a plastic funnel resting in the bowl (see sketch). It works admirably where the rim is flared, otherwise glaze collects under the rim and necessitates touching up. **JBM**

● **WHEN POURING GLAZE** onto tall, narrow-mouthed pots, I have found it difficult to balance the pot safely over the catching bowl. Also, having first glazed the inside with a white glaze for hygenic appearance, the poured glaze can splash up inside, spoiling the effect. Both problems can be overcome by sitting the pot onto a funnel, itself supported over the drip bowl which stands on a banding wheel. The rough sketch is not to scale. A hand on the foot both steadies the pot and rotates it. An added bonus is a much neater rim, needing less cleaning up. I use a plastic funnel with 5 inches diameter mouth, 7 inches high, which gives a very stable support. **LEW**

● **TRYING TO DIP** items of biscuit ware into glaze can be fiddly, and sometimes they slip from the grasp altogether. One of my students, in a brilliant piece of lateral thinking, brought into our pottery department an old wire chip basket. Small items for glazing are put in the basket and then lowered into the glaze, providing an even, fingerprint-free finish. **SP**

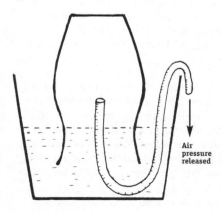

Air pressure released

● **WHEN GLAZING A** band of second colour over a first, I found that frequently, when removing the pot from the glaze, air pressure caused an unsightly splash back of glaze inside the pot.

By using a plastic tube as shown in the diagram air pressure does not build up and this nuisance can be avoided. If a piece of wire is threaded through the tube it can be bent to whatever shape is needed to suit any depth of glaze being used. **SH**

● **WHEN DIPPING POTS** in glaze we often want to get a horizontal line partway up the pot, which is hard to do by eye. If you buy a small utility level and set it on the bottom of the pot the problem is solved. If dipping bottom first, place the level on a flat surface which has been placed over the opening. These levels have two bubbles and are about 3 × 2" in size. They should be available in hardware stores. **HH**

Frank Benatt suggests the use of an upturned dustbin lid to hold glaze when there is only a limited amount and large dishes are to be covered. Ann Parkhouse has a beautifully simple system for speeding up the glazing of several pieces, especially with high-fired biscuit; Susan Bennett suggests an efficient method for glazing flat ware and Rosemary Downs advises on storing glaze.

● **GLAZING HIGH-FIRED BISCUIT** pots can be difficult and one can waste a lot of time holding an inverted pot whilst the glaze dries sufficiently to permit standing it down without the glaze running. I found a method for making this process less hazardous. Select a dozen tools with wooden handles. Next make a dozen balls of clay about cricket ball size. Stick each tool end into a ball of clay leaving the wooden end upright. When you have glazed the pot stand it upside down over the wooden handle and proceed to the next pot. By the time the twelve are complete the first is dry. It is a way of making 'six pairs of hands'. **AP**

● **WHEN NOT ENGAGED** in potting activities, Earl Hyde and I are heavily involved in creating and maintaining a garden. In fact there is quite a symbiotic relationship between the two. Spin-offs from the garden include a really useful container for glazing flat ware, especially when you are running short of glaze. During a particularly dry summer, to conserve water I stood my small flowerpots in the nursery area in large plastic trays which I kept topped up with water. Some were taken from a defunct photography department, but most came from Marks and Spencer's food hall – flimsy, clear plastic trays used to display crisps, and readily available on request. They measure 57 × 47 × 8cm. Place the tray on a corner of your table or bench and fill with the appropriate amount of glaze. To empty after use, place a bucket under one corner, and cut or pierce the container to allow the liquid to flow out. A perfect, disposable container – free for the asking.

Do not lift the tray full of liquid to empty it. If you cannot see why, try it – but experiment with water not glaze. **SB**

● **AFTER DIPPING VARIOUS** pots in the glaze slop stored in a plastic bucket, I foolishly allowed drops of glaze to dry on the side of the bucket and when glazing subsequently the dry bits fell into the glaze which then required stirring and sieving to break them down. Scraping the wet surface with a rubber kidney or even a bank card immediately after glazing to return any splashes to the mix would have avoided the problem in the first place. Incidentally, using a piece of hardboard as a lid helps prevent the glaze drying out and enables the buckets to be stacked on top of each other. **RD**

Ruth Karnac describes the principle whereby glaze can be made to flow upwards, and Russell Davis expands upon this phenomenon mathematically.

● **WHEN VISITING A** domestic ware factory at Shihwan, near Canton in China, I saw a very simple and effective method of applying an even coating of slip or glaze to the surface of a small plate.

The leatherhard plate was placed securely on the centre of the wheel-head. A small quantity of slip was then poured into the centre of the plate and the wheel was immediately set spinning fast. Centrifugal force caused the slip to spread evenly over the surface. I have tried this and found that it works equally well with small- to medium-sized bowls which are not too deep, and with larger plates, but I secure the pots to the wheel-head with three small wads of clay.

The method can be used in conjunction with wax or paper resist designs, or simply with the rims waxed. It lessens possible damage to leatherhard ware in the handling. Experience will show the best consistency for the slip or glaze. (Raw glazing only.) If too thick it will not spread evenly; if too thin, the clay will show through. It would be advisable to use a batt for anything large and leave it on the batt until firmed up enough to handle safely. **RK**

● **THE DESCRIPTION OF** the Chinese method of slip-glazing the inside of a spinning bowl given by Ruth Karnac nudged a mathematical corner of my mind. When a bowl of liquid is spun in this way the liquid surface takes the shape of a parabola, the steepness of which depends upon the speed of rotation.

Given a parabolic pot spinning steadily at the right speed for its shape (see diagram) it should be possible to slip glaze by pouring along a radius. The slip would spread out without either pooling in the bottom or flowing excessively from the rim, and could sit in the spinning bowl for as long as needed to dry it.

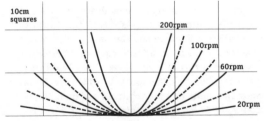

have not tried the method on a pot, but I did check the theoretical shapes by setting a washing-up bowl of water on the wheel. This curved water surface, apparently defying gravity, was a curious sight. **RD**

Two ingenious suggestions for preventing glaze spreading from the outside to the inside of a pot by John Gunn and Pat Barfoot.

● **TO GLAZE THE** inside and outside of a pot in different coloured glazes without any penetration of the outside glaze into the rim of the pot (ordinary dipping often produces an irregular and unsightly blob on the inside) simply float a very large cork or an old cork table-mat on top of the glaze and press this down with the pot as you dip it, having glazed the inside first. It effectively closes the mouth of the pot and prevents ingress of unwanted glaze. To my mind dipping is the easiest, cleanest and most effective way of applying a smooth and even coat of glaze to a pot, but how often do you find that the glaze in the bucket just is not deep enough to dip that long narrow pot in one go?

Tall narrow containers are not at all easy to come by and my solution to the problem has been to obtain a 2ft piece of six-inch PVC drainpipe, bevel one end with a Surform file, grease it lightly and then ram it into a small plastic bucket of the type that is used to contain tile cement, putty or, in institutional catering, 5lb of coleslaw or other such vegetarian delights. This seems to answer very well – no leaks and less than a bucketful of glaze can be made to cover a 20" pot with ease. Try local builder's yards for the large plastic pipe – although not too common the first yard I searched yielded the piece that I use. The larger builder's merchants should also be able to help, or you may be lucky and find a scrap length by the roadside. If you want to make a really pukka job, self-sealing end-caps for this sort of pipe are available, but of course it will add to the cost. **JG**

● **A POTTERY AID** I find valuable uses inflatable balloons; useful when glazing pierced pots of sculptures with different glazes inside and outside.
1. Glaze the inside, allow to dry and clean off any dribbles which may have run on to the outside.
2. Insert a balloon (or two in some cases), inside the article and blow it up until it seals off all the openings completely.
3. The article can then be dipped, sprayed or glazed by pouring with no fear of the glaze running inside.
4. When the outside glaze is dry deflate the balloon and remove it. Any dry flakes of glaze which do fall inside at this stage can easily be blown out. **PB**

The spraying on of glaze and pigments can give highly individual results but the technique should be approached with caution. Not only is the air filled with fine droplets but a film of glaze is deposited all around and can be an added hazard as it dries. A good face mask is the least precaution; an extractor fan a better one. The following tips should be viewed with this in mind. James Rush describes a fairly elaborate spray booth water curtain, the components of which are, however, fairly easily obtainable. The preceding hints on spraying itself are from Susan Bennett, with Earl Hyde and Earl Hyde/Dr Reeve Arenstein, Krzysztof Buras, Joseph Neville, Mart Muller (Nairobi), Ian Grant, David Powell, Doreen Costello and Tony J Moody.

● **IF, LIKE US,** you use plant misting sprays to keep your ceramic creations from drying out, you probably find they tend to clog up after a while. If wear and tear is not the problem, it is probably a build up of algae. To prevent this simply add a few drops of household bleach to the water.

Should you employ these sprays in schools, you are doubtless aware of their alternative function as water pistols. Even if swimming pools contain an even higher percentage of chlorine, better green water than sore eyes. **SB/EH**

● **RECENTLY WE RECEIVED** a commission to produce 100 circular pendants 3cm in diameter with a bas-relief design. Spraying was the best solution for applying glaze since care had to be taken not to block the small holes. The prospect of waxing so many small items was daunting – and even then they would need careful checking and cleaning before firing.

We devised an excellent method. It was fast, efficient and labour-saving – and avoided the necessity of waxing and cleaning. We draped an old cotton sheet over a large board, lined up the discs 0.5cm apart and propped the board at a slight angle to ensure no drips from the glaze fell onto the ware. After spraying and allowing the discs to dry out, we found it was possible to put them straight onto the kiln shelves with no further process. Had they been placed straight onto wood, the glaze would have pooled around the discs. The cotton absorbed any residual glaze. The final outcome was perfect. **SB/EH**

● **HAVING SPENT SEVERAL** months researching into spray guns and compressors to equip the studio with urgently needed spraying facilities, we were about to spend several hundred pounds when our helpful dentist made a suggestion. He offered to lend us a spray bottle attachment from his Electrolux cylinder vacuum cleaner to use with our own cleaner of the same make and type.

The spray turned out to be a most effective piece of equipment. We now spray various stoneware glazes, some containing a high proportion of ash over large and intricately worked areas with great ease and control, and with very satisfactory results.

My spray bottle attachment has a part number 321467/03. If you do not possess an Electrolux cylinder cleaner you may be able to obtain one second-hand at relatively low cost. If you own another brand it may be worth enquiring whether the manufacturer can supply a similar device. **SB/EH/RA**

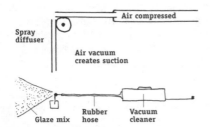

● **MY DRAWINGS SHOW** a very economical and efficient means of applying spray to a pot. One can buy a second-hand vacuum cleaner at any bric-a-brac shop, making sure that it both takes in and expels air.

Attach a length of rubber hose to the expelling end, and to this attach a spray diffuser bought from any art shop. By altering the spray diffuser nozzle a certain degree of fineness or density of glaze concentration can be obtained. By placing a turntable on a stand inside a cabinet of suitable dimensions and attaching a dust extractor at the rear, a cost-effective and quite adequate spraying booth can be made for as little as an eighth of the price charged by dealers of ceramic materials.

I have found this an invaluable means of achieving many varied and delightful glaze effects, using both raw glazes, oxide washes and normal glaze mixes. However, one should use a face mask when spraying.

Care should be taken in flushing the diffuser through with clean water when spraying ceases. **KB**

● **POWERED SPRAY-GLAZING WITH** simple inexpensive equipment has been well-described by Krzysztof Buras's recommendation of an artists' fixative spray diffuser and Bennett, Hyde and Arenstein's advocacy of the Electrolux spray bottle attachment. Both methods work quite beautifully, as I can vouch after trial, and are powered by the air blast from an cylinder vacuum cleaner. However, there are places without electricity, and times when small fiddly glazing tasks (such as dealing with tiny or small 'one-off' ceramics, or touching in finger marks on dry glazed surfaces) confront you and the prospect of assembling even the simplest cylinder-powered spray kit may appear to resemble using a sledgehammer to crack a nut.

In such circumstances, the manually operated flitgun, filled, used, emptied and washed clean in a few minutes, has its role. Many modern flitguns are made from heavy-duty plastic and corrosion-resisting metal, but even tinplate models can have their containers protected with a couple of internal coats of polyurethane varnish. Pistons should not be over-lubricated otherwise your work will be showered with droplets of oil. Any clogged suction tubes or air jets will clear with a prod from a bit of wire. A wipe from a small damp sponge cleans any glaze that may accumulate and begin to dry around the junction between tube and jet... it is rather like keeping a beloved child's snotty nose clean. Standard density studio glazes may require a little but non-critical thinning until the flitgun's action is easy and its output copious.

With flitsprays, as with any and all spray-glazing procedures, the usual safety precautions must be taken to obviate risks of inhaling nebulised glaze particles. Flitguns are expendable, but lungs are not. **JN**

● **FOR THE BEGINNER** potter, mixing up a glaze in small quantities and wanting to spray rather than brush on glaze, I pass on my own method.

Take an ordinary nail brush (wood and natural fibre – plastic does not work) and a flat wooden stick. Dip brush in glaze, shake off surplus, hold the brush about a foot from your pot, and move the stick firmly along the brush towards you: this will spray the glaze on to your pot. A large carton, placed on its side, makes a satisfactory 'booth'. Any brush seems to work as long as the bristles are close together. It needs a little practice to get the right thickness of glaze and to find the best distance between brush and pot. **MM**

● **MART MULLER'S INGENIOUS** use of a nail-brush for spraying glaze on to pots reminded me of a method I have used.

Instead of a nail-brush I use my retired toothbrushes. I would not recommend these as substitutes for a spray, as the globules of glaze/oxides vary in size and range according to the antiquity of the toothbrush. But you can get some quite attractive 'pointiliste' effects. I take the pot outside and work standing to windward. For use with oxides, it is best to have a different toothbrush for each oxide. **IG**

● **I HAD THE** problem of glazing a large sculptural form. Not having an electrical spray gun at my disposal, I came across the idea of using a pump spray gun (the old type of fly sprayer), which can be purchased from an ironmongers or garden shop. It works perfectly. **DP**

● **THIS IS AN** idea of my husband's for a small spray booth which I find very useful.

It is just an ordinary plastic dustbin with a hole cut in one side. The pot can be placed inside for spraying, either on the base or a brick or turntable, and sprayed. The residual spray is collected in the base, and can be used again. It is also very easy to wash. (For outdoor use only.) **DC**

● **POTTERS WHO USE** a spray to apply glaze will be aware of the problem of achieving an even glaze thickness. It is especially difficult to know what is happening when the glaze and body are similar in colour. I thought about adding a bright vegetable dye to the glaze mixture but none of the local health food shops, chemists or hardware suppliers could help, so I thought again. One of the things I liked best about infant school was painting – bright happy colours from tins of powder paint. Good toy shops still sell similar tins. Just add a few spoonfuls to the glaze mixture and spray away: the powder will burn away in the firing leaving this happy potter complete with well-glazed work. **TJM**

● **BOOTHS FOR SPRAYING** glaze are almost essential from a health point of view and the minimum requirement is the fitting of an extractor fan. The ultimate refinement is a combination of spray booth together with a water curtain to take away the overspray from the gun before it can be expelled into the atmosphere. This method can considerably lessen atmospheric pollution as well as reduce personal risk from the glaze. Such a water curtain can be constructed quite simply in an afternoon by any potter who has even a modest do-it-yourself ability.

The two main components are a fish pond pump with a good delivery and an old kitchen sink of the porcelain or stoneware type. Other parts are not difficult to get and consist of a piece of hessian or similar material which is draped into the sink to direct the water flow; a length of metal pipe as long as the sink, about ½" bore; and a strip of 1 × 2" wood long enough to span the width of the booth. Other requirements are a bucket or similar container together with enough rain water pipe – the cheap plastic sort is ideal – to reach down from the sink waste to the bucket. Leave this pipe loose so that the sludge can be emptied from the bucket when necessary. Also needed will be enough flexible hose to reach from bucket to metal pipe in the booth. Make sure it is the correct bore for the pump outlet. Begin by fixing the wooden strip which holds the curtain behind the spraying area in the booth at a suitable height to catch the overspray from the gun.

Next, drill a line of ⅛" holes at about ¼" intervals along the full length of the metal pipe and stop one end up completely before attaching it to the wooden support with metal strips or strong wire. Connect the pipe to the flexible hose which, in turn, is coupled to the pump outlet and this latter immersed in the bucket of water. I used 'jubilee' clips to make the hose connections for my spray unit. To avoid splashing the pots being sprayed keep the ⅛" holes turned towards the curtain and this will give a silent waterfall effect.

Plug the pump into the electricity supply and switch on. To prevent the spray gun being used without the water curtain operating I wired the pump plug in parallel (for those with little electrical knowledge this simply means that the leads or wires of the compressor were wired to the corresponding leads of the pump cable, i.e. the two earth wires were connected to the earth pin in the plug; the two live wires were connected to the live pin and the two neutral wires connected to the neutral pin) with the compressor supply so it was a case of 'all on or off'. The pump I used was a Stuart SS1 which is quite adequate for the booth we use. This type of pump must only operate whilst submerged but topping up the evaporation losses in the water container only means emptying some water into the sink from time to time.

The curtain described has now been operating quite satisfactorily for nearly a year, and judging by the sludge that empties from the container, it is quite obvious that local air pollution has been greatly reduced. **JR**

Still with spraying, Joseph Neville describes an adjustable trivet, and Eric Degg gives details of a simple spray system.

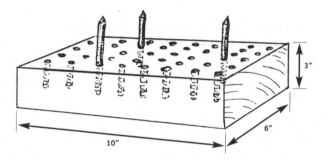

● **IT IS NOT** easy to position a ceramic piece which is large, heavy, intricately contoured with areas that tend to be masked by overhangs from the spray, and at the same time to ensure that delicate or downright fragile features are not damaged in the process. The task is rendered all the more hazardous when the ceramic in question is being raw glazed. A modifiable miniature 'bed of nails' is one answer to the problem, as shown in the diagram. The ceramic piece is supported on three upturned headless 4" nails, ¼" diameter, which have been inserted into ⅜" diameter holes, 2" deep, drilled cribbage board fashion in a heavy block of scrap deal.

The particular array of the nails is of course determined by the dimensions and the mode of construction of the piece to be glazed. ¼" diameter coach bolts can be substituted for one or all of the nails if you are worried about the risk of nail points damaging the piece. The dimensions shown in the diagram are those of the trivet I use for dealing with 'green' sculptures up to some 16" in height. Once strategically and safely positioned, the piece on its trivet claws is placed on the spraybooth's turntable and spraying commences. Any annoyance caused by glaze particles settling and blocking unoccupied holes can be avoided by thrusting a sheet of paper over the spikes and tucking the ends under the wooden base. **JN**

● **SEVERAL YEARS AGO** the art section of the college in which I work was allocated money for extra equipment in its pottery studio. I purchased two spray booths, two Tuffy air compressors and three Thomas Industries spray guns. The booths and compressors worked very well but the spray guns were such a constant source of trouble and time-waste that everyone eventually ignored them. Imagine then my recent surprise to see some beautifully sprayed pots sitting on a workbench. I looked at the spray guns but they had not been used. Having located the student responsible, I asked him to show me how he had achieved the result. He placed the pot in a booth, plugged in a compressor, fetched a jug of glaze, produced from his pocket a charcoal fixative diffuser, which he held to the nozzle of the compressor tube and sprayed the pot perfectly. When I thought how many times I had used a fixative diffuser to spray drawings in that studio without the idea of teaming it up with the compressors I could have kicked myself. At moderate cost compared with the relatively high price of a spray gun it is a real bargain. **ED**

The painting on of glaze and raw-glazing present their own problems, though air pollution is not one of them. A May and Nora Kay have tips on these techniques.

● **MORE OFTEN THAN** not the children I have taught preferred to paint the glaze on to their pots rather than dipping or pouring. Painting is particularly difficult for children. To help them paint more easily and to get a smoother more even cover of glaze I mix a small amount of wallpaper paste according to the instructions on the packet, and then add the required amount of glaze, mixing thoroughly. The glaze can then be painted on in the same manner as a 'brush-on' glaze, using two or three coats. The glaze used in this way has given very satisfactory results.

I must emphasise that only a small amount can be mixed at a time, as the glaze can only be stored in this state for a few days. **AM**

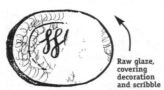

Raw glaze, covering decoration and scribble

● **WHEN UNPACKING THE** results of what appears to be a satisfactory glaze firing, it is annoying to discover that there are small unglazed areas visible on otherwise perfect dishes or plates. These can, of course, be touched up with glaze and re-fired, but this means extra fuel and time.

This tiresome problem seems to occur when the raw glaze mixture and the body to which it is being applied are very similar in colour; particularly when a transparent or opaque tin glaze is used on a white body. Small unglazed patches are not easily visible and can occur round the rims and edges of larger pieces.

A simple and easy way to ensure that the whole surface is covered with glaze is to scribble, with an ordinary soft blacklead pencil, over all the plain undecorated areas, particularly the edges and rims. Use a blunt B or 2B pencil and scribble lightly, making a definite visible pattern which will then be obscured by the glaze. Any blank patches will show and can be touched up. The blacklead fires away completely and does not seem to have any effect on the quality of the glaze firing. **NK**

Alex Robertson and Ian D Smith discuss cleaning surplus glaze from the base of pots, while Susan Bennett gives an original hint on neater glazing.

● **ONE OF THE** most tedious tasks in glazing is the wiping of the foot: I find the following practice most helpful.

Having waxed and glazed, I fix a wooden batt to the wheel-head. To this I secure either a scouring pad or a thin sheet of sponge or foam rubber by means of four drawing pins. When rotated, this removes neatly and evenly all traces of glaze from the foot. Not only do I find this speeds up the cleaning process but it eliminates the cramp which I certainly feel in the fingers of the hand holding the pot when wiping in the customary way.

Incidentally, talking of waxing, I am intrigued by the frequent references I read to the problems of preparing wax for resist work. I use a readily available latex emulsion which has the dual quality of resisting wholly or, when thinned slightly with water, lending itself to fine lines or spatter. Messing about with candles, paraffin and food warmers may be alright for the purist, but it is tough on the brushes. With an emulsion wax one can use the finest Chinese brush and simply rinse it afterwards in water. **AR**

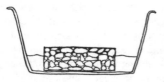

● **WHILE WORKING IN** school I needed a rapid method of cleaning excess glaze from the bases of a large number of pots. I discovered that a simple solution was to stand a large sponge in a couple of inches of water. In order to remove the excess glaze the pots were simply wiped across the sponge which was kept constantly damp. This method meant a considerably shorter time spent in 'tidying up' individual pots. **IDS**

● **LARGE AREAS OF** unglazed clay can look very unsightly on small delicate pieces of work. Earthenware can be glazed all over and fired on stilts, but stoneware and porcelain may sag and distort when supported in this way.

One solution I have found is to glaze the piece almost to the base and then to moisten the underside (saliva works better than water) and to touch it briefly and gently on to a flat bed of dry clean sand. The grains which adhere raise the object slightly – just enough to prevent it sticking to the shelf. After firing the sand can be rubbed off.

Do not be tempted to place tiny objects on to sand already spread on the kiln shelf – they are likely to sink into it.

Kiln shelves often pick up a thin coating of glaze which can cause all or part of the base of cleaned pots to stick. This method can help to prevent this by forming an absorbent barrier.

Cushions of sand placed under large pots, by allowing some movement during firing, can help to prevent warping.

A word of warning: great care must be taken when using sand in the kiln to prevent it from ending up where it is not wanted. **SB**

Ten items deal with the storage, labelling and economic use of glaze. They are from Adrian Phelps, Vivian Stanley, Stephen Grieve, Margaret Brook, Susan Bennett, Colin Cooke, Pamela Scott, Gordon Gerrard, Dorothy Ann Jones and Anne Leon. The mention of lead in the last entry suggests that it refers to earthenware glazes although the ash glaze additions make this ambiguous. Lead at stoneware temperatures is dangerous on several counts, and should be avoided.

● **GLAZE STORAGE CAN** become a bit of a problem, particularly when the cost of containers supplied by the main pottery firms are so high. I have found a suitable alternative, which is in fact identical to those supplied by the main pottery suppliers except for the brand name printed on the containers. These containers are home-brew fermenting bins, which are available in 25 litre and 15 litre sizes. They are supplied complete with air-tight lids, and cost much less than those supplied by the main pottery firms. They are available at Boots the chemist, and the brand name can be easily removed with nail varnish remover. **AP**

● **KEEPING A SET** of clearly labelled jars of glazes by the kiln is handy for touching up pots which get chipped or knocked as the kiln is packed. It saves stirring up large buckets of glaze and the exasperation of running to and fro. **VS**

● **HAVING LABELLED MY** glaze buckets for years with numbers and letters, I recently started using names of friends instead, a great *aide-memoire* to what is in them – for example Bob over Jane good – Jane under May interesting but unusual. **SG**

● **A SECOND SMALLER** bucket for each of one's regular glazes, labelled with the glaze, each with its own sponge and nearly full of water, can be very useful. When glazing, the glazed pot bases (or any areas not requiring glaze) are washed off with the sponge from the relative smaller bucket. It is surprising how much glaze can be saved this way, and when a new batch of glaze is made its smaller bucket of 'washings' is put through the sieves as well. **MB**

● **TO RETURN TO** labelling – despite all my 'tips', I still confound myself with bags of white powder. I know I can test these mystery materials, but even the anticipation of such tedium tests me to distraction. So now I write a description of the contents in permanent ink, on unfriendly non-degradable, indestructible plastic labels, which I place inside the containers as a precaution in case the external label fails. **SB**

● **I WAS INTERESTED** to read Susan Bennett's solution to avoiding the problem of unmarked materials. One system she did not mention is to mix a little of the material with water to the consistency of glaze and paint it on a round biscuit-fired tile marked on the back in manganese with the name, source and date of the material. When fired in the kiln it will be a visual and literal reminder of the material and can be stored inside the barrel or packet. If two buttons are made, one can hang on the outside. Anonymous materials can be similarly button-tested for identification. **CC**

● **NEVER THROW GLAZES** away. If you have decided to stop using them pour what is left into a special bucket. It always comes in handy for glazing the insides of narrow-necked pots. **PS**

● **AVOIDING THOSE ANONYMOUS** bags of white powder in the glaze cupboard is much more preferable to trying to work out what they are despite the useful tips given in *Ceramic Review* over the years. One golden rule is to always place a piece of cardboard with the name of the material written in black indelible felt-tip pen inside the bag, bucket or sack, no matter how small the amount – you will never remember what it is no matter how 'individual' the container. This is in addition to the label on the outside, which often dries up and falls off or becomes indecipherable. Purists may want to add the source of the material, though in my experience the next batch is likely to vary slightly. **GG**

● **KEEP ALL YOUR** scraps of glaze from tests and suchlike in one large container. The addition of oxides will often result in a useful black or dark brown, which can be applied on the inside of vessels. **DAJ**

● **GARBAGE GLAZE. SET** aside a bucket of water in which to wash off all glazing equipment, sponges used to wipe over the table or glaze spills on the floor, your hands, and any 'glazing mistakes'. When the bucket is fairly full, skim off the excess water then sieve the glaze through a fine sieve to remove small bits of sponge that may have fallen in. Test the glaze. It will probably be green. Add an opacifier such as zinc oxide if an opaque glaze is wanted. Additions of oxides should also be tried, if the green is unattractive. If lead glazes were added to the bucket make a note to use the garbage glaze on pot exteriors only. I have added ash glazes and have never had any problems, but do not add glazes that crystallise. **AL**

We all make glaze tests but only three items on this fascinating subject appeared in Tips, though these give sound advice. From Monica Russell, Bolton Technical College and Audrey Price.

● **BEING AN INVETERATE** glaze tester I am constantly running out of suitable containers. I have now discovered the perfect solution in the polystyrene cups used in my local college for serving drinks. The college throw them away: I collect them, give them a rinse, and they are excellent. The cup is half-filled with a 100g test, which is an economical and an ideal amount for dipping small tiles or pots. Reference numbers can be clearly written on the side without the use of labels, and if you are lucky enough to find the plastic snap-on lids supplied with hot drinks, then the tests can be stored in piles of three – always a wise precaution in case the test for some reason fails because of a kiln mishap.

Incidentally, I put all the test remnants in the 'ends' bucket and get quite a useful glaze which can be used for the insides of pots: as I work at stoneware temperatures this is quite safe. **MR**

 ● **SENSIBLY SIZED GLAZE** tests, say 5 × 3", may be fired on edge (to check for glaze running and appearance on upright surfaces) if they are stacked in a toast rack built from slabs, I prefer to use crank mixture for this. **BTC**

● **WHEN I AM** testing glazes, clays or oxides I prefer to throw small (2-2½") open dishes rather than using small clay squares or oblong pieces. These little open dishes are then useful for mixing up oxides or small quantities of coloured slips for brush decoration. They can be numbered and records kept about the test. I find they stack easily for storage and are not only more interesting to make but give a better idea of the possibilities of that particular glaze, oxide or clay. **AP**

James Walford lists a clever glaze adjustment guide; Darwin Turner tries out gouache colours, though he does not say if these are cheaper than oxides.

● **I TEND TO** fire at a constant temperature of 1280°C, and during the course of testing various glazes I have found it useful to have a quick rule of thumb which could help me to make an adjustment for altered materials so as to keep the glaze maturing temperature constant. For this I have evolved a points system based on a glaze temperature of 1280°C, which gives compensations for small changes to the glaze composition. To keep the glaze temperature constant the system is used so that the final points balance out. Thus:

Adding 1% China clay	+2	Adding 1% Fireclay	+1.5
Adding 1% Limestone	−1	Adding 1% Red iron oxide	−0.5
Adding 1% Elm ash	−0.2	Adding 1% Quartz or flint	+0.5
Adding 1% Feldspar	−0.5		
Adding 1% White ball clay	+0.75		
Adding 1% Red Devon clay	−0.25		

If one adds 1% china clay to a glaze, one must also add either 2% limestone or some other material which will give 2 minus points.

I must stress that this method applies for small variations only. Due to the many combinations that quartz or flint can enter into, it will be found that this is the least reliable value. Potters who use other materials will find their own points value in due course. In practice I have found that each point is equivalent to a variation of about 4°C, so that if only 1% china clay is added to the glaze this will raise the glaze temperature by about 8°C.

Now that china stone is no longer being mined, I have found the following substitution useful in cases where a glaze formula stipulates china stone:

China stone (4 parts) ....Feldspar (2 parts)
Quartz or flint (1 part)
White ball clay (1 part) **JW**

● **I HAVE RECENTLY** tried Winsor and Newton Designer's Gouache colours to decorate tin glaze to 1020°C and the results are given below:

Colour Name	Pigment Composition	Results (1020°C)	Likely Results (1250°C)
Brilliant Green	Copper and zinc	Almost zero	No comment
Naples Yellow	Reduced cadmium sulphide	Much blistered yellow	Probably burns off
Raw Umber	Synthetic iron oxide	Good brown	Probably very good
Red Ochre	Synthetic iron oxide	Streaky pale brown	Probably fair
Yellow Ochre	Synthetic iron oxide	V good; stable dark brown	Probably very good
Oxide of Chromium	Chromium sesquioxide	V good; green blisters where too thick	Probably very good
Cobalt Blue	Cobalt aluminate	Superb blue	Probably very good
Cadmium Yellow Deep	Cadmium sulphide	Almost zero	Probably burns off

It can be seen that Yellow Ochre, Oxide of Chromium and Cobalt Blue give very good colours and, as they are so convenient for small-scale productions, I see them as a very useful addition to the small workshop. **DT**

Joseph Neville gives a clever method for measuring small amounts of material.

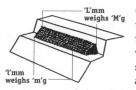

'L'mm weighs 'M'g

'l'mm weighs 'm'g

● **MEASURING MINUTE AMOUNTS** of powdered material when preparing test stains and glazes presents difficulties when a chemical balance is not available. Here is a way of employing the commonplace balance and weights scales to obtain reasonably accurate results. Pleat paper as in diagram, place on the load pan (it is rarely necessary to counterbalance) then add the minimum weight ('M'g) to the weight pan which decisively tips the balance. Now tip the powder into the centre fold until equilibrium is regained, and smooth it out into a regular prismatic column. Measure the powder's length ('L'mm). If 'm'g is the weight required, then the length ('l'mm) of powder in millimetres to be slid off and collected will be: $L \times m/M$. **JN**

The Wellington Potters Newsletter gives a useful conversion of cobalt compounds. Peter Venning writes about finding granite dust to use as an ingredient of glazes.

● **IF YOU HAVE** a glaze recipe which requires cobalt carbonate, but you only have the oxide, or vice versa, here is a conversion formula. It applies only to cobalt. Divide carbonate amount by 100, multiply by 63 = oxide amount. Divide oxide amount by 63, multiply by 100 = carbonate amount. **WPN**

● **FOR THOSE POTTERS** who want to try granite dust glazes like Penlee stone etc., I noticed a ready source of stone dust at a nearby quarry. The screened and graded stone is fed into large hoppers, under which a lorry is driven, before some ten tons of stone descends into the lorry amidst a cloud of dust. **PV**

Simple and practical, like all good tips, is that from Hilary Sutton, on keeping your glazes clean.

● **I HAVE A** small studio pottery and love experimenting with different coloured glazes. I found, however, that I spent ages washing up my sieves and brushes to remove all traces of colouring oxides to prevent specking in white glazes – especially with the all powerful cobalt oxide – until my partner suggested having two complete sets – one for white or clear and one for coloured glazes. It was further suggested that red 'warning' paint would help distinguish clearly one set from the other. The result is a saving in time and anguish – specking is banished forever. **HS**

Susan Bennett and Mike Rawlinson tackle some of the discomforts and chills of winter glazing.

● **IS YOUR STUDIO** constantly heated to a comfortable working temperature? If it is, do not bother to read on. If like mine it is not, then maybe you can benefit from my latest flash of enlightenment.

I had always dreaded glazing more than anything in cold weather when the temperature, especially near ground level, was near zero. Putting a hand into a bucket of freezing glaze was torture – thawing out was worse. I invariably throw with warm water when it is very cold but it has taken me ten years of annual suffering to solve the glazing problem. Simply decant the water off the top of the glaze before you stir it; replace with the same volume of very hot water, thus taking the chill off the contents, and preventing chilblains on the hands. Simple, quick and effective – I still cannot understand why it took me so long to think of it. **SB**

● **GLAZING POTS BY** hand in the winter months was never my favourite job, until I hit upon the following way of making life a little more pleasant.

Unless the glaze is one which settles well, I add a little flocculant to it, e.g. calcium chloride or sodium carbonate, which causes it to settle out. When I want to use the glaze, I remove all the water from the top of the bucket, measure it, and replace it with an equal volume of boiling water. When this is stirred in with a stick, the glaze is warm enough to make this task reasonably pleasant. **MR**

A final item by Ann Parkhouse leads into the next chapter.

● **I HAD BEEN** experiencing considerable difficulty with an earthenware transparent glaze bought from a commercial supplier. The glaze had a simple addition of iron oxide to produce a rich brown over a red body. However the glazed ware showed blisters varying in size and sharp around the edges.

On writing to the manufacturers it was suggested I raise the bisque firing to allow gases to escape from the ware before glazing. This I did with no improved result. Eventually I found that by slowing down the kiln when I could see the glaze starting to melt, around 900-1080°C, the fault disappeared. **AP**

Chapter 6
Kilns and firing

The actual building of kilns is too large a topic for the Tips column but many details were considered. Vincent Cooper and Paul Reid give advice on the cutting and shaping of insulating firebrick.

● **TO CUT INSULATING** firebrick I have always used either a tungsten carbide disc on a power drill, or a large hacksaw. Neither is satisfactory – the first is fast but inaccurate, messy (and produces harmful dust) and wears out the discs quite rapidly; the second is more accurate but tedious, needs a new blade every few bricks, and I find that the hacksaw frame gets in the way when cutting bricks in half.

My method, arrived at quite by chance, is to use a logsaw (light tubular frame with 24" disposable, large-toothed blade). Old blades are quite adequate and can be reversed when the firebrick has really rotted the teeth in one direction. It cuts fast, as accurately as a hacksaw, and the large frame easily spans a brick lengthwise. For the really conservation-minded, I am sure the blades could then be made into turning tools, anti-theft shelf fronts, etc. **VC**

● **WHEN KILN BUILDING,** one of the most time consuming jobs is shaping the bricks for the arch. Although a hacksaw can be used to considerable advantage to cut white-hot face bricks I suggest that a better way is to simply rub the bricks on a pre-cast concrete building block (such as the type you might use for the base of the kiln). Bricks can be 'worn' to shape very accurately using this method. Considerable amounts of dust are left and this can be used to fill cavities or spread over the top of the arch as insulation. **PR**

Problems with electric kiln elements have beset most potters. Stephen Grieve, Susan Bennett, Carenza Hayhoe, G A Stevens and Emmanuel Cooper deal with some of these. For those who do not have access to a blowlamp it is possible to switch the kiln on until the elements begin to glow, then turn it off (very important) and push the sagging elements back into their slots. There will be an all-enveloping heat in the chamber so a longer 'blunt instrument' is needed.

● **AS THE BOOKS** so often remind us, Kanthal elements become very brittle after firing: nevertheless, should an element sag or bunch up, it can easily be pushed back into place by heating to orange heat with a blow lamp and then using a blunt instrument. **SG**

● **HERE IS A** simple emergency procedure to extend the working life of a broken element when no replacement is to hand and you are desperate to fire the kiln.

Heat one side of the broken element with a blowtorch until it is as hot as you can make it, and the metal is pliable. With pliers bend it into a hook and carefully hook it around the other side of the break. This will make a connection and should give you at least another firing.

Warning: do not attempt this without heating the element. The metal is so brittle when cold, it will snap. Do not forget to turn off the electricity supply to the kiln when engaged in this work unless you are prepared to be the object of the firing. **SB**

● **A SIMPLER AND** safer method of repairing an element, rather than using a blowtorch, is to bridge the gap with a four inch coil taken from an old element and winding it to join the two ends together.

Last time this was necessary, the repair lasted for four years of at least weekly firings in my biscuit kiln. At this point, I sold the kiln and for all I know the repaired element is still in use. **CH**

● **WHEN REPLACING THE** element in my Hobbycraft kiln, I received two tightly coiled elements about three feet long which had to fit into two grooves in the kiln approximately three times longer.

Lay a piece of gauge for the required length, a knot at each end marking the length of the final element. One end of the element, together with one end of the string, is tightly clamped in a vice.

It is a simple matter to stretch the element in one hand whilst offering up the string with the other until the length of the stretched element coincides with the second knot in the string. The string may then be kept for future use. **GAS**

Simple burnout

Ends interlocked

● **ONE METHOD OF** joining together a burnt-out element is illustrated above. Stretch the wire and interlock; dab the join with water. Turn on the electricity supply, which will cause the wire to arc at the joins and fuse together. (From *Electric Kiln Pottery*, Batsford.) **EC**

Joseph Neville suggests an alternative source for switchgears, while an inventive lid for top loaders is illustrated by B Hobbs.

● **ELECTRIC KILN SWITCHGEARS** of the Simmerstat type often have a shorter working life than identical controls (240/50V, 15amp) fitted to ordinary domestic stoves, when the thermocouple in a kiln switch has to contend with intense heat, vapour and corrosive fumes. Replacement switches are readily available without cost when salvaged from a discarded electric cooker – no trivial economy, since new thermostatic switches are often quite expensive. **JN**

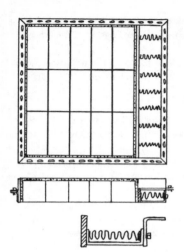

● **DETERMINED TO MAKE** a cube of Savit bricks for a top-loading electric kiln I was building, I devised this idea to hold the (removable) lid bricks in place.

Make sure there is enough compression of the springs to cater for some movement of the bricks and blanket. Keep the springs well outside the kiln. My lid is about 25 × 24" (brick area) and it is about the maximum size and weight for this idea. **BH**

Two hints on firing plates and wide-based pots from Frands Sorensen (from the Faroe Islands) and Tricia Whillock.

● **LARGE PLATES USUALLY** need care and time and, as a consequence of this, lots of room to dry out safely. Now I have found out that using wooden grills instead of ordinary shelves makes it possible to dry out plates up to at least 16" overnight.

Though my plates are rather thin I stack them 7-10 high for bisque firing. I decide the centre of the stack and place three rolls of grogged clay radially. The first (and largest if the plates are not equal in size) plate is placed on top of then and again 3 rolls placed exactly above the three first rolls and so on. Done carefully the plates are under no tension at all during the firing and I could probably fire even higher stacks of plates this way. **FS**

● **I FIND IT** best to fire such pieces on a double thickness of newspaper with a thin, even layer of fine grog on the paper. This seems to dispel any tension between the coiled wall and base, and so avoids cracks. **TW**

Rosemary Capes from Almeria, Edwin Todd and Lucy Learman have ideas to prevent lids sticking during firing.

● **FOR INSTANT RELEASE** of lids after firing, paint calcined alumina in lid sill before waxing. A sparse covering will do – it stops clay sticking to clay and dusts off easily. **RC**

● **APPLY ALUMINIUM PAINT** to the rims of casseroles and teapots so that the lids will not stick. **ET**

● **I USE A** proprietary brand of water-soluble wax resist to paint on flanges and lids and find that on this smooth, slippery surface alumina hydrate – an ideal material to prevent surfaces sticking together – will not stay in place. However, a good pinch of alumina in the liquid wax mixture does both jobs in one and works a treat. **LL**

Six hints on packing kilns come from Susan Bennett, Cynthia Wardley, Margaret Power and Martin Cowley, plus a tip on unpacking hot pots from G A Stevens. In addition to the Perspex mentioned an ordinary lathe of wood, long enough to stretch across from one shelf support to another, is adequate. Two or three different lengths are useful.

● **THIS IS A** tip with more economical firings in mind. I have noticed that many potters are shy of experimenting with kiln packing when they first obtain a kiln. I pack very tight kilns out of necessity, even ¼" saved low down can make a big difference to how much I can pack at the top of the kiln.

I take it for granted that everyone knows you use three props only to support the shelves – four being unstable and wasteful of space – and that the props on the next shelf should be placed directly over those already in place. If the tallest piece of ware is just a fraction higher than the most suitable prop, I do not add a 1" prop extension, I find some bits of broken kiln shelf – I have a large collection of thick and thin broken shelves – and I build up the props with them. I even use the flattened balls of stiff, highly grogged clay (rolled in sand to prevent adherence to shelves and props) but here you must be careful that the weight of the shelves above does not completely flatten your clay. Used near the top of the kiln these clay pads are useful to steady shelves and give a little extra height to a prop where needed. **SB**

● **THE KILN IS** almost fully packed – a final check and somehow you manage to knock the edge of a spout or handle, and the fragment disappears on to a lower shelf threatening to stick to, and ruin, another object. What do you do if you cannot reach it? Start unpacking the kiln? Wait – as long as the fragment is visibly accessible, attach a blob of clay to the end of an unravelled wire coat-hanger bent into the required shape, and manoeuvre it until it touches the offending fragment – it should adhere easily. Withdraw carefully, and proceed as normal. You might experiment with a stick or paint-brush. For tiny fragments sticky tape might help. Whatever you do, as in life in general – do not give up, 'stick at it'. **SB**

● **PLANNING THE PRECISE** arrangement of pots in the kiln has become a simple matter since I noticed that a ware board in my workshop was the exact width of a kiln shelf. I worked out spaces representing kiln shelves on the board, including the positions of the shelf props. When the board is filled with dry pots I know it is time for another firing and also exactly where each pot is to be placed in the kiln. **CW**

● **PEERING INTO A** top-loading kiln, upside-down and sideways, to ensure clearance between the highest ware and the next kiln shelf can be awkward. I have found a sheet of clear Perspex useful, placed on the props. If there is any doubt about the depth of clearance, a mark on the Perspex with a felt-tip pen over the high points makes it easy to estimate the space. **MP**

● **MY KILN IS** 20" wide and 18" from door to back with elements in the floor and sides. The following method of packing allows me to fire bowls/plates of 19" and greater in diameter. I have encountered no problems with warpage at earthenware temperatures, but be careful – a 19" bowl landing on your foot can be a health hazard.

If you have an unglazed rim, or leave a 'dry spot', pack the bowl on two shelves and then elevate the front of the upper shelf, allowing the bowl's rim to rest on the back wall of the kiln, this allows access to the small wedge shape between the shelves to sneak in a few tiny items. **MC**

● **WHEN HANDLING HOT** pottery from the kiln, leather (not plastic) gardening gloves protect from moderate heat, and also from sharp glaze spikes left by kiln stilts. **GAS**

A number of potters submitted their own ideas for cheap, easily made pot supports and shelf spacers. A highly refractory and fairly open clay will help to prevent vitrification at stoneware temperatures. Contributors are Elana Morris, Nora Kay, Susan Bennett, Alan H Bolton and Andrew Crisp.

● **I USE SMALL** pieces of old kiln batts as spacers for adding to shelf props when packing the kiln. **EM**

● **SHELF SPACERS CAN** easily be made from the odd pieces of flat clay remaining left over when making moulded dishes or plates from slabs of rolled clay. Large moulds need thicker slabs and small ones use thinner clay, so 'spacers' of different thickness can easily be made. Just cut them out of the residue clay with a small biscuit cutter or suitable tin lid – a wipe with an oily rag stops the clay sticking to the cutter – dry them between wooden boards to keep them flat; when dry put them inside any pots and include them in a biscuit firing. The use of these small flat discs added to ordinary props means that small space-saving adjustments can easily be made. **NK**

● **I REALLY ENJOY** the challenge of kiln-packing – apart from the strain lifting heavy shelves imposes on my neck and thumbs. *Ceramic Review* readers may remember my earlier tip about using bits of kiln shelf and pads of stiff groggy clay to raise shelves sufficiently to clear pots without wasting space with a full extension piece (p115). I have developed a useful refinement which avoids the risk of pads of clay compressing under the weight of further shelves and damaging ware already in place.

Simply make yourself batches of pads of varying thickness to fit over your props, and fire them to the highest temperature you fire to. They will come in useful to counteract the effect of a slightly warped shelf as well as giving you greater flexibility in economical kiln packing.

Using this method I am often able to squeeze in a full shelf of ware at the top of my arched kiln instead of having to waste the space at either side. I save and prosper – you can too. **SB**

● **BISCUIT FIRING MY** bottomed planters was a problem until I started using already biscuit fired rings (about 4" diameter by 1" high). Now I can stack them at least six high whilst filling them up with smaller pots. **AHB**

● **ROLL OUT A** sheet of fine stoneware clay to about ¹⁄₈ inch thickness, cut into strips about ¹⁄₄ inch wide, in turn chopped up into pieces 1 inch long. These are then biscuit fired, and serve as useful props for earthenware glaze firings. Even when the bottoms of pieces are cleaned of glaze (as is often the case with school earthenware firing) runs and drips can occur with over thick and inexperienced application of glaze to a pot. This method is cheaper and sometimes more convenient that the use of regular stilts. **AC**

Three submissions on the irritating business of glaze dribbles on expensive kiln shelves. Glaze can be chipped away more easily from the even dearer silicon carbide shelves (which can be used in electric kilns, contrary to some reports). The first comes from Susan Bennett; Joseph Neville supplies two suggestions.

● **TRY SPRINKLING SAND** onto small blobs of glaze which have melted on to kiln shelves, rather than attack them with a hammer and chisel. After the next high firing the sand will have soaked up the glaze and it will be much easier to clean off without damage to the shelf. **SB**

● **APART FROM ACTING** as spacers or adjusters of kiln props, as advocated by Nora Kay, suitably sized and shaped refractory thin discs prove invaluable protectors of batts from glaze driblets during glost firing. Such discs are readily made from stoneware body heavily tempered with materials like kaolin, flint or silica sand, or alumina, to the degree of nearly losing plasticity. Raw glazed ware can be appropriately placed on unfired protective spacers, but – whether green or biscuited – a light dusting of placing powder or a thin coat of batt wash should be applied to each disc's top surface before ware is placed upon it, in order to facilitate separation after firing. Once protective discs have been strategically positioned under pots, expensive batts and cherished pottery should no longer be endangered by glaze dribbles. In particular, the horrendous effects of 'glaze plucking' are sidestepped. In the event of any glaze flowing down over the base of a pot, it is an easy matter to snap away any adherent disc and to grind off glaze spurs. Any disc that has been contaminated by an ooze of glaze should be scrapped. Compare the economy and effectiveness of employing refractory spacer biscuits with the ruinous effects of coating first one surface and then the other of costly batts with batt wash; a ritual which creates a moonscape of buckled layers of kiln wash, punctuated with craters and mounds where glaze dribbles have fluxed their way right through coats of wash and placing powders, before digesting the batt itself. **JN**

● **BATT WASH AND** placing powder are made of highly refractory materials such as kaolin, flint and alumina. Kaolin and its close relative Fullers Earth are present in quite large amounts in the thick, heavy and brilliantly glossy paper which characterises superior quality publications... *Ceramic Review* for example. Four or more layers of high-grade paper strategically interposed between pot base and kiln shelf can prove as effective as any wash or powder. The paper's lignin/cellulose network burns away during the 'smoking phase' leaving its loading of refractory ash in situ as a separating medium. And once the kiln has cooled, this ash can be vacuumed away in a trice. Three cautions – apart from never vandalising CR for the purpose. Paper can only be used in electric kilns, where there are no gusts of hot gas to scatter ash, and, similarly, paper should not overhang shelving. Finally, neither paper, wash nor powder can be relied upon to defend pot bases and kiln shelves from the dire effects of massive drips and oozing on the part of glazes that are either insufficiently viscous or are badly applied. In such cases disposable and very thin refractory ceramic discs or tiles remain the sole means of mitigating the damage to both pot and the underlying kiln batt. **JN**

Batt wash and firebars are discussed by Peter Lee, Chris Southall, Bruno Manini and Susan Bennett.

● **FOR WOOD FIRING** potters. Coat your kiln shelves with three parts 20 mesh clean river sand mixed with one part white bread flour to a soft paste. Spread with a builder's trowel to cover evenly and clean edges thoroughly. This sets firmly and does not brush off during packing. After firing it falls off. **PL**

● **I WOULD LIKE** to pass on a tip discovered in the construction of our 130 cu.ft. wood kiln. Faced with the usual problem of firebars I used 3" diameter props. The bars are still going strong after three years' use. **CS**

● **HOWEVER CAREFUL POTTERS** are with their glazes and glazing it seems inevitable that sooner or later accidents occur in the kiln. Either due to glaze formulas on firing or stacking, pots get stuck to batts as if by mutual attraction.

Bits get chipped out of the batts and they end up looking like moon craters. If you brush the batt wash on, not only do you wear out the brush quickly, but the channels are merely filmed over.

I have found that by making up the wash to a thin cream consistency and applying it with a palette knife, not only are the indentations filled in but any unmixed power is easily broken down as you put it on. **BM**

● **WITH EVERYTHING GLAZED** ready to fire my new kiln to stoneware for the first time, I discovered I had forgotten to batt wash the shelves. My 12 hours of cheap rate electricity were running out – I needed a quick solution in case the glazes ran in an untested atmosphere and firing cycle. Sprinkling a layer of sand on the shelves seems a good idea, but it invariably finds its way on the the ware below.

The solution. Place a shallow container of clean, dry sand, a bowl of water and a sponge next to the kiln. Before you place your ware on the shelf, skim the base with a damp sponge and dab it gently on the sand – it will pick up just enough to raise it off the shelf should the glaze flow more than usual. It will also work well on old shelves that have become coated with a thin layer of glaze material, which causes the bases of pots to adhere and chip as you lift them – even when the glaze has not run.

Do not, however, rely on this method for totally untried glaze combinations. If you are unsure, do not risk ruining good shelves – take a piece of broken kiln shelf that will support the base of your pot with some to spare, sprinkle some sand on it and when it is in situ in the kiln, then place your pot on top. If the worst happens, you have minimised your losses. **SB**

The use of digital indicators; a simple form of kiln alarm; and a system of standardising the kiln log are described by Derek Clarkson, A M Seiko and Mike Francis.

● **POSITION YOUR DIGITAL** temperature indicator (DTI) so that it can be seen alongside a clock which has a seconds finger. This allows a very quick check on the rate of rise (or fall) in temperature, e.g. an increase of 1°C in 60 seconds indicates a rise of 60°C per hour; 1°C in 45 seconds – 90°C per hour.

A DTI is particularly useful during reduction firing at the time when making adjustments to burners, air and damper to give a reducing atmosphere. You see at once whether the temperature is still rising, static or falling and can make any readjustments immediately if necessary.

The kiln temperature can easily be seen at a glance across the studio and the connecting cable to the thermocouple can run to almost any length (useful if your kiln is in a shed at the bottom of the garden). My DTI is positioned in the studio rather than the kiln room so I can keep an eye on the firing's progress as I work. A 90° swivel of the DTI as I go through to the kiln room means I can also see the temperature whilst making adjustments at the kiln. **DC**

● **A TIP FOR** potters and technicians in business and education alike, especially if you have electric kilns that quietly switch on and off during the firing cycle, allowing you to pot on, forget them completely and thus causing untold damage and heartbreak. For as little as £10 you can invest in a digital alarm wristwatch that can be set to remind you to check on your precious charge at any interval you require, wake you up to get to that jamboree in time or even tell you it is time for Martinis on the terrace. **AMS**

● **WHEN MAKING COMPARISONS** between firing cycles with the use of my 'kiln log', to make things easier for my unmathematical brain I operate the following system.

I have a clock which I keep solely for use with the kiln. When starting the kiln I start the clock but instead of it reading the time of day, I set the clock to twelve. This translates to my 'kiln log' as '00 hours'. When the kiln has run for an hour and the clock reads one o'clock then the log reads '01 hours'. So whether I start some time in the morning or evening the kiln log always runs from '00 hours' onwards so enabling immediate comparison with previous firings without mental acrobatics, and one can see at a glance how many hours the kiln has taken. **MF**

The infra-red light from kilns can harm your eyes and L E Wells, Peter and Wendy Green, Jonathan Chiswell Jones, Bolton Technical College, John Cooper and John Lawrence all contribute warnings and ideas. But firstly, an illustration from France for a 'cone spy'.

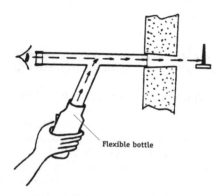

Flexible bottle

● **IN POTTERY LITERATURE** warnings sometimes appear about dust and poisonous materials; and at other times about singed eyebrows. But I cannot recall any warnings about the effect of heat upon the eyes themselves. Too much ultra-violet light can cause great discomfort (i.e. snow-blindness) but the eyes generally recover after treatment and rest; however, damage caused by infra-red light (heat) can be much more difficult to put right.

I know that generally potters do not gaze into their kilns for minutes on end, and I do not wish in any way to be alarmist; but I do feel that potters ought to be fully aware of the danger. Either limit the time spent exposed to direct heat (as when stoking a solid fuel kiln) or conscientiously use eye-shielding goggles or screen. Even ordinary window glass will provide some protection, though the ideal is a glass with a pale green tint (from inclusion of iron, the molecules of which tend to block the infra-red rays) such as is actually used by industrial furnace-men.

Sunglasses will, of course, provide some protection, but on no account use those with plastic lenses and/or frames. **LEW**

● **WE HAVE BEEN** very worried recently to see sunglasses beside potters' kilns. These are being used to see inside the kiln, but their use is dangerous. Bright light causes the pupil to contract; sunglasses counteract this effect. They cut out the light but have no effect on the amount of infra-red rays reaching the back of the eye and can lead eventually to blindness. Goggles from ceramic suppliers or shops dealing in industrial safety equipment are both effective and safe. **PG/WG**

● **WITH APOLOGIES TO** those potters who have already taken this sensible precaution, may I suggest that those firing to stoneware temperatures invest in a pair of cheap welding goggles when peering at cones. I am told that staring into hot kilns can damage the eyes, but aside from this health hazard, a pair of goggles makes it much easier to see what is going on. **JCJ**

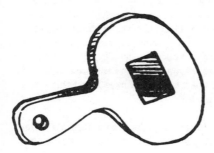

● **EYES ARE PROTECTED** and pyrometric cones rendered more easily visible if, when peering through kiln spyholes, one looks through a piece of blue glass, such as the dark cobalt blue glass used in school laboratories for observing flames. For convenience, this glass can be mounted in a piece of plywood like a ping-pong bat with a hole in it. It can then be hung on a nail and not mislaid or dropped and broken. **BTC**

● **WHEN MY RAKU** kiln was up to temperature, say around 1000°C, it proved very difficult when peering in the top to see the state of the glazes through the glare, even using a blue glass filter. In a moment of desperation, bearing in mind all safety factors, I took the unlikely step of a narrow beam torch shining in the hole at the top of the kiln. Lo and behold, the glaze (boiling at that time) picked up the beam and the surface reflected the torchlight giving a clear picture of what was happening. A torch is now an essential part of my equipment. **JC**

● **AFTER MORE THAN** forty years of spyhole gazing my optician told me I had a cataract in my eye. I started using the glass from a gas welding mask which kept getting lost. Finding an old aluminium frying pan the idea evolved of a 'Ned Kelly' cone gazer. Unless you have some metal sticky tape, plastic tape will work providing you do not gaze too long. It is a good idea to have two versions – a dark one for glaze firings and a paler one for biscuit. **JL**

Help on the difficulty of placing cones in the kiln is given by Julie Woods, Don Witts and Stephen Grieve. Joseph Neville salvages broken unfired cones by re-forming them, Juliet Breese and Anne Kenny suggest uses for fired cones and Nirmala Patwardhan comes up with a cone alternative.

● **AS MY ELECTRIC** kiln has such a small spyhole I found it difficult to see whether my cones had been placed correctly when the door was closed. I solved this problem easily by placing the cone in roughly the right position then pushing a lighted match into the clay holding the cone thus lighting the interior of the kiln whilst the door was closed. Leave the bung out to allow some air supply and close the door gently. **JW**

● **SEEING THE CONE** through small spyholes, or in awkward places, an ordinary candle cut up into about three pieces (which will last a long time) can be used. When it comes to placing the cones, place them in the approximate position, and then on the same shelf, or very near it place the small piece of candle, usually in a ½ inch prop for stability, and light it; this gives ample illumination, and, provided one is not too heavy-handed closing and opening the kiln door, it stays alight until you have positioned the cones. If you have more than one cone position then use two or more candle bits at the same time. I have found this a very useful and easy method of cone placement. **DW**

● **TO GET CONES** in the correct position in the kiln I have constructed a series of simple 'T'-shaped pieces of wood which just fit the bottom and sides of the door openings.

These are made at the correct height for the spyholes and have the lateral position for the cones marked on them. **SG**

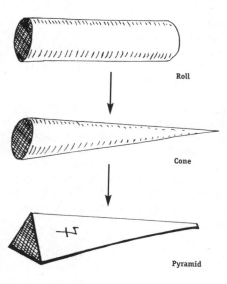

Roll

Cone

Pyramid

● **ATTEMPTS TO REPAIR** broken unfired pyrometric cones are exasperating and futile, as well as inviting bungled kiln thermometry. However, when two packs of much-needed number 7 cones arrived, and nearly all the cones proved to have broken in transit, it was imperative to attempt wholesale salvage: a task which proved easy, using a method which should be applicable to few or many fractured cones, provided they all belong to the same code and manufacturer. Never amalgamate cone fragments from different batches, code values or manufacturers. You will produce eutectic hybrids which are good for nothing.

Grind the broken pieces in a mortar and convert to a slurry with rain or ion-free water. Dry to plasticity without placing the mass on any absorbent surface which might leach away soluble fluxes. Knead thoroughly, then roll out into the appropriate number of true geometric cones, which are pressed by thumb and finger into pyramids whose dimensions should be precisely one smidgeon larger than a virgin cone so as to allow for shrinkage during drying. Smooth facets with a modelling tool before scratching the identifying code number on to each reconstituted cone. Finally, make up your mind whether to complain to the supplier or take your custom elsewhere in future. (In the event you will probably do neither.) **JN**

● **FOR THOSE USING** cones – if you make two holes in the blob of clay you stand the cone up with, some of them will make strong/good/free/unusual cup/coat hooks. **JB**

● **WHAT TO DO** with those fired cones (stuck in a blob of fired clay) – why not call them 'dragon's teeth' and sell them for charity? Interesting objects in their own right and ecologically correct recycling in action. Display them in a flat basket and kids love them. Three for £2 seems to be the going rate. **AK**

● **IF YOU HAVE** no cones and the pyrometer is not working you can improvise a cone. Take your best and most reliable glaze, pour it on a plaster slab and, when pliable, roll it in your hands quickly and stick this on to a blob of clay as you do with any Orton cone. It should melt down at the correct temperature. This I learnt in Korea from Yooa Kwang Chow. **NP**

Impatient potters are helped by Susan Bennett, those plagued by bloating clay by Nigel Buchanan-Wollaston, while Rik Midgley suggests how to avoid steam blow-outs in a gas kiln.

● **IF YOU ARE** so pushed for time that you have to fire damp pots in a bisque kiln, then lessen the risk of losing them through cracked bases or blow-outs by the simple expedient of firing them 'bottoms up' – if possible in the coolest part of the kiln. The water content escapes more easily.

I only hit on this simple solution recently and, by firing as slowly as possible, upside-down, I now lose far fewer of my 'at risk' pots. **SB**

● **IN 1976 I** was using a body made up of Hymod SMD, Hymod AT, Acme Marls Buff Burning clay A62 (a fireclay – loss on ignition 11.5%) plus sand and/or grog. At the time I was biscuit firing in a new 10 cu.ft. electric kiln and firing the glaze in a 42 cu.ft. oil-fired kiln. Spectacular bloating occurred. After blaming my glaze firing cycle for a while but gaining no better results from alterations to it, with much valued help from Russell Collins I came to blame the body. I wrote to Acme Marls suggesting that A62 was to blame and almost at once had a visit from their clay manager Mr Barker. He took away samples of the two bodies I was using, for testing, suggesting that my biscuit firing was probably at fault.

The results of Mr Barker's tests showed him to be right and that the biscuit firing cycle was too fast between about 650°C and 1000°C. Not only that, but the kiln was insufficiently ventilated at this time when carbonaceous matter should have been burning off. In fact there may even have been a reducing atmosphere in the kiln so that it could not burn off, and oxidation would be essential to allow this to happen.

If I biscuit in the electric kiln now (only occasionally) I have a ½" gap at the lower spyhole, and at the vent in the roof of the kiln, from about 650°C until the cone is over – and I get no bloating at all in the following glaze firings. Biscuiting in the oil kiln does not present the same difficulties because it is naturally oxidising and ventilated, but I still go slowly for the last 300°C, i.e. somewhere around 50°C per hour.

I have heard of many people using buff clays, which are usually some shade of grey when plastic due to their content of organic matter, and in particular Potclays Buff and Acme Marls Throwing Clay E7, who are getting serious bloating at 1260-1300°C. They are often advised to soak at 960°C, 1000°C or even 1060°C (which may be higher than they want to go), but no one mentions ventilation, which I believe is equally important. The point is that the damage is done in the biscuit firing, which is perhaps more important than some people realise. Alas, I am not offering a cure for all bloating – I wish I could. **NB-W**

● **STEAM BLOW-OUTS ARE** a problem with raw/bisque firing in a gas kiln. There may be a tendency for this to occur towards the bottom of the kiln. The atmosphere is relatively calm in the kiln during the early firing stages; however as the top warms up a hot area develops which gradually moves downwards resulting in a rapid temperature rise at the bottom.

A temporary extension to the flue will reduce this effect by increasing the draw and thus the turbulence within the kiln. I use an old two foot chimney for this; a piece of flue pipe would suffice. This extension should be removed when steam clears the flue at around 400°C. **RM**

The position of pots in a kiln will often affect the result but it is not always possible to remember which glaze is on which pot. Tony O'Donovan describes an identification system to help rectify this.

● **I HAVE GLAZES** that perform better at the top, or bottom of the kiln, as I imagine most of us have. Some glazed pots can sit around a long time and one can be uncertain as to what the glaze is, so I use a traffic lights system: a dab of red for those that like the top, a green for the bottom. Use waterproof ink, or culinary dyes, and nothing for the glazes you can recognise. **TO'D**

Oxidation and reduction, the twin poles of firing, prompt entries from Peter and Wendy Green and the Pottery Supply House, Ontario.

● **TO ASSESS THE** state of the atmosphere within a gas fired kiln at temperatures above 750°C use a straight stick of absolutely dry wood about 2 feet long and not more than ³/₄" thick. Apple prunings are good and smell delicious. Pass the tip of the wood through the spyhole and hold it there until flames appear. If the tip smoulders but does not burn, there is no free oxygen in the atmosphere; if the stick burns only in the spyhole, reduction is taking place. If the tip first glows and then burns, there is free oxygen in the kiln atmosphere. The behaviour of the flame and/or smoke is a good indicator of the atmospheric pressure within the kiln. **PG/WG**

● **TOP-LOADING KILNS WITH** Kanthal A1 elements are suitable for reduction. You will need an indicating pyrometer; propane gas in a small 1lb cylinder; and a 1" iron pipe 8" long attached to the burner assembly with plumbing fittings. The burner uses the lower peephole with a shelf located just above, substituting as a baffle and forcing the gas into and up in the kiln.

Element Conditioning: Before reduction firings are attempted, it is most important that an oxide coating is built up on the elements by firing the kiln to maximum temperature several times with just the kiln furniture in place.

Firing Procedure: Fire normally to 1093°C at which time the gas valve is opened slightly. Within two minutes a wisp of smoke will appear at the lid, and it should be just detectable. The valve may have to be regulated at intervals to maintain this condition since we have found that only a small amount of gas is necessary for good reduction. Total consumption for an average firing is just 6¹/₂ ounces of Propane. Continue firing in reduction to 1234°C after which cut the power and turn the burner off, allowing the kiln to cool normally.

Results: The results were consistently good with complete control over the amount of reduction. Adequate ventilation is essential but an open window might be enough in most cases, unless reduction continues for a long time. The element life will depend more on the top temperature at which the kiln is consistently fired than on the reducing atmosphere, and as long as the oxide coating is built up again after each reduction firing, indications are that normal element life can be expected. **PSH**

Two suggestions regarding kiln shelves come from Mike Rawlinson, who has a simple way of ensuring they do not warp, and Billy Nightingale, with a method of cleaning them.

● **KILN SHELVES HAVE** a tendency to warp with repeated firing at high temperatures. This can be alleviated by ensuring that the shelf is turned over for each firing – the problem is knowing which way up the shelf was last time you used it.

I solved this by making a mark on one side of each shelf with iron oxide, and a mark with cobalt on the reverse side. A piece of wood hanging by a string on the wall near the kiln is painted brown on one side and blue on the other. When I fire the kiln, I turn my marker to show which way up I packed the shelves, so that next time I fire I can ensure that they are the other way up. Despite regular firings to 1280°C I now have no trouble with warping shelves. **MR**

● **I HAVE DISCOVERED** that thin-nosed hammers, as used by cabinet makers, are excellent for chipping glaze off shelves if used at the correct angle, chipping as close to the shelf as possible. **BN**

The chapter is completed with a variety of useful tips. Stephen Grieve looks at propane economy and placating neighbours; Paddy Bakker moves her kiln using rollers; Derek Clarkson outlines a method for spyhole enlarging; Joseph Neville suggests a way of draught-proofing a kiln; while Mart Muller offers two tips on the use of woodchips in a sawdust firing and handling large raku pots.

● **TO PREVENT OUR** propane gas cylinders from freezing we put the garden hose on them: even cold water contains enough heat to stop the bottle freezing and allow just about all the propane to be usefully employed. **SG**

● **IF YOUR NEIGHBOURS,** like mine, are upset by the bush fire on the top of your flue during heavy reduction on long winter's nights – and tend to phone for the fire brigade – rig up a couple of electric lights near the top of the flue, thus rendering the fire invisible. **SG**

● **HAVING TO WAIT** for my husband and son to have a spare five minutes at the same time to haul my kiln away from the wall in order to change a broken element was very frustrating.

However the problem is now solved – I have put the kiln on the type of rollers that the electricity boards sell for putting under heavy freezers etc. These are adjustable and have a brake to stop unwanted movement. I can now pull out my kiln by hand. **PB**

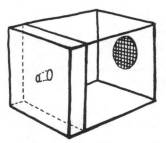

● **IF YOUR KILN** has an inadequately small spyhole, making even a slight increase in size is worthwhile and, providing the brickwork is of the low thermal mass type, it can be done quickly and easily even with coarse sandpaper, though a round file or rasp is more convenient.

The following figures relate to a spyhole in a 4½″ thick door, 15″ deep chamber, and ⅞″ outer diameter hole left unaltered. If the spyhole widens to a 1″ diameter on the inside you see an area of over 41 square inches on the back wall. Increase this to 1¼″ you see over 58 square inches, an improvement of 29%. Only ¼″ more gives 69 square inches and the improvement is over 69%.

I use a single cone placed well into the kiln and the back wall can be seen behind it. The amount of bend in the cone can be judged accurately seen against a grid scored into the brickwork $^1/_{16}$" to $^1/_8$" deep. Deeper grooves, not wider, can be seen more clearly. **DC**

● **SO AS TO** compensate for the warping of an ancient electric kiln door, the gap in closure was reduced by cementing carefully tailored strips of ceramic fibre to the hot-face brick surround, only to find that gaps recurred when the temperature rose above 1000°C. Consequently, I have for several years tucked rolls of fibreglass (salvaged from a discarded fridge) around the edges of the kiln door when firing at glazing or stoneware temperatures. Over some ten years the original batch of fibreglass has neither fused to the brickwork nor disintegrated to any marked degree. Note: when fibreglass is handled it is safe and more comfortable to wear a dust mask and household gloves. **JN**

● **TO AVOID UGLY** spots on polished pots when giving them a raku treatment in sawdust to get flame effects and darkening of body etc., I sprinkle some wood chips (gathered in the parks after the gardeners have done their trimming job and a useful machine has cut it all in to handsome small pieces for me) on top of the sawdust which I suspect to be very resinous, hence the patches. **MM**

● **TO TAKE MY** big pots (burnished) which are too heavy for my raku tongs, out of the kiln when raku firing, I use nickel wire and iron bars (building site leftovers about 1m long).

Wire around neck, not too tight to allow for expansion of clay in firing. Bars put through loops to lift pot out of kiln on to wood chippings. With bowls or neckless pots I make a sort of wire basket of two pieces of wire twisted around each other in the centre, wire joined at the top. **MM**

Four tips from Susan Bennett explore organising a raku firing, removing hot shelves from a raku kiln (with Earl Hyde), efficient kiln gloves and a remarkable claim that cracked pots can be refired to wholeness. Peter A Lee suggests using a wooden poker, Tony O'Donovan helps to prevent damage to thermocouple sheaths, Ruth Karnac looks at two methods for firing large quantities of raku tiles and Jane Bridges advises on smokeless raku.

● **WHEN ORGANISING A** raku firing you need easy access to sawdust and water. Try using wheelbarrows as containers. You can easily move them to the most convenient location. If the water becomes too soiled, it is easier to push a wheelbarrow to a drain or flower-bed and tip it up, than to manoeuvre a tin bath or vessel full of water. Similarly, if wind carries sawdust smoke towards participants, you simply wheel it to another spot.

Strong, relatively cheap barrows can be obtained from a builder's merchants. An extra wheelbarrow, filled with ice, would make an excellent cooler for cans of thirst-quenching lager, bottles of water and wine, and of course, the odd bottle of champagne to celebrate a successful day's firing. Cheers! **SB**

● **REMOVING WARE FROM** a front-loading raku kiln with tongs can be a tricky operation. Removing hot shelves can be even trickier as the tongs seem to have a habit of twisting – you lose control – disaster ensues.

During a recent firing we were gardening between firings when an urgent call went out to help remove a shelf of ware. Earl dashed to the rescue, large fork in hand, which he slid under the shelf. The prongs conveniently slipped between the props and provided a long and stable support for said shelf which was swiftly and safely removed, the ware still in place. It was then a simple movement to place it on the ground and continue the operation in the normal way. **SB/EH**

● **THIS TIP SUPERSEDES** all previous advice on the subject of unpacking kilns and handling hot ware.

It entails the purchase of a pair of Coolskin knitted oven gloves that the advertisers claim can withstand 350°C for 16 seconds while maintaining flexibility and delicacy of touch. Out with the oven mitts, stiff gauntlets, bits of towel and old leather gloves. I have not looked back. These gloves are brilliant and make handling hot ware much easier and safer for both the user and the ware.

You can also obtain gauntlets and arm guards – they are ambidextrous and can be supplied singly. They are even washable. I paid £11.99 including postage and packing in January 2000.

For further information, advice and stockists in the UK and Europe contact: Lanco Teksolv Ltd. Tel 01480 437437; Website www.coolskin.co.uk. **SB**

● **IN COMMON WITH** most potters, I inevitably accumulate seconds. I abhor waste, preferring to give those pots away to help raise money for causes dear to my heart rather than smash them up lest they reproach my 'reputation'.

I used to destroy cracked pots. Cracks occurring before bisque or glaze firing seem to worsen during the firing, and pots inadvertently knocked thereafter were deemed too fragile to pass on.

However, I recently tried re-firing filigree planters with hairline cracks incurred during careless wrapping and, to my delight, they emerged ringing true.

Pots on the verge of falling apart should not be re-fired in case they collapse and damage other ware – but it is worth experimenting with less acute cases. **SB**

● **USE A WOODEN** 'fire iron'. A stick of inch-and-half diameter (even pine) makes an excellent poker and does not cool the firebox or wear out the stoker's arm. A few are needed of course. **PAL**

● **HAVING TWICE RECENTLY** heard of people breaking a thermocouple sheath when loading the kiln, I offer a tip I have used for some years. Simply to give it a wash of iron oxide and make it readily visible. **TO'D**

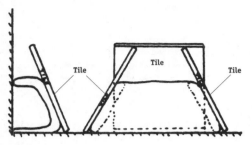

Figure 1

Figure 2

● **AS PART OF** a Dacorum and Chiltern Potters Guild Summer Event we planned to fire several hundred 4 × 4" tiles, after they had been decorated and glazed by Guild Members and visitors. This activity, together with displaying the finished fired plaque, was part of a fund-raising effort for Project Ploughshare.

It became obvious that we needed some way of holding many tiles in each kiln to improve the throughput. Two ideas were developed: Leslie Risby designed, made and pre-fired supports from Potclays Crank, as shown in Figure 1. A rectangular central support held four tiles up on edge and the side supports were placed around the kiln wall, supporting one tile each.

The second idea by Mervyn Fitzwilliam, shown in Figure 2 was a support or multi-shelf made from slices of HT Brick; the base measured 4 × 9 × 1.5" and the supports above it were the same thickness but 3" wide. A central support rod of $5/16$" diameter steel, with a nut and washer on the base and a welded eyelet at the top, held the pieces of brick in place. This unit could be loaded with 16 tiles, lifted into the kiln and the lid placed on, with the eyelet being in the central flue. Unloading was achieved by lifting the unit out, removing the fired tiles for reduction, reloading and replacing in the kiln and so on as firing proceeded. **RK**

● **THIS IS A** Billy Eccles tip for smokeless raku. Take a large metal bowl and half fill with water. Place a brick in the middle of the bowl, with a few sheets of newspaper on top of it. Prepare a small cardboard funnel and impregnate it with cooking oil and white spirit. When the pot is removed from the kiln, place it on the newspaper on the brick. Place the funnel on the pot. When this ignites, a metal bucket or tin is placed over it all, into the water, trapping any smoke inside the bucket and creating a reduced atmosphere inside. This seemed to me a good way of firing when neighbours are nearby or, like Billy, for winter firing in a shed. **JB**

Chapter 7
Tools, equipment and materials

Home-made, free and adapted pottery tools and equipment figure throughout Potters' Tips. Although specialist tools and equipment, e.g. wheels, glazing tools, kiln furniture, etc. have been included under other headings, this is still the largest chapter and includes generally useful items which can cover several techniques. The feeling of self-sufficiency and satisfaction is part of the pleasure for many potters and they have the backing of as eminent a name as the late Harry Davis who always deplored our conspicuous waste.

To start, one of the simplest and most useful of tools, clay-cutting wire, exercised the ingenuity of many. Nora Kay uses nylon; Clare Sheppard, Keith Parry and J W Barratt plump for model airplane wire; Joseph Neville finds some free wire; other ideas by D Haig-Thomas, and Darwin Turner; a nicely illustrated and useful method of permanently twisting fishing line by John VEG Mitchell; Krzysztof Buras also uses twine (untwisted this time); Ray Hargreaves and Tom Price deal with toggles; Adrian Foulds uses bicycle brake wire, while Henry Sommerville examines the different wiring options for different jobs.

● **FOR SEVERAL YEARS** I have been using nylon fishing line instead of metal wire. It is practically indestructible, cannot rot or rust, is extremely strong (average breaking point about 12-14lbs), cheap, and readily available in sports shops. A single strand is sufficient for general clay-cutting and wedging, but it needs some kind of grip at each end, both for use and to ensure visibility – the nylon is hard to see on the workbench and even worse when dropped on the floor. Old curtain rings or large buttons make ideal grips, and the cutter can then be hung from a hook when not in use.

When cutting pots from the wheel-head, a stouter cutter is required. Take two single lengths of line, each at least twice as long as the length of the finished cutter, double these in half and loop the double ends by half-hitches on to a ring. Put this ring on a hook, pull the four strands taut and plait them together, securing the end with a twist of Sellotape or insulating tape, then attach this end to another ring or button. This makes a cutting 'wire' that will last for years. **NK**

● **WITH REGARD TO** the hints for cutting wire a lot of us here in New Zealand use Modelair U control wire, which lasts for over six months provided you do not bend it. Thread the ends through large buttons making sure that wire ends are turned back on themselves so the ends will not pierce your fingers. Other countries should have similar model aircraft wire. **CS**

● **I SHOULD IMAGINE** most potters use twisted brass wire round two toggles to cut through clay, particularly to undercut pots left on batts after throwing. The trouble is that the brass wire tends to twist and break very easily. We now use, and recommend to all potters, the wire model enthusiasts use to fly aircraft. We paid a modest sum for 100ft of this (much finer) wire. It still gives the familiar 'shell' pattern, but does not leave the bases of the pots anything like so rough. **KP**

● **I HAVE A** tip for cutting off pots. I use a twisted wire which I believe is made of stainless steel. I have one which I used for a few weeks, left it hanging for a three month holiday and have used it for some time since without a trace of rust. The material that I use is model aeroplane control wire. I have the remains of a 70 foot reel with me now. It was inexpensive and should be obtainable from most model aeroplane shops. **JWB**

● **FOR REMARKABLY ABUNDANT** and free supplies of superlatively good cutting wire for 'harps' and 'frogs', potters may benefit from the largesse of telephone engineers who, after they have clambered down from their aerial labours, are prone to abandon generous lengths of grey PVC clad twin core connecting wire at the feet of telegraph poles. (A practice which may reflect BT's desire to make token restitution to victims of its extortionate charges. Alternatively, it could be atavistic: an instinctive, almost canine, compulsion on the part of linesmen to register their equivalent of 'Kilroy was here'). Do not be fooled by its copper coating – the wire is highly tensile, corrosion-resistant steel, well nigh indestructible when strung in a clay harp. What a pity to record that its extremely springy temper renders such a durable wire unsuitable for cutting pots off the wheel-head. **JN**

● **WIRES NEED TO** be of different lengths, and it is often difficult to find the right one. Whatever material is used for the wire (stainless fishing wires are best), the handles need to be thin, so that pots can be easily cut off the wheel.

  Coat-hangers provide the easy answer. The end is bent into a small loop with pliers and the length of the handle should be nearly proportional to the length of the wire. The wires can be easily held in the correct position, and one can always find the right one. **DH-T**

● **THE FIRST CORD** I used when throwing on a hump (lump) was an old and irreplaceable piece of fly fishing silk line. I wondered what I would do when it wore out or I lost it. I solved the problem with the discovery of Marlow whipping twine from a boat-chandler in Norwich. It is available in three sizes and is very good. **DT**

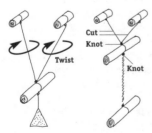

● **A TWISTED WIRE** cuts a pot off the wheel with a pleasant swirly pattern to the base of the pot.

  Fishing line, which does not rust, can be used instead of wire. Most text books say that fishing line will not give the swirly finish because it cannot be twisted together.

  Here is a technique for twisting two lines together:

1. Tie a thin piece of wood as a handle to the centre of a length of fishing line and temporary pieces each end.

2. Suspend a weight from the centre and twist the two ends in the same direction (see sketch).

3. When the twist in the two wires has developed far enough, tie in a permanent handle. Cut the temporary bits of wood off. The twist will not unwind. **JVEGM**

● **FOR A VERY** long time I have been fed up to the eyebrows with my wire clay cutter always snapping at an awkward time, usually in the middle of throwing a good pot. Many is the time I have stormed out of my studio in an almost despondent mood, until I learned about an alternative.

It was whilst I was having a lesson with a potter who had spent some considerable length of time in Japan that I was told about a very convenient substitute for brass wire, which I have found to crack and split after six months' constant use.

The substitute is three ply twine. One has to get the right sort, as the thickness is very critical. I used to get mine from a ship-chandlers, so the brand name was very old; it may indeed have been marine twine.

After cutting off a two foot length, I carefully undo it so that one of the three strands comes away. The two remaining strands are tied with a small knot at either end, and suitably adorned with a favourite stone, or piece of good wood to enable one to locate it amongst the chaos of one's throwing bench, if indeed one is a chaotic thrower. This device saves countless pounds in wasted expensive brass wire, and as the potter from Mashiko pointed out, gives one an acceptable shell or scroll pattern on the foot or base of one's pot. **KB**

● **I HAVE FOUND** that cricket bails make excellent toggles for a wire clay cutter. They have grooves from which the wire will not slide and are easy to hold and grip when in use. **RH**

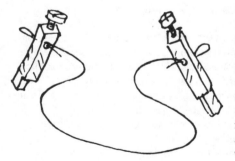

● **AS A 'YOUNG** apprentice' at Peter Ilsley's studio I dismantled an old electric plug to make this quick-fit wire cutter. The brass spikes from the plug can be screwed on to the wire in seconds (the ends of the wire having been doubled back inside, not protruding), and the weight of the brass allows it to hang well on the wheel surround. **TP**

● **IF YOU HAVE** found that single Elasticum trace wire, once so useful for making cutting wires, has become difficult to get hold of, then this tip is for you.

Take the inner wire from a bicycle brake cable (old is free, but new is still cheap), untwist two of the strands and use this to make a new cutter. If you are new to this then this is how you do it: make toggle ends from a small piece of wood or similar, wind two strands around the toggle and then back around themselves. Put a lump of clay onto wheel-head, push the toggle into it and, holding a free end in each hand, spin the wheel at top speed. As the strands twist allow your hands to come together – the wire has to be overtwisted to retain the desired twist. Pull toggle from the clay and allow wire to recoil. Wind the free end around the other toggle.

Safety note: finish off the wire ends so that they twist back down towards the toggles, as this helps to stop the free ends jabbing into your fingertips. **AF**

● **IT OCCURRED TO** me that potters need different kinds of wire for different purposes, for cutting bulky clay for wedging, a sturdy wire with large toggles is required. Almost any strong and flexible wire will survive as long as it is securely wrapped around a suitable handle – be it a champagne cork, large washer or length of smooth dowel. The wire for cutting pots off the wheel needs to be altogether more subtle. The wire needs to be strong and slightly twisted, and attached to delicate but sufficiently large toggles – wood or cork – to provide a firm grip. Metal washers are good as they weigh the wire down, but can rust. Incidentally, ensure that the ends of the wire are turned back to prevent them piercing your skin. Personally I dislike nylon fishing wire as it 'gives' slightly but it is sturdy and long lasting. **HS**

Still on the subject of clay-cutting, a brief entry by Ellen Curran and more details of the same idea from Joseph Neville, plus two more traditional 'harps' illustrated by Bolton Technical College and L E Wells. A harp from the 19th century is shown on p60.

● **CLAY CUTTER: STRING** a coping saw with tight piano wire where the blade would be. **EC**

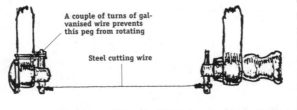

A couple of turns of galvanised wire prevents this peg from rotating

Steel cutting wire

● **MANY A COPING** saw now languishes in the toolbox, made redundant by the advent of electrically powered jigsaws and milling machines. Simply replace the coping sawblade with a length of high-tensile steel wire (odd bits are often scrapped by BT engineers after they have shinned down your neighbourhood telephone pole) and there is a clay harp complete with a comfortable handle.

Loop the cutting wire over the notches which originally held the blade's pins. Screw in the saw handle and the wire is automatically tightened.

My own rehabilitated coping saw has been in regular use as a clay harp for the past thirteen years. **JN**

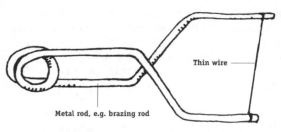

● **IMPROVED HARP: SQUEEZING** the handle will tighten the brass wire or whatever it is strung across it. **BTC**

Thin wire

Metal rod, e.g. brazing rod

● **A MICRO-ADJUSTABLE HARP,** based on the now rather old-fashioned bow-saw, is illustrated in the rough sketch (not to scale). Use steel bolts, preferably at least 8" long and ½" minimum diameter to resist the bending moment. The pitch of the thread does not matter, but the beer can rings engage nicely with Whitworth or thread of similar pitch. The holes in the hardwood beam should be ¹⁄₁₆" larger than the diameter of the bolts, so that these can rock freely as the wire is tightened by twisting up the tourniquet. The length of the beam obviously fixes the length of the cutting wire. Any springy cord may be used for the tourniquet, but nylon cord is especially good. To adjust the thickness of the cut, dimension D, slacken the tourniquet slightly and turn the bolts to raise or lower the wire with respect to the bolt tips/table top; and finally tighten by winding up the tourniquet and sliding the lever C into locking engagement with the beam.

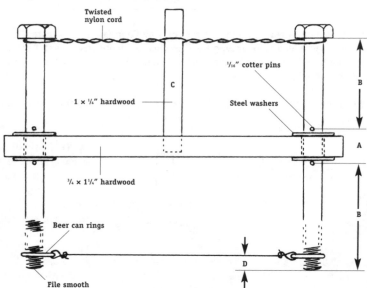

Twisted nylon cord

¹⁄₁₆" cotter pins

C

B

1 × ¼" hardwood

Steel washers

A

¾ × 1¼" hardwood

B

Beer can rings

D

File smooth

Dimension A must be sufficient to allow ¹⁄₁₆" clearance with the washers in place. The two dimensions B are equal. Initially fit the wire with the tourniquet slack but not loose, then wind up to the required tension; slacken off when not in use. **LEW**

A variety of home-made tools make up this next batch of tips, with Emily Cooke extolling the value of lollipop sticks, Susan Bennett adapting discarded mop handles, Bill Jones finding uses for all manner of everyday objects and G A Stevens examining an alternative use for a DIY sanding block.

● **I USE LOLLIPOP** sticks to smooth the walls of a pot when throwing, as an internal support when making spouts, and for removing clay at base of pot. They are excellent for getting glaze off the bases of pots, and when worn out can be thrown away without qualms. The lollipops can be enjoyable too. **EC**

● **AS ANOTHER PAINT-BRUSH** sheds its handle and departs to join its fellows in paint-brush paradise, I find myself with yet another item for the 'do not throw away in case it comes in useful' pile.

Searching in vain through the conglomeration of oddments for my favourite ornamental-groove-cutting wooden tool and drawing a blank, I grasp instead at my recently discarded plain wooden paint-brush handle. I turn the narrow end on my bench grinder until I have the appropriate wedge shape, and finish off with a bit of sandpapering. The new tool can be altered to suit my purpose – both ends can be used as there is plenty of wood on the 7" handle, and it is comfortable to hold. If you do not have a grinding wheel, you can fettle the ends with a knife. Of course you can use ice lolly sticks as tools too, but paint-brush handles are stronger, more versatile, do not get lost so easily – and salve the conscience if, like me, you do not look after your brushes as well as you should. **SB**

● **MANY HOUSEHOLD ITEMS** can be used to help make pottery. What about the wife's or husband's darning mushroom as a former for the inside of pots, using an old wooden coat-hanger to give a good curve to the inside of vases where it is possible to put your hand, or clothes pegs for the making of small lidded pots?

One handy item that I have adapted is an old anglepoise lamp screwed to the wall above my wheel with the lamp removed and a rubber marker inserted to measure the height of pots or cups when throwing more than one item. It has all the adjustments and is easy to move out of the way when not in use. **BJ**

● **A FLEXIBLE SANDING** block (a carborundum coated sponge) from a DIY store is a very efficient means of cleaning up dried green ware prior to firing – but beware of the dust. **GAS**

Two hints on sponges come from Maureen Russell and Alan H Bolton.

● **AS NATURAL SPONGES** become increasingly expensive I find offcuts of upholstery foam make excellent alternatives. Cut with a sharp knife to various sizes they serve as a practical throwing tool for mopping out: they can be used to clean glaze off biscuit-fired pots and the larger pieces are first-class for wiping down surfaces. Unlike their 'natural' counterparts foams do not rot or disintegrate quickly in water and, though without 'aesthetic' appeal, they are cheap and efficient. **MR**

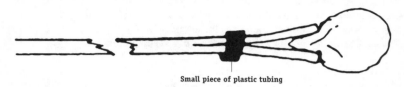

Small piece of plastic tubing

● **GREEN GARDEN CANE** split about 4" down the middle makes an ideal sponge holder. A small collar that will slide down keeps it tight. **AHB**

Alternative rolling pins are suggested by Robert Flexen and Anne Leon. Anne also contributes a needle-awl, as does Harriet Mark and Geoff Lamb, the latter with the bonus of a safety cover.

● **LAST YEAR WHEN** I took over a pottery studio at a college I found that there was no money to buy some much-needed rolling pins. I was able to make some from offcut lengths of plastic rainwater pipe filled with some cement fondue that we had. A second model was also made from larger diameter pipe by setting a length of broom handle down the centre. The pipe was lightly sanded down to avoid sticking to the clay. **RF**

● **CARDBOARD ROLLING PIN.** Mailing tubes are tough and make very efficient short-term rolling pins. They can also be wrapped in newspaper and used as forms for wrapping clay slabs around. **AL**

● **A NEEDLE GLUED** into a discarded wine cork may easily fall out and get lost in the clay. A hat pin pushed right through a cork makes a safe and sturdy pricker. **AL**

● **FED UP WITH** losing my cutting-off pin I found that a stainless steel sewing needle pushed 'eye' end into a cork was the answer. It floats in my bowl of water and does not rust. **HM**

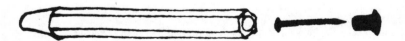

● **I HAVE FOUND** a use for a discarded ballpoint pen case and a pin. By removing the small cap at the opposite end from the pen point and pushing a pin through from the inside an effective clay cutting point is made. An added bonus is by reversing the end the cover of the pen is normally put on, the point can safely be carried in a pocket. **GL**

Everyday objects are used as scrapers by Ellen Curran, Anne Leon, Tina Woodhouse and Hugh Stewart. L E Wells describes a traditional clay plane.

● **SCRAPER: LINOLEUM MASTIC** spreader with the serrated edge bent down. Great for cleaning wedging board. **EC**

● **SCRAPING TOOL: TOOLS** with saw-like edges are used for scraping clay especially in working the coils together in a coiled pot. If you do not have access to used hacksaw blades, similar saw edges can be found on boxes containing wax paper or foil. Tear off the entire cardboard strip which has the metal on it, then cut off the desired length. **AL**

● **OUT-OF-DATE BANK CHEQUE** cards, usually made out of flexible plastic, are ideal – and free – tools. Not only do they make excellent ribs for throwing but I have found they are good all-purpose implements in the workshop. They are useful as bench and shelf scrapers as well as for cleaning glaze slop from the inside walls of the glaze bucket after glazing pots. Removing the wet glaze prevents it from drying on the walls of the bucket and subsequently falling into the slop and making it lumpy. **TW**

● **USED PHONE CARDS** make excellent scrapers – and can be picked up outside kiosks free. **HS**

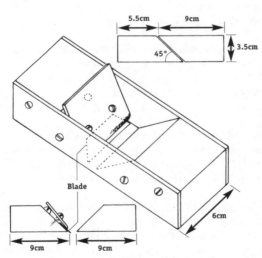

● **BERNARD LEACH, IN** *A Potter's Book*, mentions the use of a clay plane, for example for cleaning up the edges of tiles, and for cutting flat faces on round pots – faceting. By using a throwaway blade a good plane may be made up as shown in the sketch. I used a Spiralux blade, which, being 6cm wide, determines the width of the plane, the other dimensions not needing to be exactly as shown. The two blocks of wood which form the body are cut at 45° from a single piece approximately 6 × 3.5 × 14.7cm, and are joined together by pieces of 5mm plyboard screwed on either side. The blade clamp is also made from 5mm ply held by two round head screws located close to the back of the blade, and rocking on a third round head screw situated as far from the blade as possible. Adjust the blade so that it protrudes by only about 1mm. **LEW**

Bamboo gets a solitary mention by Darwin Turner; Lakshmi Murthy describes a small wire tool; Pat Beese and Rosemary D Wren suggest fettling knives.

● **BAMBOO TOOLS CAN** all be home-made, the bamboo can be obtained free from carpet shops where 8-10' poles are used to wrap carpets around. **DT**

● **I HAVE ALWAYS** had problems with finding clay tools and all my makeshift wire apparatus gives way quickly. After thinking about this a great deal I found a solution. I take an old pen, preferably a marker pen. I yank the tip out of it. Into that I insert a wire loop of any shape and plug it with a small wooden bit. The wire loop is now firm and jammed inside the pen. This always makes a perfect tool. **LM**

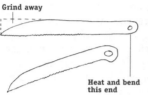

Grind away

Heat and bend this end

● **THIS TOOL, MADE** from a broken hacksaw blade, can be made by those who have access to a grinding wheel and an anvil and it is ideal for teachers who are tired of splashing out for knives which get broken or lost.

Using a grinding wheel grind a blade on the unserrated edge of the broken hacksaw blade. Heat the end with the hole to a dull red and beat a rounded end. The knife makes a much thinner cut than most commercial potters' knives, the serrated edge can be used for texturing the outside of pots, the smooth edge for scraping down and the curved end for scraping down the inside of narrow-necked coil pots. Also, the hole is handy for hanging the tool up on a nail. **PB**

● **FETTLING KNIFE: THIS** can be made from old hacksaw blade. The teeth are ground off, the blade is cut as shown in the diagram and sharpened on the upper surface only. Being very thin in section the blade does not drag the clay when cutting. **RDW**

Several turning tools were described in the Throwing section. Here are some more made from strip and wire scrap material, kicking off with two suggestions from John VEG Mitchell, further ideas coming from Valerie Snow, Darwin Turner, Chris Southall, Stephen Grieve, June Linsley Hood and Mary R Southal.

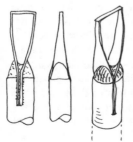

● **STRIPS OF BAKED** bean tin, dowel rod and Araldite can be used to make very effective turning tools.

Cut a 12mm wide strip of tin and bend it to the shape shown in the drawing and insert it into a saw cut in the end of a piece of 12mm dowel. Use plenty of Araldite on all touching surfaces. When the Araldite has set, taper the tip on a grinding wheel to about 2mm.

Any shape can be fabricated in this way to suit the work in hand. The thin edge of the tin cuts very cleanly into leatherhard clay. **JVEGM**

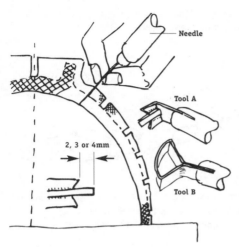

● **WE HAVE ALL** turned a pot through the base or side into space. These tools made from steel banding strip (from any building site), Araldite glue and a length of dowelling, could help. The 'V' is shaped at the end of the strip. It is bent, then glued into a saw cut in the dowelling. The depth indicator is glued to the bent strip. I suggest that three tools should be made with indicators projecting 2mm, 3mm and 4mm (if your throwing turns out rather thick).

1. Measure the thickness of the pot at various places with needle and thumb.

2. Mark these places with the thickness of clay to be removed.
3. Choose tool A to match the depth of clay to be removed.
4. Make a fair number of grooves... Change tools to suit the depth. The two 'spikes' on the tool are there to give warning that the depths have been reached...
5. Use tool B to remove surplus clay. The 'bow shape' will span over the grooves. (Note: sharpen the cutting edge.)
6. Finish turning with your normal tools. **JVEGM**

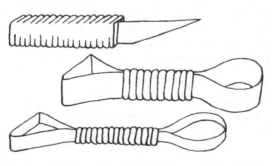

● **NO DOUBT MANY** other potters, like myself, find that the tools they make for themselves are very often the most useful.

Just in case there is anyone who has not yet discovered the versatile nature of the metal binding which is used in packing bundles of bricks here are sketches of tools which I have made with it and which to me are particularly invaluable. The knife is very flexible and thin-bladed yet only consists of a metal strip cut on the slant at one end with the other end taped with a strip of wood on either side then bound with string for easy grip.

The strip turning tools are bent from a 9" length of metal with one end square, the other rounded. The join is first taped and then bound with string. If the 9" metal strip is cut in half lengthwise it will make two finer and more delicate tools, even if it is a rather laborious process. All these tools can be easily sharpened on a stone. **VS**

● **VERY EFFECTIVE TURNING** tools can be made free from the mild steel banding used on packing cases bent to form a strong and practical shape. **DT**

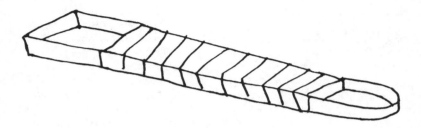

● **CHEAP TURNING TOOLS,** as illustrated above, can be made by taping steel banding strip (used for banding crates and tea chests) onto pieces of wood about $3/4 \times 1/4$" to form loops at the ends bent at one end and square at the other. **CS**

● **I MAKE MY** very simple turning tools by just twisting a loop of wire (above). Soft wire is no good and I find the best source comes from old steel braced tyres after burning – one tyre will supply enough for a lifetime.

Incidentally I find the village dump a vital source of free building and potting material. With a bit of simple segregation, for example keeping food waste away from the rest, such dumps become excellent recycling areas – every community should have one. **SG**

● **I HAVE ALWAYS** disliked 'official' turning tools, and do most of mine with a wire loop tool (one end square, one rounded) and a flexible metal kidney. It has recently occurred to me that a long-handled metal spoon is a wonderful tool for turning/fettling the inside of a narrow-necked vessel where fingers cannot reach. It will also remove any stray bits. **JLH**

● **THE SEARCH FOR** cheap but effective tools for trimming and turning is never-ending, though I often think a too dry or too wet pot is a central part of the problem. Looking around my husband's workbox I spotted a discarded Surform blade which still seemed sharp. This has proved an excellent turning tool for the sides of pots. Because of the sharp edges the blade does not require great pressure and also cuts through the lump and ridges. Not much use for turning a foot but otherwise excellent (and free). **MRS**

Rosemary D Wren, Peter Chesney, Avis Loshak, Joseph Neville, Dick Wilson, John VEG Mitchell, Adrian Foulds, Susan Bennett, Bill Jones and Margaret Cooke offer a variety of tips.

● **THE BLADE OF** a paper folder (made from hardwood) works well as a pot beater. It has a rounded cross-section which does not stick to clay. **RDW**

● **ANOTHER USE FOR** a blunt hacksaw blade – a simple and cheap pair of straight callipers made as follows in five minutes. To make a small pair, up to 6":
1. Cut blade in two with tinsnips.
2. Cut each end at an angle as shown in diagram.
3. Join together with small nut and bolt, and if possible a spring washer.

For a large pair, up to 12", repeat as above but use two separate blunt hacksaw blades.

These callipers can be painted with rust inhibiting paint, but as a bonus the steel does resist to some extent. **PC**

● **TOOLS WITH METAL** handles, and also hacksaw blades, are not comfortable to hold. We made durable handles ten years ago with strips of gummed brown paper wrapped around to build up a thick layer. We then soaked the lot in polyurethane varnish. It may also be practicable now to use gummed strip plastic as supplied for offices. **AL**

Epoxy resin   File out concavity to fit index finger

● **WHEN IT COMES** to pulling handles, practice does not make perfect in the case of a natural pull-foozler like me. Much easier to admit you are beaten and to search around for some method of producing plain or ornamental clay straps even when you cannot employ a pugmill or a wad box fitted with a suitable die. With the aid of rat-tailed pliers, shape a few inches of strong galvanised wire into an outline of your choice, then twist the spare ends into a tight spiral stem which is inserted (once coated with epoxy resin) into a hole drilled into the end of a five or six inch length of dowelling (see diagram above). Now you have your very own profile cutter to be dragged vertically through a clay coil. Gently pull back the cut edges and there it nestles... a newly hatched potential handle. **JN**

143

● **HERE IS A** simple device to measure the thickness of the base of a pot to be turned. Screw a clothes peg, via a spacer washer, to a suitable wood crosspiece. A plant stick will serve as the measuring rod.

Release dowel into thrown pot, then invert pot and place crosspiece on to the base. The distance between the end of the rod and wheel-head then represents the thickness of the base. **DW**

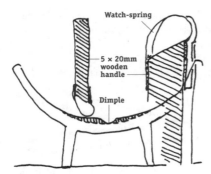

Watch-spring

5 × 20mm wooden handle

Dimple

● **A BOWL IS** sometimes left with a dimple in the centre of the base. At leatherhard stage you can turn a smooth curve with a watch-spring tool.

First find a watch-spring. Cut off the right length and shape it as shown in the sketch. Glue it to the wooden handle with Araldite. **JVEGM**

● **DOES YOUR BANDING** wheel slow down too fast? Banding wheels with light wheel-heads slow down very quickly, before you have time to complete lines. The wheel-head does not have enough momentum to keep it spinning. Solve the problem by forming a thick coil of clay into a ring and stick it to the underside of the rim. It does not need to cover the whole of the underside, and is most effective if it is right on the edge. **AF**

● **INITIALLY THE POTTERY** department at our school felt a bit threatened by the new Craft Design and Technology department. But over the years we have developed a very healthy symbiotic relationship, and benefit from many of their waste products – offcuts of marine ply and other boards for modelling, thinner strips for rolling guides, and the latest boon has been surplus dowel rods of various diameters cut to usable lengths. They are really helpful for creating hollow tubes to transform into spouts, trees, trousers, torsos, vases, etc. Depending on the eventual size required simply push a dowel rod through a solid coil lengthways and roll as if using a rolling pin, being careful to keep the walls of the tube the same thickness throughout.

This method has been especially useful for building figures – thin dowels can be used for arms and legs making the models lighter, hollow and less likely to blow up in the kiln. **SB**

● **THERE ARE TWO** items which I find most useful in my pottery. The first is a short length of hosepipe, which I use to unblock the drainpipe of my wheel, and the second is my old shaving brush, which is ideal for brushing those little sticky shavings that result from turning green pots and which stick to the most inaccessible places on the recesses of foot-rings. **BJ**

● **I HAVE FOUND** an ordinary plastic comb is excellent for smoothing down runs of glaze after they have dried. Using the comb in a cross-hatching motion seems to give the best results. Be careful not to allow the powdered glaze to fall on to the floor, but catch it in a basin of water and ideally wear a suitable mask. Do not be tempted to blow the glaze as this causes dust. **MC**

Original methods of cutting holes, large and small, in clay come from Jerry Harper, Brigitta Appleby, Anne Leon, Muriel Watson, an anonymous potter in Barrow-in-Furness, Kenneth Breese, and, if you have recently given up golf, Duncan James Smith.

● **TO MAKE A** large hole borer try plastic pipes as supplied to the building trade for water and drainage: ³⁄₄″ up to 3¹⁄₂″ might be useful and your local plumber will possibly supply offcuts about 6-8″ long. Cut a chamfer on one end using either a wood saw or hacksaw and trim with a sharp knife. **JH**

● **A SMALL BRASS** tool was used for cutting holes in teapots at the Shihwan Porcelain Factory. Its tapered form allowed the cut sections to pass easily through and the inside never became blocked up. **BA**

● **A REFILLABLE BALLPOINT** pen makes a most efficient hole maker. Unscrew the pen. Insert the pen into the clay and rotate it. When removed, the clay plug will come away inside the pen. Remove the plug with a needle. The hole will be crisp with no ragged edges. Use the small end of the pen to make holes in buttons. **AL**

● **TAKING UP POTTERY** as a pensioner I have to be as thrifty as possible with my purchases of materials and equipment, and wherever possible I devise my own tools. Looking through my overcrowded drawers I came across an old-fashioned pen with one of those lovely brass 'relief' nibs. I removed the nib and then put it in again back to front and now I have a very effective hole piercer – ideal for my teapots. **MW**

● **I HAVE FOUND** that a Nutbrown pastry cutter is a very handy tool for cutting clay. **ANON**

● **TO ENABLE YOU** to produce a variety of clean circular holes in leatherhard clay, use the clear rigid plastic tubes that are used to protect the heads of artists' brushes. Most art shops have a surplus of these as they fall off the brushes (I know from personal experience). This may seem obvious, but if you connect up several holes you can make good filigree work. **KB**

Hole cutting tool ⸺⸺⸺⸺⸺⸺⸺⸺⸺⸺   Golf club shaft

● **TO MAKE HOLE** cutters of all sizes get hold of an old golf club shaft from your local golf club's pro shop. The shafts are of hollow metal, made of joined sections which get smaller and smaller towards the club head. Each section is also tapered, allowing a cutter of two different sizes to be made at each end of each section. Hacksaw in direction of dotted lines as illustrated. File off any burrs. **DJS**

Help in maintaining smooth slips and glazes comes from John Mathieson, A H Bolton and Jean Hamilton. Meanwhile Tammy Parkes-Legge outlines a method of making a simple coloured slip and adds a glaze recipe for good measure, while S Heaton has a simple solution to the handy storage of tools.

● **BOSCH SUPPLY A** high-volume paint mixer attachment for an electric drill, which is excellent for the rapid mixing of slips and glazes. It consists of a 36cm rod with a nylon impeller at one end. As a single splash could be fatal a power-breaker is essential when using this equipment.

For more punishing work consider a more heavy duty mixer. Mine is the Piranha X66452, which is of all-metal construction; the label states that it can be used for mixing concrete. Use on a slow drill speed – it really is powerful. **JM**

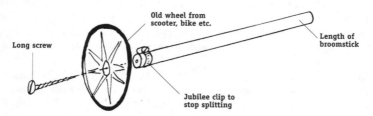

Old wheel from
scooter, bike etc.

Long screw

Length of
broomstick

Jubilee clip to
stop splitting

● **WHILE RENOVATING OUR** present farmhouse and workshop I saw the plasterer using an ingenious idea (diagram above) for dispelling the lumps in plaster. I immediately 'borrowed' the idea and have found it unbeatable for re-mixing slips, glazes etc. by pumping up and down; and the rim of the wheel is marvellous for scraping the bottom of the five gallon buckets I use. **AHB**

● **FOR STIRRING GLAZES** I find a kitchen straining spoon (the type with holes in) is the most useful tool. It gets into all the corners of the bucket well, and they can often be bought very cheaply at jumble sales. **JH**

● **TO MAKE A** simple slip that adheres to your greenware pots, take the water when you have finished throwing and let it settle. Pour off the excess water until there is liquid clay you can squirt or paint with without the clay running. You may have to sieve it to remove any lumps; you can then use it as it is or add a body stain. The amount of stain added is dictated by your preference of colour and intensity. Start with 1 cup of slip to 1-2 teaspoons of stain, mix and sieve to ensure an even colour distribution.

A transparent glaze (cone 6) I have found useful:

Wollastonite 10
Ferro frit 3134..30
EPK 25
Flint...15
Soda feldspar 20

This came from Tony Hansen at Plainsman Clays Ltd. **TP-L**

● **A CUTLERY DRAINER** makes an excellent holder for tools on the bench. Such drainers are usually divided into three and also have sloping sides thus making it very easy to select the tool – and dust on the tools drops through the draining holes. **SH**

Many potters rightly object to paying for expensive commercial sieves, especially as some designs can be difficult to clean. Plastics have simplified the construction of sieves – the lawn can be bonded on by the heat of a soldering iron. Krzysztof Buras, Jan van der Tas from Holland, Darwin Turner, Lynn Carter, Jane Lord (two entries), Anne Leon, L E Wells and Shelley Talbot all contribute valuable ideas.

● **WHILST WORKING AS** an apprentice potter at the Chelsea Pottery in London, I found a very useful tip for sieving small quantities of glaze. Joyce Morgan, their principal decorator, brought this handy observation to light. When applying on-glaze colours, there would also be the problem of nasty lumps, if, as invariably did happen, the glaze mix had dried up.

This problem was solved by the cunning use of a common Woolworths plastic standard tea-strainer. The mesh size was just right to break down the glaze back into a usable viscosity. Water, of course, was needed to render it into a liquid before straining began.

The strainer is also very handy for preparing small quantities of glaze for tests. It is sometimes very cumbersome and wasteful to use a full-sized brass or nylon mesh. After use the strainer should be washed in clean cold water thoroughly to avoid any contamination in the next glaze preparation. **KB**

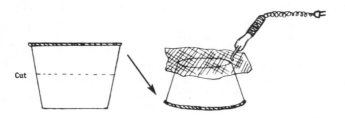

Cut

● **AN EASY WAY** to make a good glaze sieve is to take a plastic bucket, cut it as shown above and bond the sieve lawn into the plastic rim. It is simple to do and the result is strong. An advantage of this sieve is that it is very easy to clean. **JVDT**

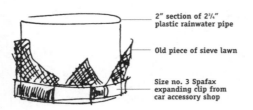

2" section of 2¼" plastic rainwater pipe

Old piece of sieve lawn

Size no. 3 Spafax expanding clip from car accessory shop

● **A SIEVE FOR** test glazes is illustrated. As a good lawn brush use Gault No. 10 stencil brush. **DT**

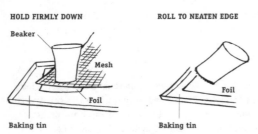

HOLD FIRMLY DOWN

Beaker

Mesh

Foil

Baking tin

ROLL TO NEATEN EDGE

Foil

Baking tin

● **A TIP FOR** making test cup lawns from damaged lawns (using the undamaged area). Get a polythene beaker or small polythene bowl (not hard plastic) and cut the bottom out of it. Put a baking tin on an oven hotplate for a smooth surface, and turn hotplate on 'high'. Put a piece of foil over the tin to keep it clean. Then hold mesh piece over tin foil and press bottom of polythene beaker on to mesh giving a few twists to weld the mesh into the polythene. This idea can be used to make bigger lawns. Trim mesh away from beaker and neaten outside edge by rolling beaker on hot tin to push edges of mesh into polythene. This really works. **LC**

● **INSTEAD OF PAYING** over the odds for a new rotary sieve, buy the individual rubber-edged meshes at the cheapest rate. Then get a two gallon galvanised bucket and knock out the bottom with a chisel right up to the rolled foot edge. Pop in the mesh and measure exactly where it fits just tight inside the bucket. From outside drill holes (eight will do) to fit ½" or 1" galvanised roofing nails with large flat head. Slip these into the holes from outside and they form a ring to hold the mesh inside – hey presto, a quick-change one gallon plus bucket sieve. Most materials run through wet with a loo brush in no time at all. **JL**

● **SOME TIME AGO** I sent in a tip about making a sieve from a two gallon bucket and the removable rubber-edged mesh from a rotary sieve. I have since found a much simpler method of making a smaller version: knock out the bottom of a one gallon galvanised bucket, and the sieve mesh can be pushed firmly and level into the bucket, clay infill round the edge if necessary. It sieves quantities of around a litre quickly, using anything from a scrubbing brush to a household 2" paint-brush. I noticed recently that someone advocated a pram wheel on a dowel to mix slip and glaze. I recommend a potato masher for light work, and a bicycle chain wheel welded to a rod for quite stiff mixtures. And finally cutting wires of various gauges can be had from a guitarist throwing away used strings, especially the wound ones. **JL**

● **AN EMERGENCY SIEVE** can be made using pantyhose, by stretching the thick panty part of the hose over a bucket. Many glazes are more interesting when passed through a coarser sieve, so even better results can be hoped for. Pantyhose can also be draped over bowls, etc., so that slabs can be draped over them and formed without sticking. This gives a delicate texture to the clay. Try covering a teacup with pantyhose. Take a walnut size piece of clay and press it down into the bottom of the cup. Press and spread the clay until it is as thin as wanted. Gather up the pantyhose and pull the small pot out of the cup. Unwrap the pot and make any small adjustments as needed. This method works well with porcelain. The rims may be further thinned by wetting the fingers and gently raising the rim between thumb and index finger. **AL**

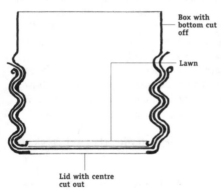

Box with bottom cut off

Lawn

Lid with centre cut out

● **THE SIEVE IS** one of the most valuable tools in preparing well-blended glazes. But whilst the craft potter may be able to afford an adequate range, the hobby potter working within a shoestring budget may find them alarmingly expensive. With the advent of synthetic fibre, excellent lawn made from nylon or similar fibre is obtainable, usually described as organdie. Stretched over a suitable short cylinder, it makes an excellent sieve. Choose the diameter of the sieve suited to the job, and use a decorators' paint-brush to assist the flow of glaze through the sieve without damaging the mesh.

If you can obtain a cylindrical metal box with screw-on lid, you can, by cutting off the box bottom and the centre out of the lid (as shown in the sketch), make a most useful sieve. The lawn is easily pulled tight before the lid is tightened up, and is quickly removed for washing or replacement. The organdie I am using is of about 65 mesh, but by putting the mix through two or three times very good results are obtained. Try your local friendly chemist for a metal screwtop ex-pill box. Or, if you are skilled in glass cutting, consider using a Kilner preserving jar with its bottom cut off (but grind down the sharp edges). **LEW**

● **FOR THOSE KEEN** on pushing clay through sieves but not so keen on cleaning up (especially children) nylon sieves are infinitely better than metal ones.

No scrubbing in water to clean – wait until dry and rumple them between your fingers and the clay drops off cleanly. They are incredibly strong and do not rust. **ST**

Jane Searle and Brian Sutherland describe methods of repairing damaged lawns without the use of a soldering iron.

● **THREE YEARS AGO** I accidentally pierced a small hole, $\frac{1}{10}$" across, in my only sieve half way through sieving a glaze. In order to finish the job I pressed a small piece of Blu Tack into the mesh from both sides, working it well in. The Blu Tack hardened and formed such an effective repair that the sieve has been in regular use ever since – and is still my only sieve. **JS**

● **WE HAVE ALL** experienced the frustration and annoyance when a split occurs in the phosphor bronze lawn mesh of our otherwise perfect glaze sieve. Hitherto I mended mine by sweating on a small piece of sheet tin with solder, but I have since discovered a far easier method which is very reliable and effective.

Cut a small rectangle of PVC about $\frac{5}{8}$" wide and 1" longer than the split in your mesh.

Mix a small quantity of Araldite epoxy resin on a tin lid or piece of card (equal parts resin and hardener the size of a pea should suffice). After thorough blending with a matchstick or similar dispensable tool, smear evenly on to the PVC and apply to the underside of the mesh, ensuring it is correctly positioned over the split.

A small wooden block under the mesh will help. The Araldite will ooze through the mesh and can be smoothed over with a piece of card.

When the Araldite has hardened thoroughly, which takes 24 hours at normal room temperature, the PVC can be peeled away and discarded. I have a 120 mesh lawn repaired nearly 12 months ago by this method and it is still in service. **BS**

Four more sieving tips from Dick Shattock, Joseph Neville, Margaret Brook and Marie-Pierre Governale.

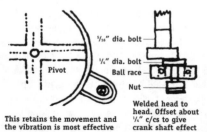

$\frac{5}{16}$" dia. bolt

$\frac{1}{4}$" dia. bolt
Ball race
Nut
Pivot

Welded head to head. Offset about $\frac{1}{4}$" c/cs to give crank shaft effect

This retains the movement and the vibration is most effective

● **I USE A** 40 mesh 12" sieve. The motor is provided by an electric hand drill. Metal frame $\frac{5}{8}$" or $\frac{3}{4}$" wide by $\frac{1}{8}$" thick MS strap. Central pivot on frame across chipboard with hole to fit sieve diameter. Metal braces bolted on to hold frame for drill mounting fixing. A 'loop' welded to side of shaker frame in which runs a very small ball race fitted to a crank 'shaft' held in drill chuck. A bolt is fixed into the wooden wall of the sieve and located between two pegs on the frame. **DS**

150

● **DRY-SIEVING CERAMIC MATERIALS** cannot always be avoided, particularly when basic glazes are mixed and stored in powder form. Few potters are equipped with vibratory sieves, and such essential hygienic precautions as good workshop ventilation, covering sieves and containers with adequate lids, and one's own snout and hair with, respectively, dust mask and a fetching paper bag hat, do not render sifting quick and easy. The main reason is that many powdered materials compact themselves to the mesh and wooden frame, and defy efforts to break up the clumping by intensifying what ideally should be a regular rhythmical jiggling and tapping. Prodding with stick or brush merely makes a tedious job all the more laborious and dusty.

This problem can be alleviated and the whole process accelerated by the simple expedient of keeping a couple of tame smooth rounded pebbles, about 1" diameter, in the sieve. As the sieve is shaken and tapped, so the lightly polished stones skeeter and ricochet. Powders are kept dispersed and gently massaged through the lawn without damage to the mesh, the wooden surround, or the potter's temper. However, do not use skeeter stones in the hemispherical type of kitchen sieve: a couple of shakes and they are in trajectory, with slightly fatal consequences if your name happens to be Goliath. **JN**

● **TO SAVE A** lot of splashing when sieving slips and glazes make a sieve holder out of an old metal coat hanger.

Cut the hanger into two after straightening it out, then bend hooks at each end of them so that they hang down inside the bucket. These sieve holders will fit buckets of different sizes. **MB**

Mini sieve ——

These bits can be tucked around the rim

Big yoghurt pot

● **TO SIEVE A** small quantity of slip I use two bits of wire. They come with bags of clay and the best ones are covered in plastic. This device goes on top of a big yogurt pot and supports the sieve. The slip is pushed through with a brush. Additionally, the device can be used as a very pretty decoration for the workshop. **M-PG**

**Free! Free! Drawers, scoops, buckets, sponges, bins and plastic containers sal-
vaged by Frands Sorensen (Faroe Islands), David White, Bob Bell, Audrey Potts,
Stephen Woodhead, Jyl Bailey, Susan Bennett (who provides two money-saving
ideas), Ken Jones and, from Newcastle, Betty Allsop.**

● **PICK UP AND** use old plastic containers to keep order in the corner of your
workshop where you make your glaze tests.

Cut like this and you have a practical
drawer with handle

Cut like this and you have a cheap scoop. Use
one for every colouring oxide so cleaning is
not necessary

This tip also makes environmental sense. **FS**

● **FOREVER IN NEED** of buckets and unwilling to buy them, building sites have
proved to be a good source especially towards the end of construction, as
umpteen finishing materials, such as putty and paint seem to be supplied in ten
gallon (rare), five and one gallon containers with wire handles and snap-on lids.
Of course, it is best to ask permission. **DW**

● **LIDDED BUCKETS OF** five gallon or so capacity can be obtained for zero cost
from fast food restaurants which are now appearing up and down the nation's
highways. Used to supply cooking oil, they need a good scrub with detergent
before use. **BB**

● **WHEN I STARTED** pottery I found the class was always short of sponges and containers. I enquired at the local chemists and found that the small to large plastic
containers that drugs came in were disposed of, as were the round sponges. They
said they would keep them for me instead of throwing them out, so in no time I
had taken several of each to school. The teacher said it helped with their budget
and also the students were able to mix up small amounts of glaze or paint. **AP**

● **WITH REGARD TO** glaze storage, I use home-brew buckets for glaze storage and
have found another advantage of using them other than the price. They can be
obtained in different shapes which will suit the type of ware to be dipped – for
example a tall thin bucket for tall thin pots and a wide dumpy bucket for wide
bowls and dishes. I have found the best selection of buckets to be found at specialist home-brew shops.

I also use old margarine and ice cream containers for storing small samples of
ready-mixed glaze. They can be easily labelled for future use. **SW**

● **AFTER READING A** tip about fermenting bins being used as a 50% cheaper alternative to pottery firms' glaze buckets, I felt I had to share my tip with CR readers.

The majority of my glaze buckets have not cost me a penny as I use buckets which previously contained tile adhesive. Similar buckets are those which previously contained textured paints, Polyfilla and emulsion etc.

They are all very strong with firm metal handles and airtight lids and hold an average 5 litres so are a comfortable size to store and move about.

These can be easily obtained from your friendly local builder, plumber, painter, glazier or DIY freak. It is also possible to find the odd one or two in rubbish skips. Either a short trip around your neighbourhood or a small advertisement in your local newsagent's window should bring them in. They will probably need a little scrub around and perhaps a couple of quid to persuade the not-so-friendly builder etc., but five minutes' effort and £2 is not bad for a whole set of glaze, clay, plaster of Paris and/or slip buckets is it? An enormous amount of money will be saved. **JB**

● **THE TINY AIRTIGHT** plastic containers with snap-on lids that photographic films come in are excellent for storing small quantities of materials like test-glazes, oxides, special colour mixes and lustres.

Travelling potters might like to concoct a lightweight toilet kit by decanting small amounts of face-cream, hair cream, shampoo, washing powder etc. into these containers as I did on a recent trip to the USA. I have never travelled so light. Had I remembered to label everything, the idea would have worked even better. **SB**

● **SLURRY IS MESSY,** but generally necessary for handbuilding. At school we tried to keep an airtight container of sticky slurry available to decant as required, but by the following day what was unused had become a useless crust that had to be prized out of a dozen plastic beakers – until the advent of lidded plastic containers, which seem to have replaced lined paper bags formerly used by our ceramic material suppliers. Small containers are perfect for preserving individual portions of workable slurry indefinitely.

Larger tubs with handles are convenient for conveying raku glazes outdoors safely, for use in situ. Keep the smaller ones, preferably washed, for pickles, prawns and pimentos to eat with your ploughman's – or potter's – lunch. **SB**

● **A GOOD SOURCE** of supply for sponges is the local chemist. Many of the containers for pills and tablets have sponges to keep them in position. The sponges are usually smooth and pliant and vary in shape and size. Many chemists discard them as waste. **KJ**

● **THIS PART OF** the world has had a vast number of restaurants, fast food outlets and delicatessens opening recently. Many buy in salads, mayonnaise, pickles of various kinds, all of which come in beautiful buckets with well-fitting lids.

A friendly word will usually result in a gift of many such containers by managers only too willing to get rid of them. The only problem is getting rid of the remains of the food but soap and water soon does the trick. **BA**

Necessitating some cash and construction is a well thought out and original dry powder bin by Maurice Carey. The only snag may be that toes might stray under the bin as it is tipped forward, as in the second illustration. Alternatively, Russell Davis suggests a simpler – albeit non-pivoting – option.

● **HERE IS A** neat and compact dry powder storage unit which is moveable for easy cleaning and refilling, and as there is no lid allows fast access in use and speedy stock checking. Any number can be made.

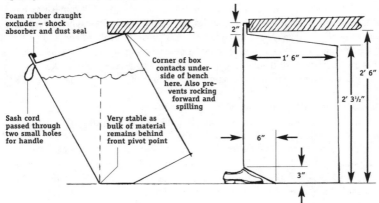

Foam rubber draught excluder – shock absorber and dust seal

Corner of box contacts under-side of bench here. Also pre-vents rocking forward and spilling

Sash cord passed through two small holes for handle

Very stable as bulk of material remains behind front pivot point

2"

1' 6"

2' 6"

2' 3½"

6"

3"

Materials for construction are for the sizes ³/₈" plywood, this is screwed to ³/₄" timber, plywood or blockboard. They can be made in any width down to 4" inter-nal; less than 4" and it is difficult to dip your hand down to the bottom. A 5" internal width will hold 25 kilos of most powders. I have designed these to fit under a 2' 6" bench but simple adjustments to height or width can be made to suit individual needs. The boxes are very light to rock forward and stable in use, having no tendency to tip forward and spill as the bulk of the contents always remains behind the front pivot point. Another bonus – when using the bench it is still possible to stand close up as the feet tuck neatly under the area cut away for the pivot. **MC**

● **LOOKING AT DUSTBINS** in a Bristol store I came across plastic multi purpose tubs, like they use in fish markets, with capacities of 45 and 69 litres: durable and cheap, but no lids. However, a plain flat lid made from any rea-sonable robust sheet material, does the job. Notches accommodate the rope handles and stop the lid from sliding about. Keeps dust and creepy-crawlies out, although not totally rainproof – and they stack.

The same approach works for those tough black 15 litre builders' buckets. The handle can be adjusted to avoid interfering with the flat lid, or just removed. **RD**

Sprays for glaze and pigments are included in the decoration chapter. Adrian Phelps suggests his alternative for helping to keep clay damp.

● **A QUITE EXPENSIVE** but really useful item is the plastic spray bottle used to keep work damp during the making process. A suitable alternative to those supplied by the main pottery firms can be found at any large DIY store with a gardening section. These spray bottles perform just as well, and cost 25% of those supplied by the main pottery firms. **AP**

Ideas for cheap damp cupboards come from Jean Hamilton, Jean Emmett, Duncan James Smith, Susan Bennett, and Sue Packer.

● **TO KEEP PRECIOUS** wheel-thrown pots made at night school safe and damp for the next week, place the pot on the upturned lid of a large ice cream plastic tub and cover with the base. This keeps the pot safe from accidental damage and just damp enough for turning the next week. At home I use old plastic bread bins for small damp cupboards; these can often be picked up at jumble sales. Also useful are the plastic lids used for propagator trays. **JH**

● **OLD FRIDGES LARGE** and small can be obtained very cheaply from the scrapyard. These will make excellent airtight damp cupboards. Take out milk, egg and butter compartments for extra space – the screws for this are usually under the rubber door seals. Replace the screws afterwards to keep the seal in place. Remove electric motor etc. for easier moving. **JE**

● **TRY YOUR FRIENDLY** neighbourhood rubbish dump and tell the foreman you are looking for a catering-type refrigerator. Rustproof, fitted with shelves and drip tray they work wonderfully well because the doors are fitted with rubber seals. **DJS**

● **POLYTHENE SHEETING IS** excellent for wrapping work and keeping it damp. However, it has the disadvantage of coming into contact with the object it covers and potentially distorting it, especially if it is very delicate. Also condensation can build up causing puddles and rivulets causing breakdown of the clay body.

Recently my partner Earl Hyde was working on a porcelain figure of a well-known opera singer. It was impossible to wrap it without distortion, so he converted a plastic sweet jar into a version of a Victorian glass dome and inverted it over the model sealing around the base where it sat on the tile with a coil of clay, thus preventing evaporation.

This method has the advantage of keeping the contents visible so no one could inadvertently damage the work. Also, the model does not have to be lifted or handled before resuming work.

Many other objects can serve as protective domes – not all transparent – i.e. buckets, bowls, flowerpots, plastic bottles, ice cream and yoghurt cartons etc. All these things are easy to come by, cost little or nothing and encourage recycling. **SB**

● **TRYING TO PREVENT** work drying out from one week to the next is not easy when a part-time student. This idea works for me.

Take a piece of board and glue a two-pint plastic milk bottle to each of the corners. Pierce holes randomly near the top of each bottle, fill with water to a level below the holes and screw the tops back on. Place work on board and wrap structure with polythene. Work no longer dries out and the bottles stop the plastic touching the pots. **SP**

One tip and three pieces of equipment for extruding clay from John Harlow, James Rush, Sue Parish and John Dix.

● **LARGE LENGTHS OF** clay shapes can be made by fitting a die of the appropriate shape on to the mouth of a pugmill. The extruded shape can be cut to required length. **JH**

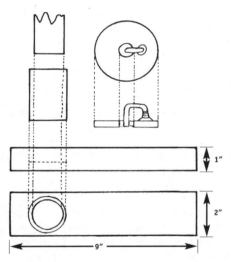

● **FIND THE NEED** – then supply it. So runs the business motto. Well, my need was to make delicate extrusions for both ceramic jewellery and ceramic buttons so, after a little thought, this need was satisfied with the help of this miniature clay extruder made from a few inexpensive materials.

Apart from the dies, the device consists of a 3" length of metal or plastic tube one inch overall diameter; a 7" length of hardwood – preferably beech – about 1 × 2 × 9". This latter will form the base of the tool. To make the extruder begin by drilling a 1" hole about 2" from one end of the wood base using a carpenter's centre bit as this makes a neat, clean hole. Do not drill right through the wood but just let the 'worm' of the bit emerge on the underside before turning the work over and drilling a ⅞" hole keeping to the original centre. With this method a stepped hole is made in which the tube can be housed; it also retains the die in place when the dowel is pushed down. The dies, of course, are the operative part of the device and can be as simple or complicated as you wish. A ready-made die in fact, is an overcoat button filed, if necessary, to fit into the hole: it will give four smooth threads of clay about ¹/₁₆" section. With the centre cut out, the same button will give an interesting cross-like extrusion. Further variations can be added by twisting the clay as it emerges from the die. Smaller buttons may be used as dies if they are placed over a metal washer of suitable size to prevent them being pushed through with the extrusion.

For button backs a slightly more elaborate die is needed. This can easily be made from a 1″ metal disc with a ³/₁₆″ or ¹/₄″ hole drilled through the centre. All that is needed to form the hollow through the extruded tube is a 1¹/₂″ round nail bent double with its head soldered to the side of the hole as shown in the sketch. The nail point is best cut off before the nail is soldered onto the washer and allowed to finish at the centre of the hole. Once one of these dies has been made further possibilities will, no doubt, spring to mind. The extruded clay tube can be cut into small lengths at the leatherhard stage and luted horizontally onto the back of the button. Simple dies giving solid extrusions can be formed from any suitable ready-made discs strong enough to withstand the pressure of the extrusion, i.e. metal or plastic. The shape of the desired section can be cut in the disc.

To operate the extruder fill the tube with soft well-wedged clay from its bottom end and secure the base in a vice or rest the 'working end' on the edge of the bench. Press the plunger down and the clay section will be extruded. Do not leave the plunger in the tube as it will be difficult to remove when the clay hardens. **JR**

● **THE FINELY PUNCHED** dies for the commercially produced hand-held clay extruders which we use always seem to split fairly quickly, and have to be discarded. Rather than pushing clay through sieves to make strands for hair and grass etc., one of our students, Julia, hit upon the idea of using a garlic press. These can be found with round or square section holes, and are strong enough to withstand constant use, even with firmish clay. **SP**

● **HERE IS A** description of a simple extruder I made from a discarded foot pump. After the boss was cut off the fixed end of the cylinder a large hole was cut in the same end leaving sufficient metal to hold the die plate in place. Then the pin that goes across the cylinder end was cut to make two studs to clear the extrusion as it came out. Discard the leather washer from the piston and away you go.

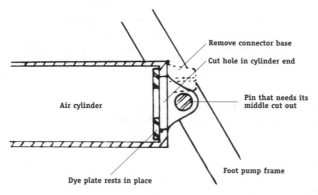

Remove connector base

Cut hole in cylinder end

Pin that needs its middle cut out

Air cylinder

Dye plate rests in place

Foot pump frame

Die plates can be made of plastic – simple but have a limited life; or large washers with a small hole – motorbikes are a good source, also bed ends.

Not a mass production tool but good for quick glaze tests and small handles. **JD**

Jerry Harper speeds up the drying of clay with a gas blowlamp.

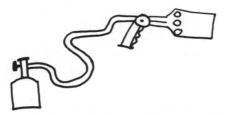

● **TO MAKE AN** Alan Peascod-style gas dryer for firming off wet pots quickly so that you can work on them immediately, or for drying off wet slip to stop a possible collapse, you will need a gas blowlamp with flexible delivery pipe connected to a hand nozzle (with interchangeable nozzles). Using a ¾" diameter nozzle drill out the gas jet using a No. 60 drill bit. Enlarge airholes at base of nozzle.

This will deliver a flame about 15" long which will envelop the pot but is not too embarrassingly large to be used in a small workshop (keep away from plastics). This will dry off pots in a few seconds as those of us who attended the Northern Potters Camp will testify. **JH**

An ingenious inner pot support is devised by Susan Bennett.

● **WHEN CONSTRUCTING A** large three-dimensional sculptural object that is not supported by a flat base, preventing distortion or total collapse can be very difficult, especially in a school environment where constant vigilance is impossible.

A group of my students recently coiled enormous vegetables – such as peppers, garlic, pumpkins – with curved or contoured bases. We used plastic bags filled with polystyrene beads to support concave areas, but soon ran out. In desperation I found some large sacks of dry sawdust we were saving for raku firings. This provided an excellent solution. To support a structure roughly 2' high by 18" wide, for example, half fill a strong bin-liner with sawdust and rest the object on top. It will find its own level; you can push the sawdust around to help fill concave areas. You can then move the object to and from the storage area with its supporting bag – thus avoiding distortion until it has stiffened sufficiently to bear its own weight – just as long as you are strong enough to lift it. **SB**

Mike Rawlinson, Torhjen Moon, Stephen Grieve and John Harlow have economical suggestions concerning the larger items of pottery equipment.

● **I HAVE FOUND** that an electric cement mixer (not as expensive as you might think) can be used as a blunger/ball mill. Simply put the clay or glaze mixture in the mixer along with a few large beach pebbles, tie a sheet of polythene over the opening, and leave it running for an hour or so.

Not only is this far cheaper than buying a blunger, but it comes in handy for mixing cement too.

If you want to see how well it works before you buy one, they can be hired for a modest daily rate. **MR**

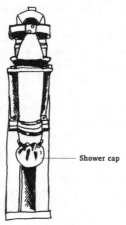

Shower cap

● **ANY READERS WHO** own a vertical pugmill will know how annoying and time-consuming it can be when the plastic covering comes away from the nozzle.

After this had happened to me a few times, I came up with the idea of using an elasticated shower cap, which stays in place at all times. **TM**

● **AFTER 18 YEARS** of subjecting ourselves to the annoying noise of our vertical pugmill, a friend pointed out that it had probably damaged our hearing. Somewhat too late therefore I have built a box of wood, lined with old carpet tiles from the dump round the motor and gearbox. This has greatly reduced the noise level so that we can subject ourselves to the radio all day. Remember to leave ventilation holes in the box. **SG**

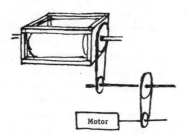

Motor

● **DIY BALL MILL:** get a five-gallon plastic drum with screw cap and fit it into a wooden frame (tight fit) with a large hinged lid with fastener. Plastic drums are light and therefore easily removed and a spare put in. There is virtually no wear on the drum. A wooden case was made and fitted with casters. **JH**

There is but a single item for potters who make their own moulds, from N Collins. Notes on plaster mixing and balloons may be found in chapter three.

● **I AM NOT** a commercial potter and any pottery I do is purely as a hobby. Recently I started to experiment with plaster of Paris and making moulds, but when it came to finding something large enough in which to house my moulds I came unstuck. I did not want the expense of buying specialised moulding equipment, so I simply acquired an assortment of cardboard boxes from a supermarket and lined them with plastic dustbin bags. Thus I had a variety of different sized containers in which to make my moulds. **NC**

Jean Hamilton, Lyndon Thomas, Susan Bennett and John Dix deal with aspects of shelving.

● **FOR CHEAP PORTABLE** shelves I use old wooden tomato boxes of varying depths which stack neatly one on top of each other. They can be used for green ware or bisque pots. **JH**

● **USERS OF ELECTRIC** kilns can easily make a drying rack over the top of the kiln with a quantity of angle iron or Dexion framing, sheets of Asbestolux and a few nuts and bolts. Such a rack saves possible damage to the kiln from the weight of the pots placed directly on what is usually a flat top. **LT**

● **PALLETS ARE OBJECTS** full of recycling possibilities. Until recently, apart from fuelling our wood-burning stove, I had not much use for them – until, that is, I set my students a project requiring vast numbers of large clay slabs. Confronted with the problem of how to store them safely, I soon ran out of cupboard space and flat boards.

Scouring the school refuse area for old shelves, I noticed some small wooden pallets, and suddenly realised I could build them up into a 'plan chest' for the slabs by knocking away the central supports and stacking them three high.

Using an existing unused work bench as a base, it worked brilliantly providing safe, compact, accessible storage and – in extremis, with the addition of a little padding – a comfy, top deck refuge for exhausted pottery teachers. **SB**

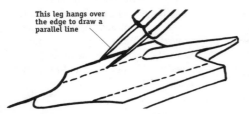

This leg hangs over the edge to draw a parallel line

● **BUYING 1" DOWEL** to fit the holes in my shelving system was going to be an expensive business. So I bought lots of broom handles and ground down a 1" flat bit to cut the correct hole size of $^{27}/_{32}$".

First colour the bit with felt-tip marker, then scribe through the film in the correct place – I used a pair of dividers. Then grind off to the lines. **JD**

One of the complaints of the public against craft pottery is the roughness of the bases. Judith Fisher, Joseph Neville and South Wales Potters tackle this problem.

● **I RECENTLY REALISED** that one can use the power of an electric wheel to smooth the base of fired pots. I cut a circle out of a sheet of silicon carbide paper, glue it on to a spare wheel batt and hold each pot against the revolving disc for a couple of seconds – much quicker than rubbing down by hand. **JF**

● **WHEN IT COMES** to cleaning up and smoothing foot-rings and bases of fired ware, there is a simple and inexpensive alternative to the abrasive disc mounted on the wheel-head, or the rotary grindstone. Most gardener's and hardware stores stock a spindle-shaped coarse whetstone whose official function is to sharpen scythes and sickles. It is some ten to twelve inches long and appears to be made of sintered materials, perhaps a mix of sand and coke. The old-time scyther used to carry it like a weapon, in a leather holster strapped to the belt. The potter should use it wet, then there is no need to don mask or goggles. A good lubricant is water to which detergent or – better still – soap has been added. An emulsified abrasive swarf soon forms, and acts as a sort of grinding-in paste. The whetstone reaches those parts that abrasive discs and grindstones cannot. It develops contours and facets which can be exploited to get at particularly awkward places. Moreover, it can help to restore a little bloom of youth to kiln furniture, especially to batts raddled by the usual sloshings of batt wash by potters who secretly yearn to be allowed to limewash the backyard privies in Coronation Street. **JN**

● **AUTOMOTIVE ENGINE VALVE** grinding compound (VGC) is great for smoothing the bottoms of pots. Just squeeze out some compound, which is like fine silicon carbide, add a little water and rotate the pot until smooth. It can be bought in a water or oil base, but the water base is easiest to wash off. VGC is great for the gallery and edges of lids. **SWP**

Breathing in clay and glaze dust is certainly not to be recommended and several potters write on the subject. There are other contributions in other sections; here Dorothy Feibleman describes her ceramic dust collector.

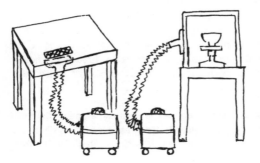

● **FOR THOSE WHO** scrape, sand etc. creating lots of dust, root out an area on worktop and screw and glue on a small vacuum cleaner attachment. Glue or position fine screen in larger rebate over cleaner attachment. Cleaner can be attached or detached, and area containing screen and attachment can be flush with worktop if you are careful, and thus not interfere with normal use of work area. There is only one company, as far as I know, which makes a small vacuum cleaner with a special attachment for silica, cadmium etc. It is Nilfisk-Advance (Newmarket Road, Bury St Edmunds, Suffolk IP33 3SR. Tel 01284 763163). It is also quiet and very powerful. **DF**

Janet Cottrell's list of general workshop tips is so various that it defied classification and so it is included as it stands.

● **I AM FREQUENTLY** amazed when I read Potters' Tips because many are things I have been doing for years and imagined that everyone else knew all about them, for example using fishing line to cut pots off the wheel-head and tile adhesive buckets for glaze bins.

So I had a look round my workroom to see if there were any other things which may not be as obvious as I thought. I came up with the following:

• Plastic sweet jars, thrown away by many shops, for storage of dry powders and small quantities of glaze.
• Apple corer for making holes.
• Mapping pen nibs for tiny holes.
• Bits of broken comb for sgraffito – break out the teeth to get the pattern you want.
• Pastry brush for slip.
• Wire and roller cheese cutter for faceting leatherhard pots.
• Manicure 'orange sticks' for small modelling tools.
• Hat pin pushed through a cork for a potter's needle – it floats too.
• If you can get hold of an old roller blind the heavy wooden dowelling makes excellent rolling pins, cut to the length you require. **JC**

Kathleen Creasey suggests a way of making holes in beads.

● **WHEN MAKING CERAMIC** beads, instead of waiting until the clay dries to leatherhard stage before laboriously drilling the hole and possibly distorting any decoration or even splitting the bead, try this quick and easy method. Place the newly shaped soft bead on an upturned polystyrene food tray, and pierce it with a suitably sized potter's pin or a fine knitting needle (remember that the hole will shrink as the clay dries). Push the pin gently through the bead and the polystyrene; it can then be withdrawn without distorting the bead, which can be left to dry to leatherhard stage, and a finer pin could be inserted through the hole to facilitate holding the bead should carving or further decoration be planned. **KC**

Although this group includes 'materials' very few entries come under this heading. Gouache colours and granite dust appear in the glaze chapter and here are observations on gum tragacanth and vinegar by Dee Batter-Hatten and Eric Degg.

● **TO PRODUCE A** solution of gum tragacanth (binder) in three minutes flat is too simple. To one teaspoonful of gum tragacanth powder, add one tablespoonful of alcohol, not 100% pure, but commercial methylated spirits or 90% alcohol. Then simply add water as needed, approximately 100-150cc. The solution becomes very warm but the gum is immediately in solution. Methylated spirits or commercial alcohol are best, in distilled water, but surgical spirit produces a white opaque solution which smells of wintergreen. I prefer the alcohol, which is marvellous, and takes less than a minute to make. Tap water is inclined to separate out, water on top – gum below. I am always horrified to hear of the hours people spend soaking in cold water, heating etc. and then the result is a mess. **DB-H**

● **EVERY POTTER REALISES** the strong affinity which exists between pottery and culinary processes, and the many items of kitchen equipment used in the workshop make the relationship even more obvious. Making pots in the kitchen can make for useful chemical discoveries too.

Some fourteen years ago I was repairing a very dry green ware pot at the kitchen table and had put a few drops of water on a plate into which I intended to dip a soft-haired brush to prepare the broken edges for welding together. Becoming absorbed in the problem of supporting the piece I inadvertently dipped my brush into vinegar left on an adjoining plate. I realised my mistake as the smell assailed my nostrils, but, having applied vinegar to the pot, reasoned that to add water as well might not be a good idea. After a moment's reflection I carried on with the repair using only the vinegar.

I was surprised how rapidly and effectively the clay became slushy and how easy it was to weld pieces together and conceal the damage. With water repairs I often found that the surface of a repair developed small cracks that had to be reworked. This repair was perfect both before and after firing. I introduced vinegar to my pottery classes and it has been used for countless repairs every since. Almost every repair has been completely successful, including damage I would not have considered repairing with water. One bonus has been the appetising smell it produces.

It is important to keep the vinegar in an airtight container and to not contaminate it by dipping dirty brushes into the storage container – it can quickly become mouldy, develop a putrid smell and become less effective. I have not been able to discover why vinegar works so well. Perhaps it simply penetrates the dry clay structure more rapidly and completely than water. **ED**

Tips on repairing cracks come from the Waikato Society of Potters, New Zealand; Dot Stephenson and Geoff Walker.

● **VINEGAR AND DRY** body clay makes a thick slip for cracks in wet or leatherhard pieces (which have become hard, but not dry).

Sugar, dry body clay and water makes a thick slip for cracks in leatherhard pieces and green ware.

Zircopax and calcined EPK with water and a few drops of sodium silicate makes a thick slip for cracks in green ware.

One part Zircopax and one part silica with water makes a thick slip for cracks in bisque ware.

Powdered bisqued body clay, grog with vinegar and a few drops of sodium silicate, makes a thick slip for bisque ware.

Ceramic supply stores also carry patching material – these as well as kiln cements will work on green or bisque ware. All usually contain sodium silicate.

Where dry body clay is called for, it is understood to be the same clay body as the piece to be patched. The best procedure is to rub the elixir well into the crack and then sand it smooth. If the piece is still wet, slow down the drying by covering in plastic.

When trying this method of repair remember that whenever sodium silicate is used in a light-coloured patching material, it will turn dark grey. It will also dry and fire hard, making it difficult to apply a glaze. **WSP**

● **THAT PRECIOUS PIECE** is almost finished and a part comes away in your hands. A crack develops in the final drying and patching with vinegar only makes it worse. Reach for the paperclay – it really works. You need only keep a little in stock, just enough for disasters, and keep a little bottle of vinegar too. Make a slip of your body clay, about the consistency of double cream. Add water to some sheets of double tissue loo paper to make it the same consistency. Combine the two, 4 parts clay slip to 1 part paper mush (a little bleach or Milton stops it smelling musty). Soften the broken/cracked edges with vinegar and fill with paperclay. This method will often work with small cracks in bisque ware too if you are lucky, only in this case wet the edges with water before applying the paperclay and polish it in firmly. **DS**

● **TAKE A SMALL** piece of almost dry clay, only just distortable when poked with maximum finger pressure. Push this piece of clay into a mound of sugar of approximately the same volume (it does not matter what type of sugar, but caster sugar works more quickly). Keep pushing/kneading this little lump into the sugar until something miraculous happens: you should finish up with a ball of quite soft clay within a few minutes. The tip is that the resultant plastic clay can be used to fill cracks in dry but unfired pots.

Apparently the old potters used this mix to fill cracks and the like in large thrown pots. I have tried it on special pots over the years and it really works.

I have no idea of the chemistry behind this, but I have amazed some very experienced potters over the years with this little party trick. **GW**

Identifying wrapped pots, especially in educational environments, is an abiding problem. Belinda Swingler comes up with a solution.

● **IN ORDER TO** distinguish one plastic-wrapped piece of work from another on the store shelves, especially if a pupil is absent, I have used some wooden clothes pegs and on to the flat side stuck narrow-width masking tape. On this I have written the pupils' names with waterproof pen. Different colours can be used for different classes or projects.

When people leave or move up a year the tape is pulled off and a new piece applied. Also some awkwardly shaped projects when wrapped need plastic held at many different points, so again clothes pegs come to the rescue. **BS**

The last entry in this chapter features designer dustbin liners from Susan Bennett.

● **AT THE END** of a day's enthusiastic throwing I leave the studio looking like a hippopotamus emerging from a mud bath. I do not normally bother with overalls so all my clothes go straight into the machine and I leap into the bath. Sometimes, just when our laundry arrangements fail to provide any clean protective clothing, I need to look instantly presentable in the middle of a working session. Recently, in desperation, I donned a large plastic bag and wore it belted as a smock. Black dustbin liners can look quite stunning. Dry cleaners' bags will do, but heavier duty dress manufacturers' bags are better. You can dispose of them after use, or recycle them to cover pots.

It strikes me that it would be useful for pottery teachers in schools to keep a few bags aside for emergency use. My young students' overalls disappear with alarming frequency. I tried to initiate a scheme involving fathers' old shirts, but none are ever available at the moment of need. Maybe a few sessions of bin bag wearing would provoke a more responsible attitude.

While on the subject of polythene bags, do look out if you are ever in a rag trade area. Dress manufacturers throw out sacks of large plastic bags – and hangers for that matter. Come to think of it, maybe there is a market for fashionable disposable protective clothing. **SB**

Chapter 8
General

This chapter includes those tips which could not easily be inserted elsewhere. They are all extremely useful, however, and illustrate the versatility and wide interest of the potter.

Bolton Technical College tells us something about weights (though we no longer have the halfpenny), Roy Hubbard helps with weight-lifting, M Trickett sends a three-in-one letter, Ken Jones offers an alternative to carborundum stone, the New Zealand Potter outlines four tips, Alan Ashpool proposes a long-lasting glasspaper, Sue Packer an alternative apron and Jerry Stovin has a tip for cleaning plaster slabs.

● **IT IS USEFUL** to know that a 2p coin weighs $\frac{1}{4}$oz, 1p half that at $\frac{1}{8}$oz, and $\frac{1}{2}$p $\frac{1}{16}$oz. Very convenient for weighing small amounts when those little weights go missing yet again. **BTC**

● **POTTING OFTEN INCLUDES** moving heavy or bulky items. Old skateboards can be very usefully recycled as low loaders for bags of clay, bottles of propane gas etc. **RH**

● **LIGHTWEIGHT CLOTHES PEGS** hold polythene sheets together to cover drying pots. An old shaving brush is ideal for applying slip when joining pieces of clay. An empty salt container is a useful holder for grog – it keeps it clean and you do not have to put clay covered hands into the grog. **MT**

● **A SUBSTITUTE FOR** carborundum rubbing stone can be made quite simply and quickly. Using a fine grogged clay make a small block (of any specific shape) and allow to dry. When dry rub the surfaces with a moist sponge. The softer clay particles are wiped away leaving the grog raised on the surface of the block. Obviously, the more clay that is taken off increases the surface texture, so one can have a variation on the same block. Fire in the hottest part of the kiln. **KJ**

● **MAKING GROG: TO** make grog, grate a lump of plastic clay on an ordinary kitchen grater. Bisque fired in pots it makes very uniform grog, eliminates screening and produces practically no dust.

Oozing clay: When joining two clay pieces together, some of the slip often oozes out. If it is in a hard to reach place, try using a small watercolour brush to wipe the excess slip away. The bristles do not damage the clay piece but do absorb the slip, and the brush is easily cleaned.

Beanbag mould: With a sheet of plastic draped over its surface, a beanbag makes a versatile form for drape-moulding large bowls or platters.

Making a foot-ring: To get a foot on a coiled pot, cut out two bases the same size. Put one piece on the working surface and cover it completely, top and sides, with thin nylon fabric (or cling film). Place the second base on top, then build the walls with coils starting outside the lower base piece. When the pot has finished and has reached the leatherhard stage, the lower base will lift out easily and leave a very neat foot-ring. **NZP**

● **A COARSE GRADE** of wet and dry glasspaper has been found to last at least a hundred times longer than a similar grade of sandpaper when used for rubbing dried clay forms. It also lasts very much longer than emery cloth. It is particularly good when used as a flat sheet for smoothing down dried tiles or pot bases. A dust mask should always be worn when using it. **AA**

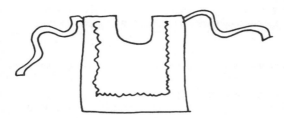

● **WHEN FIRST LEARNING** to throw I seemed to go home from evening classes wearing more clay than I had thrown. My tip is to stitch two bath towels together along the length for 18" or so. Sew a tie in each of the two top corners. The 'apron' protects legs and front while throwing.

Now that I am less messy, my latest tip is to wear a thick cotton pedestal mat (that fits around the bottom of a lavatory) with optional ties. I wear it as an apron and it works beautifully. I do not recommend the 'shag pile twist' for obvious reasons. **SP**

● **THIS TIP IS** useful for studios where student classes follow each other closely on the same day. When cleaning plaster wedging slabs, avoid washing them down and thus rendering them useless for wedging, kneading or drying the next class's clay. Keep them fairly dry by crumpling a ball of newspaper and rubbing the traces of clay left on the slab. Gripping the newspaper with both hands, push it away from you against the slab. The clay will form into crumbs which can be brushed off the slab into a bowl and recycled. **JS**

A novel method of fixing tiles from Alberta by J B Cunningham, a perfect working surface from Frank Draper, Bill Jones finds a use for film cassette pots and Susan Bennett explores the adaptability of kick stools.

● **I AM A** student at Alberta College of Art and recently completed a ceramic mural for my living room. My instructor suggested that other potters might be interested in my method of securing the tiles.

A panel of ¼" hardboard was screwed to the wall and the tiles fastened to this using strips of Velcro glued at the top and bottom of each tile. This material, most often used in clothing, has lots of strength and at the same time allows some bedding when surfaces are not perfectly flat. **JBC**

● **IN TRYING TO** produce some economical work tables for the school pottery we used, purely by chance, a type of chipboard produced with a resin glue and intended for wet floors such as kitchens and bathrooms. It goes by the trade reference of V313.

I have always despaired of children trying to control decent slabs by using cloths, and the V313 solved the problem. One can roll out directly onto its surface with no hint of an adhesion problem. In two years of use the surface has remained perfectly flat, and there has been no release of wood chips at all – in spite of being sponged three or four times a day.

We took the precaution of putting a softwood edge around the 25mm thick board and we have had very serviceable work tables which have simply developed a better working patina the more they have been used. Almost a perfect surface for potters. **FD**

● **IN THE MAKING** of plaster stamps and drum dies for incised markings I have found the use of film cassette pots ideal.

Filled with plaster the cassette case can easily be removed, either in part or whole, to reveal a small drum which can be carved as necessary. The pots are also useful for keeping underglaze colours or slips in their original state, being both waterproof and sealed as required.

My local photo developer keeps them for me – most places have a large box of discarded containers under the counter. **BJ**

● **I RECENTLY ACQUIRED** a kick stool as used in libraries and supermarkets to access high shelves.

Hitherto, I had struggled in my studio to lift pots on to or off inaccessible shelves, having to guess how far to push a board, being far too short to ever actually see what was happening.

The bonus has been that the top of the stool is exactly the right height to stand a glaze bucket on – it saves bending to floor level. Moreover, if you just raise the bucket a little, you can push it around on the stool to exactly where you need it, without having to take all the weight yourself – sacks of materials can be moved in the same way. Once you release the weight, the wheels deactivate.

The stool is light enough to grab with one hand when the phone goes, to position conveniently for a bit of a sit-down. It has proved so versatile in my studio, we now have several in the art department at school, where they are very popular and useful. They can be ordered from an educational supplies catalogue – large department stores stock them too.

Try a kick stool for yourself – you will kick yourself for not have acquired one sooner. **SB**

Mending holes, making holes, and stopping up holes from Martin King, M M Crump, Edwin Todd, Denis Hopking, and Sue Varley/Susan Bennett.

● **HOLES IN PLASTIC** or enamel buckets can be repaired with a blob of epoxy resins, such as Araldite. These resins usually work chemically by mixing two solutions. If this is done on a bit of cardboard with a matchstick no expensive knives or plates will be ruined. **MK**

● **THE DIFFERENCE OF** a millimetre greatly affects the fit of a candle in its socket. Try leaving a slightly beaded inner rim which can be fluted quickly with a small tool held vertically. Quicker still is the application of three sharp little pimples of clay placed slightly lower down out of sight or a few discreet scratches with a hacksaw blade. If necessary rub the glaze off the sharp ridges before firing. Your candles will screw into place firmly. **MMC**

● **WE MAKE LOTS** of candle shades with holes in them, and the holes have a ring about them. To make these we fashion a tool out of an old hacksaw blade.

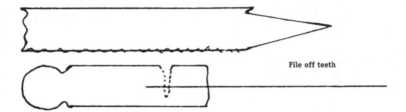

File off teeth

Heat the blade first to dull red to soften it and then cut and shape it. We make four sizes. Make a groove in a short piece of wooden dowel and jam in the blade. If necessary bore a hole and drive in a brad. **ET**

● **AN EASY AND** very efficient method for making neat and clean holes in beads and sausages of clay for necklaces or whatever, is to use the head of a masonry nail. Push the head in first – this will take with it a knob of clay, leaving the ball or bead holed and undistorted. **DH**

● **HAVE YOU EVER** desperately needed a plug and all you could find was a chain hanging into the sink? If it happens to you again and endless searching proves fruitless, make your own.

Take a lump of stiff clay, wrap it in thin polythene and wedge it into the plughole. It will work for quite a long time. If and when it becomes ineffective, simply make another. If it leaks a bit, smear a coil of clay around the edge. **SV/SB**

Another mixed bag: John VEG Mitchell examines a method of measuring thickness, Duncan Davis and Brian Cooke find useful containers by recycling food buckets while Susan Halls travels to McDonald's in search of spoons.

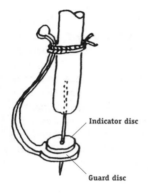

Indicator disc

Guard disc

● **PUSH A NEEDLE** tool through a 1cm diameter rubber disc cut from a car inner tube. Push this needle and disc into the base of a clay pot and the disc will slide up to record the thickness of the clay. However, the disc is just as likely to stick to the clay and slide off when the needle is pulled out. A second larger disc placed underneath the first disc will guard against this (see diagram). If the second disc sticks and moves, the first disc remains to show the pot thickness. It gives a result... first time. Make sure the second disc is attached to the handle or you will spend a lot of time fishing it out of the pot. **JVEGM**

● **PASSING MY LOCAL** delicatessen the other evening I found a pile of white plastic buckets stacked inside each other. They had clearly been used for cottage cheese and suchlike, and though needing a thorough wash made excellent containers for glazes. I thought this was a great find and plan to make regular visits to what is now my favourite deli. **DD**

● **HAVING TAKEN TO** heart your recent tip about scrounging buckets from delicatessens, I found an owner only too pleased to pass them on (in a variety of sizes) to a good home. I discovered that the tubs, or buckets, usually used for storing oily food, required a thorough wash immediately. Soap and water are okay, but good old-fashioned scouring powder (Vim or Ajax) worked much better. Incidentally, two buckets placed inside each other were overlooked and the trapped food remaining rapidly went sour and rotted – but even that could be scoured and saved. **BC**

● **CONVENTIONAL SCOOPS AND** spoons can make the weighing out of small oxide quantities a frustrating task. McDonald's have the answer. Their miniature plastic spoons (supplied with tea and coffee) make the perfect utensil for the job. You may even find them on the pavement outside. **SH**

The safe storage and identification of materials and pots is important in the studio and even more so in the classroom. Michael Skipwith, Susan Bennett, J Kollov, Paul Reid, the North London Collegiate School and John VEG Mitchell have some ideas.

● **FROM TIME TO** time you may wish to identify a tool or object etc., as being left or right. Two ideas from the world of sailing – red sticky tape (port) to indicate left and green (starboard) to indicate right. Alternatively, for metal, wood or clay use a centre punch to mark once (starboard, right) or twice (port, left), from the sound signals one for starboard, two for port. **MS**

● **DO YOU SHARE** your studio with a kiln? If so this tip could save you money and needless frustration.

Although this is an undesirable situation, you can at least escape bodily from the unhealthy effects of fumes and intense heat generated while your kiln is performing – but have you considered the effect of its outpourings on the contents of your studio? It is so tempting to stick rarely used packets and bits of equipment on the top shelves out of the way. But remember that heat rises, carrying fumes with it. When you finally reach up, the packet you encounter is likely to disintegrate between your fingers, the label faded and crumbled beyond decipher. Mechanical parts emerge rusty, dusty and corroded – my wall clock succumbed totally.

The atmosphere is cooler and relatively fume-free nearer the ground. So avoid the expense and frustration of hoarding ultimately unusable items – for a longer shelf-life, store nearer the floor. **SB**

● **WRITE YOUR NAME** on the side of some wooden clothes pegs and take to classes. When you wrap your work in polythene at the end of a session the pegs will keep it all in place snugly so no air can creep in. Also, as your name is written on the pegs, when others are hunting through the cupboards for their work they will not disturb yours. **JK**

● **ONE OF THE** problems which faces me as a pottery teacher is how to keep work damp for a week in between lessons.

I do have a damp cupboard but I find this insufficient and therefore extra wrapping in the form of polythene was what I used previously. For the past year I have found that the best containers for small articles of work are Pell trays. I simply place damp paper towels in the bottom of a tray, put the children's work inside and then cover with an inverted tray. **PR**

● **KEEPING STUDENTS' WORK** damp, safe and identifiable in a school pottery can be quite problematic. In our school, three part-time teachers work with over 200 children during a week. Storage space is limited and work often has to be left out and yet kept damp.

Clipping clothes-peg name tags on to the polythene cladding is a helpful aid, but irksome to look at each time – so we evolved a colour code system. Each teacher has a colour – green, red, blue – and their students attach the relevant coloured peg to the outside of their wrapped work. This prevents prying hands from delving into anonymous mounds and damaging other students' work, or worse, leaving it semi-unwrapped and liable to dry out. A further aid, to both identifying individual work and preventing drying out or unwelcome probing, is masking tape – a relatively cheap item which students use to hold the polythene together like a parcel, and which can be clearly labelled with a marker pen. This system provides double indemnity and has proved very successful. **NLCS**

● **AT THE END** of evening classes there is often more work needed on your pots. The advice is to cover it with a plastic bag and work on it next week.

The following week, your pot is leatherhard, and distorted from the weight of the plastic bag. You can avoid this. Use a cut-down cornflake packet to relieve the weight from the plastic bag. Cut off the top and bottom of the packet, shape it into a wall, well clear of your pot, then cover the whole lot with the plastic bag. Very obviously label it with your name on the outside of the packet to ward off your fellow evening class potters. **JVEGM**

Caroline Bousfield Gregory puts forward three useful tips, Julia Nicholson offers a remedy for stuck lids on jars, Merion John Warren converts his kiln into a temporary oven and Bill Jones suggests ways of dealing with black mould.

● **1. LEAVE SLOPPY** clay for recycling on a piece of canvas, or other strong cloth, on a thick board to dry. As the clay dries, the cloth can be peeled away and the clay rolled up for kneading.
2. Try kneading clay on a sloping surface – sloping away from the body at approximately 30° – much less of a strain on the wrists.
3. When scraping down leatherhard coil pots use a wet stainless steel scourer wrapped round the fingers to scrape rims and tight curves that cannot be reached easily with a steel kidney. Then use a damp sponge to smooth the surface. **CBG**

● **WHILST WORKING WITH** a group of disabled adults I found that the screw-on lid on a pot of glaze was well and truly stuck. I was searching for some tool which would help me remove the lid when a visually impaired member of the class suggested a simple solution. It worked, and here is the low-tech solution to the frustrating problem of a tightly fastened lid.

Wind an elastic band around the outside edge of the screw top. This enables you to get a good grip. Twist firmly and the problem should be solved. It has also worked on a container of PVA glue, where even the technician was having difficulty removing a very 'stuck' screw lid. Alternatively you can use a rubber glove. **JN**

● **LAST CHRISTMAS MY** wife remarked that our oven would be unlikely to accommodate and cook all the food needed for our four sons, the very recent wife of number three son, girlfriend of number four, my sister and my mother, the main problem being a sufficiently large turkey, and that she hoped we were not expecting a particularly prompt lunchtime meal.

I have found the accuracy and reliability of my Cambridge 40-1 controller, coupled to a Potterycrafts P4949 top-loader kiln, to be beyond reproach, and glibly claimed the turkey for my own. Armed with Delia Smith and a foreboding of disaster, I repaired to the kiln room at 7.30am Christmas Day morning and set the requisite co-ordinates. The turkey at 1pm was crisply browned perfection. However the meal was unfortunately delayed somewhat by the uncooked roast potatoes, delayed by my turning the oven off whilst putting the clock to the correct time and inadvertently setting the delayed action timer. My forebodings had come home to roost. **MJW**

● **WITH REFERENCE TO** the dreaded black mould, I have found it in paperclay, and also in porcelain, T material and in other clays, but it is most unsightly in white clays. It can pong a bit as well.

I control it by using normal household bleach when washing down my wheel or buckets but the problem with this is that the bleach also contains washing–up liquid. To control it in the water used to mix clay use sterilising tablets (the kind used for babies' bottles) – pop a couple into the mixing water and it will kill the mould. If you have left some paperclay in a bag then press a few finger holes into the clay and add sterilising solution to soften the clay. To avoid this only mix as much clay as you intend to use.

Be aware that the mould will grow on wet wooden tools and in sponges, as well as in wet cabinets, so always use plenty of bleach when cleaning or putting water into trays in the cabinets. **BJ**

George Marriott suggests a new use for old floor cleaners, Susan Bennett/Brian Rose and Michael Skipwith deal with plastic bags, Kenneth Breese finds a use for polystyrene packing and Jerry Stovin suggests a remedy for mislaid specs.

● **GET ON GOOD** terms with your local school's caretakers – they use circular scouring pads on the floor cleaning machines, and frequently discard part-worn ones. After cutting up with scissors, these make ideal pads for cleaning up dry pots ready for biscuit firing. **GM**

● **ONE WOULD NOT** imagine that knowledge of aviation could bring much joy to the potter's lot, yet this tip gleaned from my brother could have many useful applications.

He is a busy film cameraman. He often flies in small aircraft and drives frequently to varied and unfamiliar locations. Observing how pilots mark out their routes, he adapted the idea to road navigation. He selects the relevant pages on his atlas and covers each with a transparent plastic sleeve. With a crayon he boldly marks the main features of his route – road numbers, directional arrows, major locations. Thus, at a glance, he can navigate alone. Once the journey is completed, he simply erases the markings, atlas unscathed, nerves unshattered.

Another application could be for keeping stock records – simply list regular items on a permanent sheet and adjust the numbers on the plastic cover. My glaze recipe book need never have become a tick-infested mess had I slipped a sleeve over the page and ticked each ingredient off on that. In future, memos, messages, sketches, orders – there must be endless uses – all will end up on plastic sleeves. **SB/BR**

● **CLEANING PLASTIC CLAY** bags for re-use. If, as I do, you keep your clay in 25kg plastic bags, when it comes to cleaning the inside, instead of washing them out, which is messy and time and water consuming, turn them inside out and place over a bucket or suchlike and leave them to dry out. Then when dry, 'concertina' them, closing or averting your eyes as the clay shoots off at great speed. **MS**

175

● **IF YOU HAVE** the occasion to add pressed decoration to a pot with a narrow aperture whilst at leatherhard stage, fill the pot with polystyrene packing chips. This prevents the side being distorted and when dry they can be tipped out and used again. **KB**

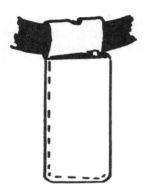

● **AS THE YEARS** and myopia (or presbyopia) creep up on defenceless potters and they spend several years repeatedly misplacing their glasses, one resort is to hang the case by a string round the neck, where they inevitably get involved in the throwing. Ten years ago, when an erstwhile friend asked if my pendant specs were my pacemaker, I devised a holster to hang from my hip. Decidedly macho. At Walter Keeler's demonstration day for London Potters, I was delighted to see that he had cut slits in an open-ended spectacles case and threaded it on his belt for the same purpose. It is easy to tweak the glasses out, even with a slurried hand, and manoeuvre them over one's ears. **JS**

Two tips to cure leaking or seeping pots. Mart Muller in Nairobi uses wax. Robert Fournier, meanwhile, finds a varnish helpful.

● **IT IS AS** if the devil plays a game with me. Most of my vessels do not leak but sometimes those intended to hold liquid for longer periods, such as vases and pitchers, have a bad habit of leaving rings of humidity on the table.

I tried yoghurt and waterglass but neither worked. I have now found a solution. I melted candle leftovers, added about a quarter of paraffin to it and put the leaking pot (after preheating) in the mixture (the bottom of the pot unglazed). Ten minutes is enough to fill the pores, excess can be wiped off.

It even worked with a pitcher with a turned bottom which was glazed and still leaked a bit. I put it in the mixture and also put some inside the pitcher and left it on the stove for half an hour. After cooling I got rid of the wax inside by using hot water.

Of course one should try to find better fitting glazes but then I have had this problem with very reliable glazes once in a while, and it is a shame to discard a nice vase just because it sweats. **MM**

● **FOR NON-DOMESTIC PIECES,** especially the occasional water-garden, the whole inside surface can be coated with polyeurathene, pouring it in, swilling it round, and pouring out the excess, leaving it to dry on its edge so as not to get a pool in the bottom. The customer should always be told, of course, that any piece has been so treated. **RF**

A brief entry on the tricky business of transporting pots from J Kyanston, and tips on packing pots from Janet Hamer, Freda Earl, the organisers of the Fletcher Challenge Award (New Zealand), Susan Bennett, Walter Keeler and Carol Ray Niño.

● **TRANSPORTING POTTERY, FIRED** or unfired, in one's car can be hazardous. To stop items sliding or moving about use cushions stuffed with polystyrene beads. They are ideal for supporting or resting pots or boards with pots on; it can save many a heartbreak – simple but very effective. **JK**

● **FOR THOSE CERAMIC** shapes which will not pack with geometric neatness like pots. Scrunched news-paper which by itself marks the work, pushed into polythene bags, will support and protect awkwardly shaped sculptures. Easily adapted in size and no hassle if not returned. **JH**

● **WAITROSE'S BANANAS COME** packed in a stiff, solid plastic foam which is much better than bubble wrap for sending small pots through the post. It tears into strips (is there an easy way to cut through bubble wrap?) It is a superb insulator too for sitting on cold pottery floors. I am afraid it is ecologically awful but it is all destined for the rubbish tip and, provided you do not encourage your supplier to use the stuff by offering to pay for it, your conscience can stay clear. **FE**

● **THE BEST METHOD** for shipping work by any means is probably a box within a box, i.e. the work placed tightly with packing material around it securely inside a container of rigid or fairly rigid walls and then this container placed within another padded box of rigid material. See diagram below.
• Pad any extrusions, e.g. handles, on the work with extra packing and tape in place.
• Have at least 50mm (2") space between work and inner box and the same for the outer box.
• Allow no movement of work within the packing material.
• If in doubt – add more packing.
• If only one box is used – make it of rigid material and allow more space between work and box e.g. 100mm (4").
• Pack everything as though it is going to be dropped from 5,000 feet. **FCA**

Outer box made of wood or rigid cardboard or plastic drum etc.

Packing materials such as polystyrene pieces, tightly wadded newspaper, wooden blocks etc.

Inner box of rigid cardboard, fibreboard etc.

Packing material – polystyrene, beads, chips or nuggets, shredded or tightly wadded paper, tightly packed straw or other fibre

● **PREPARING POTS TO** be sent by post is time-consuming, costly and nerve-racking – and it is not always easy to find boxes. Here is a tip inspired by my horticultural exploits.

For light delicate items, envelop in bubblewrap, tape well. Create a strong lightweight tube by inverting two suitable plastic flowerpots. Tape together with pot inside. For extra security, envelop this in more bubblewrap and create an outer protective tube with two larger plastic flower pots. Tape together and wrap as usual.

A good example of cross-fertilisation – and also a good way to send plants, especially pot plants. **SB**

● **I HAVE AT** last found the perfect solution to the mountains of bumph that falls through my letterbox – the paper shredder. This not only disposes of the unwanted paper but produces excellent packaging for pots – a sound investment that is also environmentally acceptable. And the paper packaging is much more user and environmentally friendly than polystyrene. Shredders can, I think, be set against tax and cost as little as £80. **WK**

● **WOODEN BOX NEEDED** to transport ceramics? After a few trials and errors, I have found this to be the easiest method:

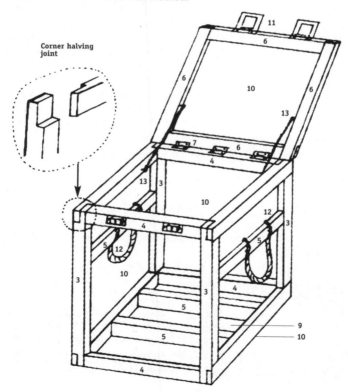

Corner halving joint

1. Measure the height, width, and depth of the ceramic piece(s), and add 10cm to all measurements, which will be the finished box size.
2. Saw 2 × 3cm battens to required lengths, all joints to be nailed.
Frame:
3. Join four battens with corner halving joints for each of the two sides.
4. These sides are joined by four battens sawn off straight across to the required lengths.
5. Nail two battens into base and one each into sides.
Lid:
6. Join four battens with corner halving joints, each 1cm longer than top of box measurements, to allow for addition of the panels.
7. With mallet and chisel make recesses to receive three to four hinges in lid and box and screw on hinges.
Cover:
8. Cut plywood to required sizes, two for base, four for sides and one for box lid – all panels pinned.
9. Use one plywood base for inside floor, cutting out four corners same size as cross-section of battens and nail in.
10. Attach the remaining plywood panels to outside of box and lid.
11. Attach two suitcase fasteners to lid and box.
12. Make holes through plywood panels at sides and tie thick string or cord handles, winding around battens no. 5.
13. Fix ring head screws to inside of box and lid, attach string to prevent hinges being damaged.
14. Line with polystyrene and/or bubble wrap.

These boxes have successfully transported my ceramics halfway round the world on a number of occasions. **CRN**

Advice for dealing with the effect of fumes from electric kiln firings from Robert Fournier and, with a more lasting solution, Susan Bennett/Earl Hyde.

● **THE FUMES FROM** firings, including those in electric kilns, will slowly render the window glass of the kilnroom opaque (think for a moment what this also indicates for the effect on your lungs). A wipe over with 3-in-1 oil will restore transparency, but not permanently. **RF**

● **PEARLY GATES MAY** be a sight for sore eyes, but pearly windows can really dampen the spirits, especially in our climate.

Recently we had most of the glass in our studio windows replaced. It was fairly expensive, but it was worth it for us, as the studio is set in very pretty gardens which were hardly visible through windows which had become opaque due to constant attack by kiln fumes. The problem had been aired in *Ceramic Review* but no one had come up with a cure, or a means of prevention.

The new glass let so much light in that the rest of the studio looked drab and in need of redecoration. It was while varnishing the woodwork that Earl hit on the idea of coating the remaining pearly panes with clear varnish. The transformation was immediate. Apart from slight streaking caused by the brush strokes, the windows are now clear again, they let in the light, and provide us with views of long-forgotten corners of our land. After several months the effect is unaltered, and even if it proves necessary to re-varnish the windows at regular intervals, the cost is negligible compared to replacing the glass. We used Ronseal clear outdoor polyeurethane wood-preserving varnish. Similar products would probably produce equally good results, maybe better – so varnish the tarnish for a clearer perspective on life. **SB/EH**

Making supports for test tiles can be tedious, but Jeanett Grube's method can be used many times.

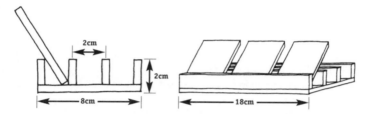

TO MAKE MY trial holders more stable and at the same time save space in my kiln I make them wider so that I can put more trials in one trial holder. I make all my trials 7 × 5 × 0.5cm and therefore I have 6cm between each department.

For example by making a trial holder that is 18cm in length with three rows and using slabs which are 0.5cm thick I can have nine trials in one trial holder. **JG**

Water supplies, hot and cold, are briefly discussed by Shelley Talbot and Mr Lahiff.

● **HAVING A 40** cu.ft. kiln busily radiating heat and an unused 100 gallon tank, we harnessed them to produce adequate hot water for three sinks.

The tank stands on the kiln. Cold water is fed into the top, controlled by a ball valve. An overflow pipe is also fitted.

The hot water pipe leaves the tank at the halfway level and coils several times directly on top of the kiln to gain a boost.

We only supplied the piping, lagging and the ingenuity. **ST**

● **CLOSED WATER SYSTEM** (this avoids connection to mains water drains, and planning permission).

Two old sinks and a washing machine pump are required. The waste water drains into first sink and clay settles to the bottom, water eventually rises over pipe in plug and repeats process in second sink. Any final waste collected in U-bend. Water then pumped back to tank. All parts obtained free except microswitch for motor, bought at modest cost. **ML**

Chapter 9
Health and safety

The final chapter deals with aspects of the health and comfort of the potter. A group on hand care, recipes and protection, from George Marriott, John Dix, Rosemary Capes, Nora Kay, Chris Southall, Claire M Wise, Judith Rivers and John VEG Mitchell.

● **FOR TREATING THOSE** painful cracks and splits around the fingernails, use Calendula ointment, a soothing homeopathic remedy.

For everyday protection ask your dispensing chemist for a mixture of glycerine and soap linament. Inexpensive, and a little goes a long way. **GM**

● **IN MY EARLY** twenties I contracted dermatitis from engineering oils with which I had been in contact. Successive doctors treated it with cortisone, very nasty stuff – it attacks the kidneys. Contemporary medicine often has a negative approach – two wrongs make a right, and the only advice ever offered was to avoid immersion.

Since then I have been using remedies that a medical herbalist gave me and they are the only things to have ever cleared the dermatitis. The simplest is just fresh lemon juice rubbed into the hands before an application of Vaseline. The other is made from the whole flower-heads of calendula (marigolds). Vaseline is melted in a saucepan with as many flower-heads as possible, heated gently for about ten minutes until the petals become crisp. Then the infusion is strained and left to set. Do not boil or over cook as it destroys the essential vitamins. The calendula ointment makes a good barrier cream as well as a dressing. Interestingly Vaseline by itself depletes the skin of vitamins. **JD**

● **JOHN DIX ON** hand cream for Potters' Tips has beaten me to it. I was going to send this idea for the tips from the kitchen, but perhaps this will help his dermatitis, or indeed anyone with dry skin. As there are very few oil glands on the hands moisture is easily lost. To prevent such loss a natural vegetable oil such as olive, corn, soya etc. will act as a barrier as well as keeping the skin soft and supple. Olive oil is what the Romans used instead of soap and today's Spanish labourers use it for cleaning cement stains or plaster off tiles and woodwork; also they rub it into their hands at the end of the day.

Vinegar and lemon juice provide the acid mantle which the skin needs. I shake oil and vinegar together and rub in before and after working with clay. It is far more effective than any hand cream I have hitherto used. Oil and vinegar is also good for suntanning without burning. Seal fat (Eskimos) bear fat (Indians), goose grease (from my childhood I seem to remember), vegetable oils – all have proved themselves, whilst an unidentifiable concoction in a fancy bottle is often inefficient for hard-working hands. **RC**

● **IS THERE ROOM** for yet more information about reliable, cheap and practical hand creams for potters? I can most strongly recommend this, which was suggested by the helpful dispensing chemist in our local branch of Savory and Moore.

It is Hydrous Ointment BP (sometimes known as aqueous cream), an unscented, smooth, white, buttery substance used as the basis of most medicated and cosmetic creams; and it forms an excellent barrier and protection cream for all pottery tasks, wet or dry. It is packed in 500g screw-lidded plastic pots – and should not be very expensive. A jar of this size lasts me for almost a year; it seems to keep indefinitely, and is little affected by extremes of temperature.

Perhaps you too can find an old-fashioned, sympathetic dispensing chemist in your locality. **NK**

● **CUTS ON HANDS** and fingers can be very annoying and painful when throwing. I find that painting them with plastic skin, sold as New Skin or Collodion, enables me to carry on as usual. **CS**

● **AFTER SUFFERING SEVERAL** years of nails worn thin by throwing I have found a very good way of keeping them strong.

I wear a bright coloured nail varnish which gets worn away instead of the nail, and as soon as I can see the varnish wearing thin I apply a couple more layers of protection. **CMW**

● **THIS TIP WAS** given to me by an old stonemason who gave us invaluable advice on restoring our old limestone barn which is now my workshop.

At the end of the day, after working with dirty and abrasive materials like plaster, lime, cement, clay, glaze, gardening etc., try this to clean and soften hands. Pour about one dessertspoon of granulated sugar into the palm of the hand with about the same amount (or slightly more) of any vegetable oil – I like olive oil. Massage well into hands. Rinse under a warm tap, enough to get rid of the sugar but leaving a film of oil on the hands. **JR**

● **DO YOU GET** sore hands after throwing many pots? Try Thermolene New Skin – a friend, Allison, used it with success. **JVEGM**

Help in the alleviation of more general aches and pains is provided by Veronica Pawluk, and of the discomfort of chilly, wet arms by A S Allan and Maria Jones (from Canada, so she knows about these things), while Susan Bennett discovers the healing properties of clay.

● **BY THE VERY** nature of their work – hands constantly damp, feet on cold hard floors, elbow joints strained, painful backs etc. – potters are very prone to lumbago and various other forms of rheumatism. A few years ago my doctor gave me a wonderful tip which initially cured a rheumatic thumb and very severe lumbago.

Obtain a bag of sharp sand either from a builder, seed merchant or best of all the seashore. Put some in a roasting tin or cotton (not nylon) bag or both and heat in the oven to the hottest bearable temperature without causing too much pain or damaging the skin. Envelop the affected area as completely as possible with it. For the feet, for instance, place them in the tin with the bag and for the back place the bag underneath at night. The treatment must be continued until the pain has vanished, and for about three weeks afterwards. **VP**

● **THE PROBLEM OF** cold arms and short cuffs that, even when rolled up, tend to become covered in clay by constant pushing up while working can be solved this way.

Cut the feet off brightly coloured old socks and place the sock over the rolled sleeves. These do not slip and can be removed at the end of the day leaving clean sleeves and warm arms. **ASA**

● **CUT THE SLEEVES** off discarded rubber gloves to keep sweater sleeves and arms dry and warm. **MJ**

● **BEFORE WINTER SET** in with a vengeance, I carried out great clearances in the pond. The next day I was stricken with an unbearably itchy rash on both hands and wrists. Sleep was almost impossible, and unconscious scratching was spreading the rash. Despite treatment with cortisone cream and antihistamine for over a week, it persisted and worsened. I could not work.

Then a friend reminded me I had often told her how healing clay was for the skin – I invariably forget my own tips. That night I covered the affected area with thick cool slip made with Valentine's stoneware (I imagine any smooth relatively pure clay would do) bound my hands and arms in Egyptian mummy fashion, and retired, perchance to doze – fitfully. The clay seemed to relieve the itching. I slept. Next morning, surrounded by the aftermath of an apparent volcanic eruption, I awoke. The clay had dried and cracked off, revealing skin well on the way to recovery. Very soon all was normal.

I offer this economical, non-toxic remedy as a possible alternative to more costly therapies. Investing in a pair of long cotton evening gloves might save on the laundry bill. **SB**

Dealing with stress is, for many of us, a continuing problem. John Shirely has a novel technique for 'centring the self'.

● **IN THESE DAYS** of constant stress one needs to take time out to relax. I have found the following exercise to be a great aid. Firstly, you will need a ball of clay no bigger than a tennis ball, a comfortable upright chair and a quiet space. You will have your eyes closed for the whole of this exercise – if you think this will be difficult use a blindfold. Sit comfortably, holding the clay in your lap. Relax your whole body, starting from the top of your head. Take each part of your body in turn, concentrate on it and feel it relax until you reach your toes. Take your time; there is no rush – your whole body has to be relaxed. Now bring your attention to the ball of clay. Notice how it feels, the temperature of the clay, its firmness and strength. Take your time to fully experience the ball of clay in your hands. Still with your eyes closed, start to make a pinch pot with as round a form as you can. Pay attention to the clay, feel the shape, the thickness and evenness of the pot. Again, take your time, do not rush, the process should take between twenty minutes to one hour. Imagine it in your 'mind's eye' – do not open your eyes – 'see' the pot through touch. When you think you have finished your pot and are pleased with the 'imagined' form, open your eyes. Does the pot resemble the image in your 'mind's eye'? Now your eyes are open spend some time really studying the piece. What would you have done differently if you had been able to see? I find this exercise an invaluable process to get in touch with myself from time to time. Enjoy it. **JS**

Sweeping compounds to allay the raising of dust from the pottery floor may seem a luxury but there is no luxury like clear lungs and potters need to take this aspect of their work seriously. Details from Charles Montague and Michael Maule.

● **I AM WONDERING** if any of your readers have difficulty in keeping the workshop floor clean. For years I used damp sawdust which certainly kept down the dust while sweeping, but did little to remove fine dust which, as it dried, was easily blown about. Incidentally, though sweeping generally is not to be advocated, gentle soft strokes, making sure to keep the broom on the floor surface at the end of each stroke, do not flick up dust.

A friend recommended the use of a proprietary workshop sawdust heavily impregnated with oil. I found that this on my wooden floor not only gave a clean sweep but also 'polished' the floor and kept dust from flying about. It contained so much oil I found that it could be mixed half and half with ordinary sawdust before use. **CM**

● **READERS MAY BE** interested to know of a firm that produces sweeping compounds suitable for various types of floors: Dusmo Farinol, Michaelmas House, Royal Oak Way North, Daventry, Northants, NN1 5PQ. **MM**

Long sessions in more or less static positions can be painful and harmful. Notes from Jerry Stovin and Mike Rawlinson suggest time/motion systems for general work and pottery layout, which could save many an aching back and be of great value to enthusiast and professional alike.

● **WHEN ANNA LAMBERT** mentioned a dicey back (in her Potter's Day), I felt a sympathetic twinge. In order to remind herself to stop and stretch hourly, may I suggest that she keep an oven timer (with a quiet tick) near her and, after each alarm, to reset it for another hour before doing her stretch. If her activities might take her out of earshot, may I recommend one of those timers that hangs around the neck.

May I also pass on one of the most useful things I ever learned on a potting course – when John Solly feels the tension rising in his back, he gives a firm vigorous rub at the point of contraction (in the small of the back in both his and my case). It is wonderful how it loosens the knot and prevents a muscle spasm rising. (P.S. I learned many other useful things from John.) **JS**

● **THE EXPERTS TELL** us to design our workshops efficiently so we do not waste time walking from one end to the other. However, this assumes that we are efficient machines, which we are not. When I worked out the layout of my new workshop I did the opposite and placed my drying racks as far as possible from the wheel. Although I may spend a few minutes a day walking up and down with planks of pots, it does mean I get a short walk every few minutes which helps to prevent stiffness and fatigue associated with long hours at the wheel. **MR**

With the increasing awareness of food-safe glazes in mind, the Alberta Potters' Association outline a simple method of checking for acid release; Plainsman Clay offer advice on formulating safe glazes.

● **GLAZES ARE GLASS** and we tend to think of them as timeless, indestructible. However all glass leaches to some extent when it comes into contact with water or acids, especially if the contact occurs over a period of time or the acid is hot.

You can do a quick test on glazes containing metal oxide. Fill a glazed container half full of vinegar and leave it for several days. Dry the item and compare the colour and gloss of the surface above and below the vinegar surface line. Any difference indicates that the glaze is subject to leaching. There is a way that you can amplify the result. If your glaze is white or transparent add a little cobalt and do a vinegar leaching test on it. Excessively unstable coloured glazes can easily turn white with an overnight vinegar leach. If yours does, you need to adjust the chemistry of the glaze base or choose a more stable base.

See www.ceramic-materials.com/cermat/education/12.html for more information on making your glazes safe. **APA**

● **THE TRAFFIC IN** glaze recipes is having a net effect on functional ceramics in education, hobby and industry. It is fostering a culture that runs counter to the idea of understanding and controlling our materials and recipes, it breeds ignorance of oxide and material sciences and the true nature of the ceramic process. Weak, leachable, difficult-to-clean, crazed, shivered, and leaching glazes hurt the reputation of the pottery and the ceramics industry.

We recommend a 'base glaze with variations' model. When a base glaze is well understood it can be improved over a period of years. When it is improved, variations based benefit also. Imagine a base that is nice to use and apply; never cracks on drying; does not settle out; is reliable; cost effective; resistant to leaching, crazing, and cutlery marking; is gloss and temperature adjustable; and is easily opacified, coloured and variegated, etc. This is not dreamland, it is possible, but only if you focus on one good base glaze. Would it not make sense to transplant the 'mechanisms' from new glaze recipes into your base rather than bring new recipes with their new materials and problems into your studio?

You can find base recipes on our website for a gloss and a matt for cone 6 www.ceramic-materials.com/cermat/education/114.html and cone 10 www.ceramic-materials.com/cermat/education/218.html. **PC**

And finally, Colin Cooke offers valuable advice when using discarded coffee beakers.

● **GIVEN THE CURRENT** concern with health and safety in workshops, it has been regularly recommended in your column to make use of discarded polystyrene coffee beakers collected from canteens. An excellent idea but one fraught with danger if the glaze contents are accidentally swallowed instead of the coffee. If all glaze beakers are marked with a broad red line round the top with felt pen it will act as an alarm signal to prevent accidents. **CC**

Index

Contributors

Alberta Potters' Association
A S Allan
Hugh Allen
Stan Allman
Betty Allsop
Brenda Angel
Brigitta Appleby
Dr Reeve Arenstein
Janet Armstrong
Hannah Arnup
Pauline Ashley
Alan Ashpool
Association of Potters of
    South Africa
Jyl Bailey
Edward Baker
Paddy Bakker
Pat Barfoot
J W Barratt
Paul Barron
Ben Bates
Dee Batter-Hatten
Richard Baxter
Phyllis Beeching
Pat Beese
Bob Bell
Frank Benatt
Susan Bennett
Chrissie Bentley
Pauline Beresford
Audrey Blackman
Alan H Bolton
Bolton Technical College
C R Brampton
Alice Bree
Kenneth Breese
Juliet Breese
Jane Bridges
Briglin Pottery
Margaret Brook
Pete Brown
Nigel Buchanan-Wollaston
Jan Bunyan
Krzysztof Buras
Andy Burt
Rosemary Capes

Graham Carey
Maurice Carey
Lynn Carter
Jon Catleugh
Murray Cheesman
Peter Chesney
Jonathan Chiswell Jones
Alison Clarke
Peter Clarke
Derek Clarkson
Dean Coates
N Collins
Robin Colville
Brian Cooke
Colin Cooke
Emily Cooke
Margaret Cooke
Emmanuel Cooper
John Cooper
Vincent Cooper
Pat Cormack
Doreen Costello
Janet Cottrell
Martin Cowley
Kathleen Creasey
Andrew Crisp
Peter Crotty
M M Crump
Jane Cullett
J B Cunningham
Ellen Curran
Mary Davies
Duncan Davis
Russell Davis
Edward Dawes
Eric Degg
Peter Dick
John Dix
Peter Dixon
J R Dowling
Rosemary Downs
Ian Doyle
Frank Draper
Jonathan Dring
Anne Duffy
Douglas Eaglesham

Freda Earl
Jean Emmett
Anna English
E M English
Jane Fairbanks
Dorothy Feibleman
Alicia Felberbaum
Ray Finch
Judith Fisher
Robert Flexen
Vivienne Foley
Rein Follestad
Adrian Foulds
Robert Fournier
Mike Francis
David Frith
Borax Fritz
Gordon Gerrard
Judy Glanville
Peter Godfrey
Marie-Pierre Governale
Ian Grant
Peter Green
Susan Green
Wendy Green
Caroline Bousfield Gregory
C M Grieve
Stephen Grieve
Jeanett Grube
Eliza Grummett
John Gunn
D Haig-Thomas
Susan Halls
Frank Hamer
Janet Hamer
Jean Hamilton
S Hardwick
Ray Hargreaves
John Harlow
Hank Harmeling
Jerry Harper
M A Hatfield
S Hayes
Carenza Hayhoe
S Heaton
Margaret Hinchcliffe

B Hobbs
David Hobbs
Noirin Hobbs
Bonnie K Holland
Dennis Holloway
Danny Honig
Denis Hopking
Roy Hubbard
David Huddy
Lyn Hudson
Anne Hughes
G Hunt
Kathleen Hunter
Earl Hyde
Sylvia Hyman
Ken Isherwood
Les Jamieson
Tlws Johnson
Bill Jones
Dorothy Ann Jones
Ken Jones
Maria Jones
Ruth Karnac
Nora Kay
Walter Keeler
Anne Kenny
Martin King
Margaret Kneer
J Kollov
J Kyanston
Mr Lahiff
Geoff Lamb
John Lawrence
Lucy Learman
Peter A Lee
Veronica Lee
Ruth Lehmann
Anne Leon
Eileen Lewenstein
June Linsley Hood
David Lloyd Jones
Jane Lord
Avis Loshak
Janet Lundie
Ruth Lyle
Jean Maffey

Bruno Manini
Gary Marconi
Harriet Mark
George Marriott
William Martin
Richard Mason
John Mathieson
Michael Maule
A May
J B May
Alison McKay
Ivan McMeekin
D Metcalff
Rosemary Metz
Rik Midgley
Midland Potters Association
John Miller
John VEG Mitchell
K A Mitchell
Charles Montague
Michael Montague
Tony J Moody
Torhjen Moon
Elana Morris
Jean Morse
Margaret Moseley
Mart Muller
Lakshmi Murthy
Peter Naylor
John Neville
Joseph Neville
New Zealand Potter
G W A Newton
Julia Nicholson
Billy Nightingale
Carol Ray Niño
North London Collegiate
    School
Veronika von Nostitz
Tony O'Donovan
Organisers of the Fletcher
    Challenge Award (New
    Zealand)
Sue Packer
Judith Palmer
Ken Palmer

Sue Parish
Tammy Parkes-Legge
Ann Parkhouse
Keith Parry
Nirmala Patwardhan
Veronica Pawluk
Ron Payne
Adrian Phelps
Ted Pitman
Plainsman Clay
Potters' Society of
    Australia
Pottery Supply House,
    Ontario
Audrey Potts
David Powell
Margaret Power
Audrey Price
Tom Price
Bo Ratcliffe
Tim Ratcliffe
P H Rattray
Mike Rawlinson
G L Reeve
Christa Reichel
Paul Reid
Mary Rich
Judith Rivers
Alex Robertson
Brian Rose
Karen Roskell
James Rush
Maureen Russell
Monica Russell
Pamela Scott
Jane Searle
A M Seiko
Dick Shattock
Clare Sheppard
John Shirely
Michael Skipwith
Duncan James Smith
Ian D Smith
Valerie Snow
Henry Sommerville
Frands Sorensen

South Wales Potters
Mary R Southal
Chris Southall
Pat Southwood
Philip Stanbridge
Maureen Standring
Vivian Stanley
Dot Stephenson
G A Stevens
Hugh Stewart
Charles Stileman
Jerry Stovin
Brian Sutherland
Hilary Sutton
Belinda Swingler
Shelley Talbot
Jan van der Tas
Lyndon Thomas
Edwin Todd
M Trickett
Terence Turnbull
Bill Turner
Darwin Turner
Sheila Tyas
Tony Valintine
Sue Varley
Hugh Veater
Peter Venning
Waikato Society of
    Potters, New Zealand
James Walford
Geoff Walker
Cynthia Wardley
Merion John Warren
Hugh Watson
Muriel Watson
Edna Weldon Davies
Wellington Potters
    Newsletter
L E Wells
Tony Wells
Franz Westerveld
Tom Westman
Carol Wheeler
Tricia Whillock
David White

Pam Williams
Dick Wilson
Bob Winokur
Paula Winokur
Barry Winslow
Claire M Wise
Don Witts
J H Wood
Sheila Wood
Stephen Woodhead
Tina Woodhouse
Julie Woods
Rosemary D Wren
M Young

Notes

Share your own practical tips with an international
community of potters by sending them to Ceramic Review for
publication. Email editorial@ceramicreview.com or post to
Potters' Tips, 25 Foubert's Place, London W1F 7QF.